Author biogr

Daniel Mersey was born in 1974 in the aptly named Tintagel House, in Edmonton, London.

He read Archaeology at the University of York between 1993 and 1996. The thrilling world of discovering previously unknown treasures in distant lands awaited. Sadly, reality is seldom as exciting as fantasy, and far from a career of self-inflicted Mummies' curses and recovering the Lost Ark in the heat of the desert, as an archaeologist he has excavated in such exotic places as Cambridge, Peterborough, Yorkshire and Wales. He is now an editor and writer, but still takes an active interest in field archaeology. In addition to editing and rewriting other peoples' work, Daniel has over one hundred writing credits of his own. His previously published work includes *Legendary Warriors: Great Heroes in Myth and Reality* (Chrysalis, 2002). Off the written page and onto the airwaves, Daniel has also written comedy for radio.

He is also a Contributing Editor for the *Castles of Wales* website and has undertaken work for several museums, cataloguing archived material, assessing displays and access, and providing explanatory text.

Daniel currently lives on the south coast of England with his partner and seven guitars.

Excalibur Rises Into View

ARTHUR

KING OF THE BRITONS

From Celtic hero to cinema icon

Daniel Mersey

summersdale

ARTHUR KING OF THE BRITONS
From Celtic hero to cinema icon

Copyright © Daniel Mersey 2004
Illustrations by Deanna Tyson 2004
Sword on cover © Spiral (www.spiral.org.uk, 01634 401274)

Summersdale Publishers Ltd
46 West Street
Chichester
West Sussex
PO19 1RP
UK

www.summersdale.com

Printed and bound in Great Britain by J. H. Haynes & Co. Ltd

ISBN 1 84024 403 8

Contents

ARTHUR

KING OF THE BRITONS

Arthur King Of The Britons And Guinevere His Queen

Chapter One

King Who?

If you really did pick this book up and think 'Who is this King Arthur then?' don't worry. This question has passed many millions of people's lips over the past 1,500 years. Fortuitously, most of those who have asked were glad they did so, uncovering details of one of the most exciting periods of British history and a whole host of the world's most exciting legends in the process. Many historians and researchers have tried to pin the tail on the historical donkey, conjuring up all sorts of theories along the way. Far too many modern researchers have tended to champion one candidate as *the* King Arthur. Doing so has often proved a thankless task, and in pursuit of their goal writers will far too often ignore the evidence that does not support their pet theory. Approaching this book as a 'biography' rather than as a 'solution' allows me to present as wide a picture of the historical and literary Arthur as I may in a book of this size, and hopefully fills in some of those gaps that others have neglected to explain. What this book isn't is a dense academic tome for the expert Arthurian reader to learn more from; what it is, hopefully, is a great place for us lesser mortals to find out more about one of the most famous characters from folklore: a popular history of Arthur.

There are two very distinct King Arthurs to consider – the Arthur of children's stories, literature and folklore, and the Arthur of history. The two are very different, but both are the subject of this 'biography', which charts their rise from their earliest incarnations right up to the modern day.

The essence of King Arthur

Arthur's name first emerges from the shadowy history of the fifth and sixth centuries AD. The strong controlling hand of Roman government had crumbled away in Britain and, as happened in so many other parts of the former empire, post-Roman riches were there for the picking by ferocious, foreign barbarian tribes. A handful of passing references in the Celtic languages suggest that Arthur was a native British warlord who fought back against the enemies of Britain. Stories of Arthur's supposed historical feats (and some superhuman deeds also) became popular and spread throughout the surviving British and, later, Welsh cultures by the tenth century.

Five hundred years later, Arthur had become a byword for medieval kingship – both good and bad – and over the flourishing epoch of medieval romantic and chivalric writing, he came to stand for everything that was just and virtuous in the medieval world. What's more, medieval writers were passing these fantastical tales off as real history – concepts of 'fiction' and 'non-fiction' writing were very different in the medieval world to today's black and white view. Stories about Arthur and his court became so popular that Alanus de Insulis, writing in the latter half of the twelfth century, noted that anyone who said that Arthur was dead would almost certainly have a volley of stones thrown at them (Alanus wrote shortly after a poet named Wace popularised the theory that Arthur was not dead, just sleeping).

In a nutshell, the story of Arthur as dramatised by popular medieval authors – and built upon by modern authors – is as follows:

Arthur was born into a divided kingdom where the Britons and their enemies were fighting bloody wars. Arthur's father, Uther, was the leader of the Britons and Arthur was born illegitimately to him after the powerful and enigmatic sorcerer Merlin helped him deceive the wife of the Duke of Cornwall. When Uther died leaving no obvious heir, the British nobles continued to fight among themselves for dominance. Merlin announced that the leader of the Britons would become evident through a challenge – he summoned the nobility to a site where a beautiful sword stood magically embedded in a stone; whoever could draw the sword, Merlin decreed, would rule the country. The foremost British nobles tried but all failed; yet Arthur, as yet unknown to all to be the son of Uther, succeeded.

Although Arthur had led his early life as the lowly squire of a just knight, his charisma and leadership qualities evidently shone through when he took the royal throne – the enemies of the Britons were expelled and Arthur set about restoring order to his realm. As Arthur grew in power, he married the beautiful Guinevere, and bold knights flocked to join his court. As his court grew, Arthur founded his famous round table where no knight would sit more prominently at the table than his fellow warriors, not even Arthur himself. Merlin took Arthur to the Lady of the Lake, an enchantress who lived under the water's surface; the Lady of the Lake presented Arthur with the magical sword Excalibur.

The kingdom of Britain flourished under Arthur's rule and Merlin's guidance. One day Arthur had a religious vision and turned his attention to finding the Holy Grail. The Grail chalice had been used to collect blood pouring from Jesus' wounds on the cross, and locating it appealed to Arthur's sense of Christian devotion. Arthur's knights set out to find the Grail, each undertaking a number of difficult tasks, often highly symbolic in their nature. The majority of Arthur's knights died on their quest for the Grail, yet Galahad and Perceval succeeded in finding the holy chalice (or at least a vision of it); even so, they failed to bring it to Arthur.

The valorous knight Lancelot was Arthur's champion: the defender of the King and his wife Guinevere. Eventually, the King's wife and champion fell in love, and Lancelot left to live in exile. Guinevere was later to do the same. The affair between Lancelot and Guinevere, and the waste of Arthur's knights' lives on the Grail Quest symbolised the decline in Arthur's kingdom after his initial successes. Whilst Arthur was engaged in a military campaign overseas, his illegitimate son Modred (more about his contentious background in Chapter Three) seized power, usurping Arthur's throne and stealing Excalibur's scabbard, which magically granted protection from injury to its wearer.

Arthur returned and gathered his loyal forces to oppose Modred. The two armies clashed at the Battle of Camlann. At the end of a long bloody fight Arthur, with his few remaining knights, spotted Modred and his retinue across the battlefield. Arthur and his son met, and delivered fatal blows to each other (Excalibur's scabbard evidently did not work for the King's evil son). Modred died outright, and Arthur lay mortally wounded. The King was placed on a boat and sailed away to the mysterious island of Avalon, where he was laid to rest. Some said that Arthur was 'the once and future king', and that he and his loyal knights lay not in death but in sleep, ready to ride out once more when Britain was beset by crisis.

After the medieval period these tales of Arthur's reign continued to be told, although the stories did not evolve any further for some time. This can probably be attributed to the influence of Sir Thomas Malory's superior account of Arthur, *The Death of Arthur*, which was printed in book form by Thomas Caxton in 1485 and quickly gained popularity.

However, the chivalric and romantic empire of Malory's Arthur, where chastity and bravery mattered above all else, enchanted Britain's other great empire builders: the Victorians. Victorian Britain had a romantic movement of art and literature growing within it, and the legends of Arthur appealed to the writers and artists involved. So the Victorians – whose rewriting of history included the sudden appearance of horns on Viking helmets and many other well-attested poetic creations – picked up on the medieval version of Arthurian fiction and allowed it to run its course into the modern world. In the twentieth century, a trend of retelling Arthurian stories set in the correct historical context (the fifth and sixth centuries) emerged. Modern cinema has not overlooked the challenge of Arthur, either, and Clive Owen recently appeared in a Hollywood blockbuster about the historical Arthur. It would seem that popular legend, just like popular music and fashion, runs in circles, and just as he was in the medieval world, Arthur is now once again ready to stand at the pinnacle of our entertainment industry.

Today, many people only remember the tale of how Arthur drew the sword from the stone. Some will perhaps know a little about the Grail Quest, and how Arthur died after receiving a mortal blow from Modred. Most people recollect that before he died Arthur returned his magical sword Excalibur to the Lady of the Lake. Not so many people remember the rest of Arthur's glorious reign beyond its beginning and end, where he and his knights undertook many great quests. And more still do not realise that Arthur's famous sword Excalibur and the Sword in the Stone are not one and the same, but in fact separate weapons. Even fewer people know the historical background to the legend.

The world of legends, myth and folklore

Legends, myths and folklore. People often use these three terms interchangeably, but all three have their own unique definitions.

Myths are stories about gods, goddesses, supernatural events and fabulous creatures, and how humans interacted with such a world. As such, tales that we now see as myths generally derive from earlier religions – such as those of Greece, Egypt and the Norse world. The gods and creatures featured in myths were once believed to have existed by the people of those cultures, and helped to explain why their societies worked in the way they did. The difference between a myth and a religion depends upon whether you believe that the religious tales are true – myths, it may be said, are simply unfashionable religions.

Legends, on the other hand, are based more fully on history. This isn't to say that a legend needs any great amount of historical fact, and the historical setting of many legends can now be proved incorrect. Magical powers, fabulous beasts and the supernatural may all still play a part in legend, but exist alongside the heroes in a world sometimes tied down to specific dates. The best known tales of King Arthur fit mostly into this category – many writers give dates for Arthur's birth and death (usually in the fifth and sixth centuries AD), but then introduce medieval social values and knights in shining armour (both historically inaccurate for this period of history), and then set the King and his knights against a variety of dragons, wizards and giants. Sagas – so beloved of medieval Germanic and Scandinavian writers – also fit into this category.

Folklore, or folk tales if you prefer, are traditional stories primarily functioning as forms of entertainment rather than the more sober role of myths. Folklore is often localised, bringing the flavour of that specific region to the story. Again, magical creatures and events may feature, but the stories don't aim to instruct the audience. Fairy tales sit quite happily alongside folklore, although the phenomenon of fairy tales sprang from the Romantic movement of the nineteenth century. Many of the early Celtic Welsh and Cornish stories about Arthur should be considered as folk tales.

On the whole, many modern stories involve elements of all three, and it's not worth getting too caught up in deciphering myth from legend from folklore; as you read about Arthur in this book, you will see that folklore plays a part, legend a far stronger part, but that myth takes a backseat (except, perhaps, in the Grail Quest).

Myths, legends and folklore all developed for their own reasons; to instruct, to provide explanations or to entertain – today, most people see all three purely as forms of entertainment, though.

Arthur Inc: A worldwide phenomenon

Tales of King Arthur spread from their relatively humble origins in the feasting halls of early medieval British and, later, Welsh nobles, to become popular in the chivalric courts of medieval Europe. The French, Italians and Germans were entertained with stories of the greatest king of Christendom, and gradually Arthur's legend spread even further afield to Eastern Europe and the Middle East. Popular European legend travelled to the Americas and further flung corners of the world and, now cemented as a hero of legend, fantasy and the cinema, a quick search for the name 'King Arthur' on the Internet will bring around 295,000 entries to your fingertips.

Arthur the coat hanger: A wardrobe of heroes and gods

Some of Arthur's warriors and courtly followers are almost as famous as the King himself. Many such characters deserve this recognition, as they are figures of legend and folklore in their own right, plucked from their own tales and transplanted into Arthur's court. Others were once true characters from history, whose real identity and personality were removed so that their names could be used in Arthurian legend.

A few characters probably originated as ancient Celtic gods and goddesses; these early pagan figures were incorporated into the Christian Arthurian world as part of Christianity's well-attested drive to swallow up other religions' memories into its own (rather similar to the way that many Christian churches were built on the site of older, pagan shrines). Kay, Bedivere, Guinevere and Morgan Le Fay may possibly be identified as the Celtic deities.

Other characters, such as Lancelot, Galahad, Gawain and Perceval were probably heroes of folklore and literature in their own right before being incorporated into the immensely popular stories of Arthur. In modern terms, this is rather like a football team signing a new star player, bringing the strength of skill of the newcomer into the club and hopefully attracting some more fans at the same time.

A few of Arthur's followers can be identified as sharing their name with a historically attested figure. For example, Urien and his son Owain, who fought so well against their Saxon enemies in the northern British kingdom of Rheged, are remembered in Arthurian legend as the two knights Urien of Gore and Ywaine. Peredur was a sixth century British prince of York, but was listed by Geoffrey of Monmouth as being one of Arthur's nobles; Peredur later evolved into the famous character Perceval. Tristan, a knight both in Arthur's court and of independent British folklore, can tenuously be identified as the Briton commemorated on a famous Dark Ages standing stone in Cornwall; his father in legend, King Mark, may well be mentioned on this stone too. However, like Urien, Owain and Peredur, Tristan may originally have had origins in the north of Britain, as the Pictish prince named Drust. And finally Merlin, the great sorcerer who advised and aided Arthur so often, may have been created from the memory of a historical attested figure named Myrddin: a late sixth century northern British poet who went mad after the Battle of Arderydd in 573. The characters who occur in Arthurian legend often have little in common with their historical predecessor apart from a name; this may well be true of Arthur himself. However, in the great King's case we can't even be sure that a historical leader of that name really existed in the first place. But if he did, just like the others, he probably bore little similarity to the king of legend.

The ability of Arthurian legend to incorporate characters from other stories or cultures has helped to ensure the longevity of Arthur's name through time and across the world; the tales are pliable enough to be adapted to cultural or regional taste. Modern authors are still doing very much the same thing. For example, Bernard Cornwell makes Sagramor a north African warrior (Sagramore – with an 'e' at the end – was a well established knight in Arthurian legend, but had no African connection before Cornwell's work). And there is no shortage of movies that have incorporated the idea of a 'ordinary Joe' from the modern world being miraculously transported back in time to Arthur's world.

Knowing your Angles from your Armoricans

Throughout the book, you will notice that reference is made to the Britons, the Saxons, the Picts and several other cultures and time periods. As you read on, everything should gradually fall into place and you'll know your Angles from your Armoricans. However, here's a handy guide just in case you're getting a bit confused:

Armoricans

British emigrants who settled in Brittany in the early medieval period; this term means more or less the same as the Bretons, and I've only used it if a character from Arthurian legend is said to be from Armorica.

Anglo-Normans

The ruling classes (and therefore the cultural designation) of England from the time of William I's conquest in 1066 to the death of King Stephen in 1154. In this book, I use the term mostly when referring to the medieval chroniclers who wrote of Arthur.

Anglo-Saxons

This term is used sparingly, and it shouldn't be confused with the Saxons listed below. In this book, Anglo-Saxon is used as shorthand for settled Christian English kingdoms from the late sixth century onwards. Before this – and throughout most of the Arthurian period – I've referred to these original 'English' as Saxons.

Bretons

The people of Brittany, who had strong cultural and kindred ties to Britain in the Dark Ages and medieval period. Brittany was originally carved out from the rest of modern day France by British immigrants in the early medieval period.

Britons

The Britons were the native inhabitants of the British Isles when it was conquered by Rome in the first century AD. With the demise of Roman authority at the start of the fifth century AD, in the lead up to the Arthurian period, the Britons defended themselves once again. Eventually, with the lowlands conquered and turned into England, the surviving Britons became known as Welsh, Cornish and, when the Britons of the last northern kingdoms were swallowed up by their northern enemies, they became Scots by default.

Dark Ages

Not a people, but a period. More correctly, the period spanning roughly AD 410–1066 should be referred to as the early medieval period, but in the context of this book, Dark Ages avoids any confusion with the early part of the 'true' medieval period.

Franks

The Franks were the inheritors of most of Roman Gaul, or, more familiarly, modern France. It is likely that the Franks maintained strong links with the southern Saxon kings (indeed, a number of Franks were probably amongst the original 'Saxon' invaders), but stuck to what they knew best – conquering and defending large tracts of Europe.

Irish

The Irish, in their purest form, were the inhabitants of modern Ireland, who raided the western coast of Britain with a fair amount of success. They also settled in coastal areas of Wales, and in south-west Scotland, where the people of the kingdom of Dal Riata became known as Scots. The Irish shared some cultural heritage with the Britons (and later with the Scots, Welsh and Cornish).

Picts

The Picts were the original natives of modern Scotland: in essence, they were the northern tribes of the Britons. The Picts are often referred to, even in modern times, as 'the mysterious Picts' and the truth is that we know little of their customs or history, as no one has ever discovered any written records for them. Most scholars would suggest that the Picts were not very closely linked to the other indigenous cultures of the British Isles (the Britons and Irish). They eventually merged with the Irish Scots of Dal Riata to create Scotland.

Saxons

Throughout this book, you will read about 'the Saxons'. In the context of Arthur, the Saxons should not be considered one set of people. I've used it as a generic term for the many invading and raiding continental Germanic tribes who arrived in Britain over the space of a couple of hundred years. Most of the tribes had remained unconquered by Rome and, to begin with, many were fiercely pagan. Traditionally, three tribes came: the Angles, the Jutes and the Saxons themselves, but in reality, there were probably a lot of others too. They are different to the Anglo-Saxons mentioned in this book, but the Anglo-Saxons may be considered their mature, Christianised great-grandchildren.

Scots

The Scots originated in Ireland, and this term only refers to those Dal Riatan Irish peoples who settled in Scotland, sowing the seeds for the future kingdom of Scotland alongside the native Picts. Some Dark Ages and medieval chroniclers referred to all Irish as Scots.

Arise, Sir... er?

The origins of characters in Arthurian legend are diverse; some names began as a Welsh name, others as Irish, Latin, or from other parts of Europe. Just to confuse the unwary reader, different authors have used many variations of names in their own Arthurian tales. When a character is mentioned in legend, I've used the easiest pronunciation available or the spelling as used by the author of that particular work, whilst keeping the name in a recognisable form to the original. When referring to historical figures, I've used the most commonly accepted spellings. Different translations of personal names have been passed down through time and it is not always possible to say which is correct; in Appendix A, I've noted other commonly seen spelling variations that you might come across in other Arthurian books.

Appendix D contains a quick guide to Welsh pronunciation, if you're particularly open-minded. As a start, a word that many people mispronounce is 'Celtic' – say it with a hard 'C' ('Keltic') rather than a soft 'C' ('Seltic'), otherwise you'll be speaking about one of Scotland's most celebrated football clubs rather than one of Europe's most celebrated cultures. The same goes for Celtic personal names you read in the book – pronounce them with a hard 'C' too.

I have also chosen to present the names of the many medieval works on Arthur in modern English. Most of these works were originally written in French or Latin, but I felt that it was in keeping with the purpose of this book to present the names of works in a readily readable fashion. After all, we're not Classics snobs here.

Arthur, Dux Bellorum

Chapter Two

The Historical Arthur

The handful of references that can pass as partially reliable history, or perhaps more accurately folklore that dimly recalls history, and that have survived into the twenty-first century, suggest that Arthur lived in the late fifth or early sixth century AD. This is plausible – these two centuries are popularly known as the Dark Ages, by virtue of the fact that so little knowledge of what happened at this time has survived to this day.

During these two centuries, Britain was a very different country to today. For example, England, Wales, Scotland and Northern Ireland did not politically exist as we would recognise them now. To understand why, it is important to consider what happened in the decades immediately before Arthur's supposed lifetime, and the centuries before them. For four hundred years before Arthur's time, Britain had been part of the Roman Empire, and the end of this relationship early on in the fifth century left the inhabitants of Britain at a historical crossroad – should they continue with a Roman way of life, or reinvent themselves? And how were they to deal with the threat of the many new invaders waiting to visit with nasty, sharp, pointy spears? It proved an important period in the making of modern Britain.

Our sources
To decipher what actually happened 1,500 years ago, it is important to know who told us what at the time, and what historians and archaeologists have been able to find out since (as well as what they're not able to find out).

The crucial fact to remember is that we have very few reliable, securely dated written sources. If you went shopping at the Supermarket of History, you could pick up all of the truly useful contemporary items for Arthur's period and still queue at the 'Ten items or less' checkout.

What you won't find in this chapter is a series of solid, accurate dates. Why? Because we do not have them. Very few relevant manuscripts detailing Britain's history during the time when Arthur may have lived have survived. There were, of course, no newspapers and certainly no newsreel footage for this period, and the introduction of the printing press was still a thousand years away. Instead, the few written records we have were jotted down by contemporary writers – mostly religious men such as monks – and so reflect their views on what constituted important history, the accuracy of which may fall short of today's standards. Nevertheless, writers such as Gildas and Nennius (who we'll meet properly in Chapter Four), the eighth century Anglo-Saxon writer Bede, the occasional continental scholar with a passing interest in Britain, and even a few poets and bards, preserved the few ideas of what happened that we have today.

We do not know what was once written down and has now been lost – Geoffrey of Monmouth famously claimed to have used an ancient British book to aid him in writing his influential *History*. It may even be that writers such as Bede, who lived a couple of hundred years after some of the events about which they wrote, had access to such material, or they may just have written down the traditional oral histories of their people.

Many of the early documents that have survived to this day are not the originals. Like the Celtic stories of Arthur, the original texts were copied down, and sometimes translated, at a later date, and under such circumstances we must throw ourselves at the mercy of these later scribes, hoping that they copied accurately and translated correctly. It is also sometimes difficult to know how honest some of the later scribes were – interpolations and contamination from other sources can still sometimes be picked out and, just as in the modern world, forgeries cannot be ruled out.

Some researchers have gone overboard in their interpretation of the available sources, to the extent that several decades of history can be accounted for by over analysing one or two scanty sentences that may provide something less pure than straightforward history. Yet, despite the potential problems of working with such insubstantial and possibly inaccurate sources – and with so few relevant texts available, the chances of cross-checking facts are almost laughable – modern scholars and researchers have worked with what little we have to produce a narrative of British history in the Dark Ages.

Many of the key documents are outlined in Chapter Four; they mix possible historical anecdote with pure fantasy at will, and we can no longer be sure which parts of the surviving sources can be relied upon and which parts should be dismissed along with the stories of giants and wizards. The work of the Anglo-Saxon Bede, who wrote his *History of the English Church and People* in the eighth century should be considered along with the Britons' own sources, and draws at least partially on the earlier work of Gildas. In addition to Bede, the 'view from the other side' was also recorded in *The Anglo-Saxon Chronicle*.

The Anglo-Saxon Chronicle includes a fair amount of information on the years of the Arthurian period, some of which seems possible and some of which seems inherently unlikely. Place names cannot always be verified, and we can only guess at the information neglected by the chroniclers (there is an absence of Saxon battle defeats, for example, and the geographical areas reported on are quite restricted for certain periods). Added to this uncertainty, the *Chronicle* was not written down until a few centuries after its earliest recorded events, and, although it must have drawn on earlier Saxon oral history, there is no reason to expect it to be any more reliable than the equivalent British sources. Nevertheless, *The Anglo-Saxon Chronicle* broadly defines the old school view of British history at this time. The style of entries included are demonstrated by the following examples based on translations of the *Chronicle*:

AD 446: The Britons plead with Rome for help against the Picts. When refused, the Britons turn to the Angles instead

AD 449: The Angles arrive at the request of the British king, Vortigern. They arrive in three ships at Ebbesfleet, and they successfully fight the Picts on the Britons' behalf. Other kinsmen arrive from the Jutish and Saxon peoples. Hengist and Horsa were their leaders, and they first fought and killed the enemies of Vortigern, and then turned on the Britons destroying them with fire and sword.

AD 455: Vortigern fights Hengist and Horsa at Aegelesthrep. Horsa is killed, and Hengist and his son Aesc receive the kingdom.

AD 456: Hengest and Aesc fight a successful battle against the Britons at Crecganford (probably Crayford), driving them back to London.

AD 465: Hengest and Aesc fight the Welsh (as the *Chronicle* describes the Britons from this point onwards; ironically the word means foreigner) near Wippedesfleot and kill twelve Welsh nobles.

AD 473: Hengest and Aesc again defeat the Welsh; it is noted during this entry that the Welsh fled the Saxons as one flees fire.

AD 477: Aelle arrives in Britain, with his three sons Cymen, Wlencing, and Cissa. They land in Cymensora (probably Chichester) and kill many Welshmen. The remaining Welsh flee into the Weald.

AD 485: Aelle defeats the Welsh again, on a bank near Merecredesburna.

AD 488: Aesc receives the kingdom (Hengist, presumably, has died) and rules Kent for thirty-four years.

AD 491: Aelle and Cissa besiege Andcrida (Pevensey fort), and kill all of the Britons inside.

Providing a different type of evidence to the written, historical sources, is the data thrown up by archaeological excavation. Whereas written documents tend to show us the big picture – the names of kings, the battles fought, the important clergy of the time – archaeology helps us to decipher how people really lived, and can highlight potential biases in the written evidence. Archaeology is, in many ways, the micro to our written sources' macro level evidence. And the archaeological record is growing all the time – in the past decade, at least three significant Saxon royal burial sites have been discovered and excavated, and with each excavation we have more data to learn from.

In addition to solid history and archaeology, researchers often use folklore and regional tradition to fill in the gaps. The use of such material is problematic, as parts of a tale may clearly be mythical, whereas other sections of the same story may hint at the truth. Yet to ignore such traditions completely could be to overlook some vital and otherwise forgotten clue; the trick is to identify which parts of a tale might be true, and the best way to do this is to see if they correlate with archaeological or more robust historical testimony.

Another useful tool for historians faced with the nearly blank canvas of the British Dark Age is to compare Britain with events in Europe at the same time. Much of what had been the Roman Empire was subjected to similar power struggles and tribal migrations, and we even know that events such as Yellow Plague hit Europe in the centuries between the fall of Rome and the rise of medieval states. Some events were far better documented in Europe than in Britain; for example, the aforementioned plague is vaguely referred to in British Isles sources, although without confirmation from continental sources, we might not have known much about it. Yet comparing Britain to other European regions during this period is not simple – as an island, a different set of problems, people, and processes would have arisen in Britain compared to those on the mainland continent. The rise and fall of new regimes in France and Italy (as two examples) was more frequent than appears to have been the case in Britain; without the delineated border created by an island's shore, the continent was subjected to far more cultural movements than probably occurred in Britain, and with this, each successive wave washed over the last. If anything, Britain was probably more conservative than its neighbours, as it mostly remains today.

Historians are reassessing the various sources for British history in the Dark Ages all the time, and new theories and rebuttals occur frequently. Archaeologist Ken Dark has even proposed a radical yet believable scenario of Romano-British continuity within Dark Ages Britain, thereby going against almost all of the traditional viewpoints. Another great example of this is a modern suggestion that the early Scottish kingdom of Dal Riata was not actually founded by Irish warriors settling in the area in or around the year 500. This had been the commonly accepted history since the days of Bede at least (and he wrote way back in the eighth century). However, recent analysis of the material culture gathered by archaeologists does not show enough similarity between the personal belongings of the people in the area of Dal Riatan settlement and those of their presumed homelands in the northern part of Ireland. Instead, it may be possible that the Dal Riatans were a unique native people of the area, different from the Picts, Britons and (across the sea) Irish cultures around them. But for the sake of this book, I have kept the more traditional view of Irish immigration as the theory has not yet been fully fleshed out.

So, in short, there is not one reliable, unchallengeable source or series of sources for what was happening in Britain in the run up to, or even during, the decades in which Arthur is believed to have lived. But, by piecing together the various sources available, attempting to read between the lines, and by tying in the available archaeological evidence, it is possible to create our own sequence of events. The one thing to remember is that, most of the time, we cannot be absolutely sure what happened. And with that vote of confidence, on to the history we go…

Roman Britain's invention, rise and fall

Before approaching Arthur himself, it's useful to look at an overview of what had happened in Britain before his time; it helps explain why British history shaped itself as it did during the Dark Ages.

Britain was thrust into the historical limelight when Julius Caesar came to the island in 55 BC. Before Caesar, very few classical writers gave a second thought to the rather cold and rainy island on the very edge of the Roman Empire. The inhabitants of Britain at this time were a mixture of recent immigrants from mainland Europe and the peoples who inhabited the islands before them.

There was no national sentiment, and the concept of England, Scotland, Wales and Ireland simply did not exist – and wouldn't until several generations after the Arthurian era. There was no national infrastructure, and the Britons lived a rural lifestyle, owing loyalty and patronage to their tribal chieftains, who in turn offered protection and a sense of belonging. Kingdoms varied greatly in size – some the size of a modern British county, others the size of several counties – and power.

The Romans returned in AD 43, when an imperial invasion force was despatched across the Channel by the Emperor Claudius. The Roman conquest of Britain progressed with remarkably few set-backs – Bouddica's famous revolt was quickly crushed, as was that of Caracticus, and the mysterious Druids (presumed to have been an elite sect of British leaders, possibly assuming some religious duties too) were slaughtered in their sacred groves on Anglesey. These were really just teething problems, to be expected as the natives adjusted to a much improved way of life as the inhabitants of a Roman province; at least, that's how the Romans would have seen it. 'Romanisation' mixed subtlety with brute force – a blend of showing the natives the benefits of Roman trade, towns and social structure, backed up with legions of well-trained, well-led soldiers in case the gentle persuasion didn't work. By the reign of Hadrian in the early second century, the majority of lowland Britain was settling into life as a Roman colony, and the rowdier, generally untamed tribes of Wales and Scotland were contained in their homelands. Rule from Rome allowed trade with Europe and the Mediterranean to prosper, and Britons quickly started to settle in urban communities around the key Roman military installations and centres of government. For the first time in history, the majority of Britain was governed as one province, rather than existing as a kaleidoscope of smaller kingdoms.

As the new Roman towns began to flourish, and an infrastructure was put in place to allow lowland Britain to function as one political area rather than many for the first time ever, Britain was a rather untroubled outpost for the be-sandalled soldiers and officials of Rome. In the southern and western parts of the country, hundreds of villas were built by rich landowners; some villas were the rural residences of these rich civilians, others were little more than glorified farms, but both were indicative of a blossoming economy and the continued Romanisation of lowland Britain. It seems that the Romans even allowed a number of British nobles to retain their social status. Close to the borders of Roman Britain, these nobles may have ruled as warlords sheltering the civilized areas beyond against external threat, whereas those who lived in Roman towns would have held posts in local government. Christianity arrived in Britain and the Empire officially became Christian during the reign of Constantine; it is recorded that three British bishops attended a council at Arles in 314. Even so, pagan worship still continued.

As mentioned earlier, in the North and modern day Scotland, and in the highland areas of western Britain, the Romans were less successful; the tribes in these areas appear to have had less sophisticated societies than in the continentally-influenced south, and adapted less readily to the lifestyle created by the Roman Empire. Equally importantly, the difficult terrain of northern and western uplands made military success less straightforward for the Roman army. Most areas eventually came under the influence of the Empire, but the north of modern Scotland was never fully assimilated or conquered by Rome, and neither was Ireland; this would become a problem for Roman Britain in the long run.

Just how 'Romanised' Britain ever became would have largely depended upon whom you were asking. A first century British farmer who lived on the bank of the River Thames would have been greatly affected by the development of Roman London and the roads and villas in the area. His great-grandchildren would have lived happily in the city, probably using a mixture of Latin and British speech, and considering themselves to all intents and purposes 'Roman'. On the other hand, a British shepherd living in the Welsh hills would probably have noticed little change in his life apart from the occasional sighting of a Roman patrol, and throughout the Roman period it is likely that the shepherd's descendants would have lived a relatively un-Romanised life.

As Roman Britain flourished, so it became a target for tribes outside the direct rule of Rome. The larger towns were fairly safe from raids – they were usually well garrisoned by the army – but the rich farmland and bustling small towns must have looked easy pickings, as the Roman army could not hope to detect and repel every raiding force entering Britain. Pictish (unconquered tribes in modern day Scotland) and Irish raiders caused problems, and the Roman authorities built Hadrian's Wall in the second century (between modern Newcastle and Carlisle), the later and short-lived Antonine Wall (further north) and a series of coastal forts down the west coast in the late third century to defend against such raids. A number of British leaders even decided (with, we must presume, Roman permission) to refortify the hilltop forts first built by their ancestors; within the wooden and earthen walls of these forts, the local population could shelter in times of strife.

At some point in the third century, Roman Britain's stability was further threatened: Irish and Pictish raiding continued from the north and west, but now they were joined by newcomers on the south and east coasts. These new pirates were Saxon raiders from the continental mainland, who themselves had never been conquered by Rome. A series of forts were built along the eastern and southern coastline to counter this new threat, and were named The Saxon Shore after their would-be assailants. Despite this, raiding continued, and in 367 a so-called 'Barbarian Conspiracy' took place, where it appears that the Irish, Picts and Saxons colluded to overpower the imperial defences through a series of pre-planned attacks. Two important Roman military leaders were killed and Britain was temporarily plunged into chaos before reinforcements arrived from the continental mainland. A further period of refortification occurred after this, and by the late fourth century, many Roman towns had their own city walls (remnants can still be seen standing today in cities such as York and Chichester).

From this point in history onward, the Saxons appear frequently as a main threat to Roman Britain and its post-imperial successors, but who exactly were these Saxons? Many different histories of this period suggest that there were three 'Saxon' tribes – the Angles, the Jutes and the Saxons themselves. Traditionally, the Angles were said to have landed in the North and in East Anglia (hence the name of this area of the island), the Jutes in Kent, and the Saxons along the south coast, spreading rapidly to the Thames Valley. In actual fact, these three tribes would have been just a few of the diverse cultural groups and clans who arrived in Britain:

Franks, Danes and many other Germanic peoples travelled in their longboats from their homelands in the north-west of Europe.

In addition to arriving on British shores as raiders and pirates, Saxon people also arrived at the request of the imperial government. Military policy changed in the later empire, facilitating an influx of non-Roman warriors to be employed on a large scale as mercenary soldiers. Drawn from the unconquered lands surrounding the huge empire, this new style of Roman army included many Saxons, and archaeological finds show that a large number served in Britain. As an example of this, the two high ranking Roman leaders who were slain in the Barbarian Conspiracy were named Fullofaudes and Nectaridus, which are both Germanic names.

The third and fourth centuries saw a gradual decline in the wealth and prosperity of Roman Britain; at certain times during this period, the entire empire was politically and economically fraught, and Britain fared little better or worse than the rest of Rome's continental possessions. On two occasions, Britain became separated from the rest of the Empire in political revolts in the late third century; throughout the later empire, many different military and political leaders were appointed 'Emperor', usurping their opponents and making claim to their own, independent empires. At one point, seven individuals all claimed to be Emperor at the same time. This combined with a breakaway religious movement that had originated in Britain, gained the province a reputation for unrest.

In 383, another disaffected general decided to rebel. His name was Magnus Maximus, and he was based in Britain; many British and, later, Welsh royal houses claimed descent from him, and he features in later Welsh folklore as Macsen Wledig, so it is highly likely that he was a popular man in the province. Despite such fond memories, Magnus Maximus depleted Britain of a considerable part of its garrison, and marched to stake a claim on the continental mainland, leaving much of Britain woefully under-defended by Roman troops. Magnus Maximus would not have intended to conquer the whole of the Roman Empire, which stretched over vast tracts of mainland Europe; instead, he probably wished to carve out his own empire within the Empire, perhaps consisting of Britain and the provinces in what are now modern France and Spain. His army defeated that of the Emperor Gratian, and Magnus did indeed hold sway over the western side of the Empire until his death in 388.

During Magnus' continental campaigning, Pictish, Irish and Saxon raiding probably continued in Britain; as an experienced general (experienced enough to defeat other Roman armies in battle, at the very least), Magnus would have made some arrangements for Britain to be defended in his absence. If he had not done so, Magnus might have quickly found himself in a situation where he was faced by rival Romans to the east and disgruntled Britons to the west. Evidence suggests that he undertook campaigns against the Picts before setting off on his European adventure, to warn them off further attacks whilst his main army was away. Yet the most probable source of replacement for the army from Britain he took with him were hired mercenaries. Magnus Maximus probably invited more Saxons in to defend Britain on his behalf; as explained above, later imperial policy favoured the employment of tribal warriors *en masse*, paid from imperial coffers to defend against other less friendly tribes. It also seems likely that Magnus made arrangements for some of the less Romanised, more warlike northern and western British nobles to defend their own island; these warlords would have been the founding rulers of the later, post-Roman British dynasties, and this would perhaps explain his popularity in Welsh and British folklore (and the reason why so many British and, later, Welsh royal lines traced their lineage back to Magnus Maximus himself). One of the British warlords employed in this way may well have been Cunedda, who moved with his warriors from the Edinburgh region to defend the coast of north-west Wales from Irish incursions. The departing Roman general may also have established another such warlord in southern Scotland, and perhaps even an Irish warband in south-west Wales, to defend the area from less friendly Irishmen.

Nevertheless, marching to Europe with the bulk of his field army must have left much of Magnus' Britain exposed to further raiding; tribal warriors were obviously of use, but alongside Magnus Maximus' departing legions also disappeared their military infrastructure and province-wide defence strategies. Even so, during Magnus' period of rule on the continental mainland, and beyond his death right up until the years 396–398, no recorded imperial re-garrisoning of Britain took place, so his policies must have worked fairly well. One of the units that Magnus had marched into Europe with, which had previously been stationed in Caernarvon, was later recorded as serving in the Balkans, so it does not appear that there was ever any need to return the original units who had been garrisoned there back to Britain.

When imperial intervention did occur again at these later dates, it was overseen by the talented general Stilicho (himself a Vandal serving the Roman authorities). He launched attacks on the Picts, Irish and Saxons who had raided and started to gain footholds in Britain. Stilicho was an experienced warlord, which was not surprising: across the Empire, as well as having to contend with rebel generals and usurping emperors, the armies of Rome were fighting against barbarian hordes such as the Goths, Vandals, Huns and more Saxons. Even those two most politely named barbarian tribes – the Alans and Franks – were causing problems. The serious threat caused by these marauding tribes saw the withdrawal of imperial troops from Britain once again in 401, heading off to fight in Italy. Given the rapid redeployment of British-based Roman soldiers, it has been proposed that the static defences of Hadrian's Wall and the coastal forts along the western, southern and eastern coasts were depleted at the expense of keeping a highly mobile field army ready to travel to military hot spots (led by a general entitled the Count of the Britons). This field army, consisting of infantry and cavalry units, probably numbered in the region of 6,000 men.

The next decade was to be one of the most important in the history of Roman Britain, yet we know so little of the events today. It appears that the gradual decline of the economy continued, probably accelerated by the uncertainty surrounding the defence of Britain. And then, in 406 and 407, a succession of three new rebelling, would-be emperors thrived in Britain. Their names were Marcus, Gratian and Constantine (recognised as Emperor Constantine III). Campaigning on the continental mainland, each of the three must have depleted the army of Britain even further, and Constantine probably led most of them to a premature and bloody death fighting in France and Spain: he was executed by imperial troops loyal to the Emperor Honorius in 411.

During this time, as the three usurpers each struggled and attempted to gain a foothold in Europe, it appears that the Britons threw out the administrators of Roman government from the island, and then set about defeating the Pictish, Irish and Saxon raiders who beset their towns. At least, that's what a Greek historian named Zosimus recorded not long after the event. Without further details (and there are precious few solid facts when it comes to the history of Britain at this time), we can speculate that a majority of high-ranking Britons loyal to the true Emperor, Honorius, expelled Constantine's governors. Or perhaps, sensing that the Empire was on its knees, a group of British nationalists decided that it was time to break away from Rome and go it alone, defending themselves with British warriors, Saxon and Irish mercenaries installed by Magnus Maximus. It may even have been that Constantine or another of the usurpers ejected those officials who supported Honorius, and set his own cronies up in their posts. We simply no longer know what happened, but in effect, Britain had finally become independent once more by the year 410, and was setting about defending itself from all comers. Honorius even wrote to the local councils of Britain, telling them to look after their own defences from now on. Why he wrote to them rather than the military commanders or head of civil administration is not known; perhaps the breakaway Britons had reverted to regionalised government based on old tribal divisions, or perhaps it was the local leaders who had expelled the overall governing authorities. But what Honorius did make clear was that the Britons were not to expect any immediate help, as they had in the aftermath of the earlier British-based usurpers' defeats.

Independent Britain

So Britain was by itself, separate from Roman rule, and alone again on the edge of a failing Empire. The Britons did not wake up one day to discover that the Romans had suddenly left. It had been a gradual wind down in the previous decades (perhaps even centuries), and it even seems as though the Britons elected to break away from the Empire themselves – a move others had tried before and failed in their attempts.

Yet despite their new-found independence, the Britons did not revert back to their pre-Roman lifestyle the minute the Romans had gone, daubing themselves in blue woad war paint or dashing around in chariots. The complex relationship between Rome and Britain had developed since Julius Caesar's first contact in the first century BC, and many urban Britons would have had a long line of ancestors brought up in a Romano-British tradition. Technically, free male Britons had been allowed to call themselves imperial citizens from the early third century onwards – they were equal to any other citizen of the Roman Empire after this date.

But in that typically British way which still persists to this day in certain regions, not all Britons would have considered themselves to have belonged to anything other than their old tribal name. Remember the British farmer and shepherd used as examples of the degree of Romanisation earlier in this chapter? The extent to which Roman rule affected the lifestyle of the Britons depended greatly upon their geographical location. At a basic level, those who lived close to Roman towns and forts would have probably considered themselves to be more 'Roman' than 'British'; those who lived in isolation probably felt the reverse. So, despite throwing out the officials of Roman government, some of the Britons would still have considered themselves to some extent to be Roman – perhaps just 'independent' Roman. Other Britons, those living on the fringes of the Romanised world, may never have really considered themselves Roman anyway, and could well have seen Britain's independence as the ideal stepping stone to reasserting their own self-implemented rule. As it was to turn out, in one of those cruel twists that history sometimes throws up, the more Romanised areas were the first to fall under the influence of foreign invaders, and later British culture developed from the areas that had been traditionally less influenced by Roman rule. In 410, though, the upper hand was still with the Britons rather than any foreign invaders, and the Britons continued to rule their lands retaining Roman methods of organisation and culture.

How the Britons governed themselves in the early years of independence is difficult to judge: there is virtually no surviving evidence to help us. Historians usually assume that a centralised form of government continued, differing from earlier Roman rule only in that the Britons governed themselves in isolation from the rest of the Empire, and without answering to a non-British emperor. In this respect, whoever ruled independent, post-Roman Britain was effectively an emperor on a micro-scale, governing the regions of Britain rather than provinces across Europe. It may even be that Britain had become decentralised – Honorius' letter to the Britons in 410 might hint at this – and that a series of kingdoms sprang up immediately when Britain threw Roman rule out. In all probability, centralised government did continue (as the evidence that follows suggests), but it is also likely that a few rogue leaders (those who had never become fully Romanised) broke away to form their own small kingdoms on the fringes of Britain's post-Roman ruler. We do not know who ruled post-Roman Britain in the early fifth century, but one name survives from folklore: Vortigern.

The name Vortigern roughly translates as 'High King', and given that Vortigern makes appearances as the ruler of the whole of the formerly Roman province in traditional British history throughout most of the fifth century, it is quite possible that this was an honorific title rather than a personal name. Geoffrey of Monmouth picked up on Vortigern's name and in his *History*, the medieval writer outlined the traditional tale of Vortigern and early post-Roman Britain, assuming him to be one man rather than a composite of many. Geoffrey's tale is outlined in Chapter Three, and Vortigern's role in British history is examined later in this chapter. Whether Vortigern was one man or several, and whether he really existed or not, someone appears to have governed the province as a whole, basing their rule on Roman principles.

Aside from the traditional British and, later, Welsh memories of their history in this period, we have precious little information to assess. The split from Roman rule took Britain outside the immediate sphere of Roman interest – their historians had their time fully booked trying to record the violent comings and goings in the provinces still governed by Rome (Rome was sacked in 410 by the Visigoths, and a period of great chaos both preceded and followed this). Conflict between various claimants of emperorship, combined with a flagging economy and the establishment of formerly 'barbaric' tribes as formidable political entities were keeping the historians' quills wet and ink pots empty.

Despite the Roman view of Britain as a mere side show, a few mentions were made of the rogue island. Two accounts of visits by St Germanus exist, one in 428–9 and one in 445–6. Although the records of his visit were mostly concerned with ecclesiastical issues, enough was written to pinpoint some political aspects of life in Britain. Firstly, Germanus arrived on his first visit to combat the rise of a Christian splinter group known as the Pelagians. Throughout the later Empire, although Christianity was the official religion of Rome, various forms existed, and pagan cults were even still tolerated. Despite this, the Pelagians must have been viewed with some concern for Germanus to be despatched. It is possible that the Pelagians were influential in Britain's initial break away from the Empire, perhaps indicating that they were a British nationalist group, although this may be overplaying the movements' real motive, which really might have been as simple as being a different way of worshipping. We simply no longer know. Most importantly, Germanus' arrival indicates that there were still links between Britain and the continent, and that continental Roman church officials maintained an active interest in Britain after it became independent. Germanus' group appear to have travelled freely in Britain, and at this time (the 420s), Britain appears to have been fairly peaceful and the Britons were governing themselves in a state of order. If they had not been, we can be fairly sure that Germanus' biographer would have made a sly dig at the incompetent Britons. Town life continued as before, and Germanus healed the daughter of an official who claimed some form of imperial power; this again suggests that the Britons were governing themselves using an earlier Roman model, at least in the area that Germanus visited. In fact, we can be fairly sure of the region visited by the saint on his first visit; he made a pilgrimage to *Verulamium* (St Albans), just north of modern London. The South-East was highly Romanised in the days of the Empire, and the evidence of Germanus' visit suggests that it still was at this time. We cannot really be sure if the rest of former Roman Britain was faring so well; it seems reasonable to assume that inland areas such as that visited by the saint were pretty safe from marauding pirates, but that the fringes of the island – both along coasts and further to the north around Hadrian's Wall – were less peaceful. These borderlands must have acted as a buffer between 'civilization' and 'barbarity', and were probably overseen on a local basis by warlords and their warrior bands. This theory fits adequately with what we know of Magnus Maximus' defence policy in the late fourth century. Cunedda (who Magnus probably relocated to an area of modern north Wales from modern southern Scotland) and his successors would have operated in this buffer role, as may have a leader called Coel Hen along Hadrian's Wall. Coel Hen is better remembered as the Old King Cole of nursery rhyme fame, but appears to have been a powerful leader in northern Britain in the first decades of the fifth century; many later northern British dynasties were to claim descent from him.

Germanus himself encountered raiders on his first visit. We cannot be sure exactly where, but away from the peaceful scenes of town life, the saint led the Britons to a victory over Saxons and Pictish raiders. This victory, known as the Alleluia Battle, took place in a valley, where Germanus encouraged the Britons to ambush their enemies, all rising at once to shout 'Alleluia!' three times in unison, the sound of which startled the pagan Saxons and Picts into flight. Welsh tradition identifies the battle as having taken place near Mold in Wales, although a valley in the Chiltern Hills, closer to St Albans, is just as likely. The way in which the battle was won is almost certainly hagiographic interpretation, but it was not unknown for holy men to accompany warriors into battle (several thousand British monks were supposedly slaughtered at the later Battle of Chester in 616). Other raids must also have taken place, such as that remembered in the story of St Patrick, who was originally a Briton plucked away into Irish slavery at the age of sixteen. But on the whole, it seems as though the Britons were adequately fending for themselves.

Despite the seemingly 'business as usual' message created by the tale of Germanus (such as town life and government continuing as before, and the repulsion of raiders by the Britons), archaeological evidence suggests that not everything was quite right. Near the start of the fifth century, Britain's own pottery industry fizzled out, and during the 420s, coinage appears to have ceased to be in common usage (the last coins to arrive in Britain in any numbers had come in 402). The declining economy of the previous centuries seems to have finally ground to a halt at this time. Even so, municipal authorities were still functioning – here archaeology backs up the tale of St Germanus – as one of the main streets in Roman Lincoln was still being resurfaced well into the fifth century, the forum at Cirencester appears to have continued to be used, and phases of rebuilding were undertaken in St Albans and Wroxeter. One area of St Albans even seems to have had a new water pipe set down in the fifth century.

During the first couple of decades of the fifth century, it was not only St Germanus who crossed the Channel on imperial business. Some sources suggest that the Roman army, perhaps accompanied by government officials, returned once or more in the 410s and 420s. We do not know the reasons why; it could have been to assess the potential for the return of Roman rule. They might possibly even have returned as envoys of peace, offering an alliance between the independent Britons and the crumbling Roman Empire: the Britons seem to have been succeeding in what the rest of the Empire couldn't do, namely fighting off unfriendly invading tribes. Or perhaps they were begged to return by a group of pro-Roman officials; such pleas certainly took place in the fifth century. A reference in *The Anglo-Saxon Chronicle* for 418, which records the Romans gathering together and hiding their hoards of gold, may be a reference to such a visit, where the Roman government attempted to take with them anything of value on a final visit. Whatever the motive for the reappearance of Roman representatives, no re-integration into the Empire took place, and the Britons continued to stand independently.

By the time of St Germanus' visit in the 440s, Britain appears to have been in a state of deterioration. Up until this point, where it was noted that the saint met with an official not referred to by a Roman title but simply as a leading man of the region, most of Britain was probably still centrally governed. Some fringe areas may have seen the formation of small kingdoms, less Romanised, and employed to protect the borderlands against enemies, but, in general, Britain seemed to be managing no worse than it had under late Roman rule. That was all about to change. Dramatically.

The Saxon Wars

We will never really know if Vortigern, made famous for his incompetence in later Welsh folklore and Geoffrey of Monmouth's vastly influential *History*, was really just one man or whether the name was a title given to the centralised ruler of Britain in the early post-Roman years. What we do know is that Vortigern (or the Vortigerns, if a title it were) was blamed as the catalyst of the downfall of his nation. How true the story is we cannot be sure, but within the story told by Geoffrey of Monmouth, some historical facts probably do shine through.

The story so often told about Vortigern, how much of which was true we cannot now know, is as follows:

The armies of the Britons were no match for the marauding Picts and Irish, who raided deep into the wealthy farmlands of sub-Roman Britain. The Britons pleaded with the Roman rulers on the continent for aid, but were told to look after themselves. In desperation, the British leader Vortigern decided to fight fire with fire – he hired Saxon mercenaries from their European homelands, asking them to rid Britain of its marauding nightmare, in return for fertile land. By doing this, Vortigern was simply following a precedent set by the Roman emperors, who also employed mercenary warriors to fight for them or to live in buffer zones between peaceful Roman subjects and howling, pagan barbarian tribes.

Vortigern employed the Saxon king Hengist and his brother Horsa, who arrived with three boatloads of warriors, settling in Kent and taking on adversaries across the land (Picts and Irish – they left their British employers alone, of course). This might have happened in the 420s, or perhaps in the 440s, depending upon how the dates have been calculated. Everything went well to begin with – the Saxons were great warriors and despatched many raiding warbands to early graves with ease. Hengist sent word back to his homeland and more warriors arrived – single-handedly, the Saxons ended the Irish and Pictish threat while the Britons cowered behind the walls of their towns. As more Saxons (accompanied by two other tribes – the Jutes and Angles) arrived, the more land they needed; it's possible that plague also struck Britain at this time, affecting the town-dwelling Britons more than their rustic Saxon allies, but placing even more emphasis on the importance of owning food-producing land. Vortigern refused the Saxons more land; he needed it for his own people, and was in all probability a bit taken aback by the number of Saxons who had flooded into Britain.

Enough was enough for the Saxons. They needed more land and, being of coarse warrior stock, decided they would take it by force. A full scale rebellion took place in 449 (or perhaps even as early as 429, depending upon different interpretations of how to read the dates given in the original sources), and the Saxons coped far better than Vortigern's Britons. The Britons called a truce to discuss terms of peace, and the Saxon leaders smuggled weapons into this meeting, slaughtering the cream of British nobility in an event to be remembered as 'the Night of the Long Knives'. A cruel streak in Hengist's nature allowed Vortigern's life to be spared – he was sent back to the Britons, whom he lived among in disgrace, finally dying in a fire in his palace, a broken man.

In the wake of the Night of the Long Knives, Hengist and Horsa swept across the lowlands, and joined with other Saxon leaders to push the Britons back into the highlands of Wales, the South-West, and the hills of Cumbria (some even fled to mainland Europe, carving out their own kingdom in modern day Brittany). Any Britons who did not flee were slain by Saxon warriors or taken as slaves, and all the time, more Saxon families arrived from mainland Europe. British place names, language and customs disappeared from lowland Britain, and the remaining Britons soon forgot their Roman heritage and took on older Celtic customs which had never been forgotten in the hills of Wales and Cumbria.

And that, for the moment, is where we shall leave the traditional history.

Modern studies have shown that the final part of this story does not appear to be true – most Britons probably continued to live in their homelands under Saxon rule, and archaeological examples of genocide are few and far between. Throughout this chapter, references are made to 'the Saxon kingdoms formed', or to how 'the British lost control' of certain areas. It used to be imagined that when a region became, for example, 'Saxon', the Britons (or Irish or Picts) who had happily lived there beforehand were wiped out or fled elsewhere. This idea was supported by the startling revelations of early writers like Gildas, who gave the impression that you couldn't walk more than a couple of yards without tripping over yet another beheaded Briton. Gripping stuff though this may have been, it now seems likely that it simply wasn't true. Sure, some warlords may have decided to slaughter their newly conquered people out of hand: Saxon history remembers the seventh century British warlord Cadwallon in such a way, although these sources were understandably biased. We even have the occasional mention of similar incidents in documents such as *The Anglo-Saxon Chronicle*, which records that the Saxon warlord Aelle slaughtered all of the Britons he found inside an old shore fort at Pevensey in 491. But the very fact that such scandals were mentioned at all suggests that they were the exceptions. In all probability, the change from 'Briton' to 'Saxon' rule probably affected only the nobility – the ruling dynasty and the tier of nobles immediately surrounding them. Modern genetic tests (of both DNA and tooth structure) support the idea that the population of Britain was, before the modern era, mostly a constant. The flight of British nobles to modern Brittany around this time also suggests that conquest displaced only the upper echelons of society, rather than the population at large. This opens up the potentially confusing situation where British warriors could fight for the Saxon king who held sway over their homelands, against a rival British or Saxon king, and vice versa. The whole subject of cultural identity must have been confusing at times, and it seems sensible to imagine that later Anglo-Saxon and Welsh culture was a diluted mix of earlier Saxon and British ideals.

How much of the 'traditional' history is true, and how much is pure legend we do not now know. The Saxon revolt may have taken place in a small geographical area, or it may have been widespread, depending on exactly how far Vortigern's influence spread. It seems as though Vortigern ruled the majority of the former Roman province, although if Britain fragmented into smaller kingdoms earlier than is widely accepted, his story may only tell of the downfall of one kingdom. Having said this, the weight of opinion does suggest that Vortigern was at the head of the whole nation, and as such, the story remembering his life probably contains snippets of the truth behind the Britons' fall from power in their own country.

Before the Saxons arrived as hired spearmen, whether by Vortigern's invite or not, at least some of the Britons realised that they needed help in repelling the Irish and Pictish raiders. But instead of turning to other mercenaries, Gildas tells us that the Britons launched an appeal for help to the Roman warlord Aëtius in 446. He vividly named this event 'the Groans of the Britons'. This plea fell on deaf ears, and it seems that at least some British leaders invited Saxon mercenaries to fight on their behalf. At some point, seemingly soon after they arrived, a number of the Saxon warlords staged a coup against their British employers, taking land for themselves and their warriors.

Regardless of how widespread the revolt by Saxon mercenaries was, British leaders had to contend with incursions from the Picts in the North, the Irish to the West and the Saxons along the southern and eastern coasts. The onslaught of attacks, primarily that by the Saxons, appears to have caused Vortigern's rule to become displaced. This action probably saw a power struggle flare up between the other British leaders, and any unity probably disappeared as they clambered over each other to take each other's holdings.

At some point in the fifth century, it also appears that a number of warlords broke away from centralised rule and formed their own kingdoms. Different leaders probably formed their own kingdoms at different times, rather than one year signalling the end of centralised authority, and less Romanised areas may well have broken away early on in Britain's independence, although the downfall of a Vortigern-like leader may have acted as a catalyst. By the time of Gildas (in the sixth century), Britain was completely in the hands of these 'tyrants' (a term which was probably not as negatively suggestive as it is in modern usage). The backgrounds of these tyrants were probably quite varied – some may have been wealthy warriors who had been employed to hold the frontiers, other could have been rich landowners who took control away from central government using their own private armies. Certainly, in the eyes of Gildas, from the unification of Britain that his reference to a 'proud tyrant' (probably Vortigern) suggests, through the intervening hundred or so years to his time of writing, the central, dominant power of the Britons had fragmented into a handful of smaller, weaker kingdoms.

We do not know the names of all of the British kingdoms from this time, or where their borders were. It seems likely that many Roman cities would have been the founding sites for the new dynasties, and that the important civic figures within these cities took control. Cities such as London, Silchester, Chichester, Cirencester, Lincoln, Wroxeter, Chester, York and Carlisle may all have been the seats of kings. We know that the south-west tip of Britain, Devon and Cornwall, formed the kingdom of Dumnonia, and that several kingdoms sprang up in Wales, including Gwynedd in the North, and Gwent and Dyfed

('Demetia') in the South. The northern British kingdoms were fairly large, and were destined to survive for much longer than some of their southern counterparts: Rheged, Strathclyde, and Gododdin were to produce a fine collection of British folk tales in future centuries. Other northern kingdoms fared less well, the Pennines-based Elmet being swallowed by Saxon kingdoms, and Bernicia and Deira passing into Saxon hands at a relatively early date.

It may well be that the ineffectual rule of Vortigern (or of one particular Vortigern, if it were actually a title) created such divisions and the formation of kingdoms. Whatever the true cause, civil war flared up between the Britons, and they soon started to use Saxon mercenaries to fight their own British kinsmen. Saxon warlords could only benefit from such a role, and probably took firmer footholds in their own territory at this time; traces of Saxon enclaves in the Thames valley, parts of East Anglia and along the south coast can be seen from the mid-fifth century onwards. The continental *Gallic Chronicle* records that by 441, Britain was under the domination of the Saxons. Although this probably refers only to the southern areas that were directly in contact with the continental mainland (British areas which do show signs of Saxon growth at this time), the reference would appear to broadly tie in with the concept of the Saxon revolt and subsequent, temporary power they held. The date, if more reliable than those shown in native British sources, would suggest an earlier date for Saxon intervention than the traditional 449, possibly pushing us back to 429 or a date in the 430s or early 440s. It is even possible – probable even – that several such mercenary Saxon warlords were employed, and the differing dates may reflect rebellion by various bands in diverse areas. Nevertheless, Saxon warlords were making inroads into British territory.

Civil wars between the newly founded British kingdoms, combined with external pressures from the Irish, Picts and, to an ever increasing degree, the Saxons, probably caused Britain to descend to the edge of anarchy. Until this point in the mid-fifth century (possibly as early as the 420s and 430s, but more likely in the 440s and 450s), the Britons had managed to handle their own affairs, and keep independent Britain afloat.

Gildas' depiction of mid- to late fifth century Britain was of a corrupt, plague-ridden region spiralling into economic decline, with crumbling cities and land torn apart by war and famine. Plague is also sometimes suggested (the mid-sixth century saw the arrival of Yellow Plague in

Britain, but it is possible that earlier epidemics had spread from the continent). Yet the evidence uncovered by archaeological excavation in many areas suggests that things were not as bad as Gildas' apocalyptic description; it is unlikely that there were many instances of cities being entirely raised and permanently abandoned. Urban life does appear to have declined, but there are few suggestions that a mass abandonment of cities took place suddenly, with burning buildings and bodies in the streets Hollywood-style; rather that over the late fifth and sixth centuries, a gradual decline took place. In all probability, life continued for most people more or less as it had before, with violence and destruction only occurring during periods when ravaging armies passed close by.

Urban life certainly continued in cities as such St Albans, Silchester, London and Caerwent, amongst others, where evidence of ongoing occupation has been discovered. Wroxeter, in modern day Shropshire, even went through a phase of rebuilding, although admittedly the new timber buildings of the post-Roman period would not have looked so glorious as the masonry of Roman construction. Towards the end of the fifth century, towns were still the sites from which British kings ruled, and this may even be reflected in the name of at least one kingdom: Gwent appears to be a corruption of the Latin name for Caerwent: *Venta Silurum*. Town life may have been an enfeebled version of the urban centres that had flourished a couple of centuries before, and some of the cities may have felt distinctly like a ghost town, but it's still a far happier picture than Gildas portrayed.

Although mid- and late fifth century Britain was probably not as violent as once thought, wars were still fought, and the Britons were still at each other's and their external enemies' throats. It was in this dark hour that a saviour arrived. No, not Arthur, but Ambrosius Aurelianus (elsewhere called Aurelius Ambrosius), the son of the last Roman governors of Britain, who defeated the enemies of the Britons. In addition to Gildas' brief but influential reference to Ambrosius, who – curiously enough – the bitter Gildas definitely saw as one of history's good guys, we can again turn to the traditional view of British history to fill in the gaps:

Ambrosius reminded the Britons how to fight, and succeeded in pushing the Saxons back to the eastern side of Britain over the course of a military campaign, presumably in southern Britain. Ambrosius may also have been opposed by the son (or sons) of Vortigern, and defeated them, too. The Ambrosius and Vortigern family rivalry has often been seen as a civil war between pro- and anti-Roman factions within the British nobility, although in reality there is little evidence to support this.

As with the other traditional views shown in this chapter, we are no longer in a position to judge how much of the story is true, and how much was constructed from half-remembered names and dates. On the whole, Gildas appears to know something of the century before his own lifetime, and it is reasonable to believe that Ambrosius, a successor to some form of Roman authority, recovered British initiative for a while. This revival is usually roughly dated to 460–480, the dates of which don't quite add up if Ambrosius' mum and dad were Roman governors before 410, unless Ambrosius was in his sixties when he came to prominence. It seems more likely, however, that his parents were Romanised Britons holding some authority in the years of independent, post-Roman rule.

Ambrosius' leadership appears to have allowed the Britons to regain control of areas that had briefly fallen under the influence of Saxon warlords. The town life that is supposed to have rapidly decayed may well have reflowered, and the Britons – perhaps with a victory by Ambrosius over the Vortigern dynasty – concentrated their efforts on repelling foreign invaders instead of each other. Gildas, our main if potentially biased source, seems to believe that some good came of Ambrosius' deeds.

The Age of Arthur

And with Ambrosius arrives Arthur. Although some writers disagree, a general consensus agrees that the late fifth or early sixth centuries were the years in which Arthur would have lived, if indeed he ever did live at all. There are no solid references to him beyond the dates outlined in Chapter Four – frustratingly enough, this is the period of Dark Ages history that we have the least information on. His deeds were written down at a later date, and many of them were clearly fantastical.

The traditional story was thus:

Ambrosius was brilliantly supported by his talented cavalry leader. This commander's name was Arthur. When Ambrosius died, Arthur continued where his former commander left off, uniting the rest of the Britons and leading them to a series of twelve great victories against the Saxons, culminating with the famous victory at Mount Badon, dating to the decades around 500. Arthur was a Christian, and attributed his success against the pagan Saxons to his religion; on his shield, he carried the image of the Virgin Mary.

Victory at Mount Badon led to a generation of peace between the Britons and the Saxons. The Saxons licked their extensive wounds in East Anglia, Kent and other eastern coastal regions, while Arthur set about restoring now long-forgotten Roman virtues. Unfortunately his success led to jealousy amongst other British nobles, and he was eventually killed in civil war at the Battle of Camlann, often dated 542 (alternative dates do exist – Badon is sometimes recorded as being fought in 490 and Camlann in 515). Arthur may have been killed at Camlann by a British noble called Medraut, a relative of Arthur. With the death of their last great leader, the Britons capitulated to Saxon dominance.

It's a neat story, and plausibly explains how Roman Britain became Saxon England within the space of a couple of badly documented centuries. Unfortunately, this traditional history has hardly evolved from the work of the twelfth century writer Geoffrey of Monmouth. And Geoffrey's work also includes tales of dragons, giants and an alternative world placing ancient Britain at the centre of European high culture. Having noted this problem, a few glimpses of historical highlights do actually shine through, and it is possible that Geoffrey's *The History of the Kings of Britain* does include some true, factual episodes from the Arthurian period.

We do have the list of battles that Nennius claimed Arthur had fought – with the exception of Badon, none of these can be securely identified outside of Arthurian folklore. So what did happen in this 'Age of Arthur' that still makes us think that the great man might actually have existed?

To be honest, not a great deal. We have the dates from *The Welsh Annals* suggesting that Arthur's victory at Badon was fought in 518 and that he died in 539. Some scholars have questioned these dates, placing the events a decade or two earlier or later – as previously mentioned, another commonly cited date for Badon is 490. Neither of these dates can be reliably confirmed in any other sources, yet nor can they be proved false.

Most debate about the deeds of the historical Arthur focuses on the list of twelve battles given by Nennius in the ninth century, who claimed that Arthur was the victor in them all. We do not know if this was true, but many researchers have spent plenty of time attempting to identify where these battles may have taken place. The list of battles, with some of their possible sites (many other sites may once have had the same names but have now changed, making this an even more troublesome task), is as follows, although none of the suggestions can be safely confirmed:

Battles as named by Nennius	Other information	Possible locations
River Glein	*Nennius:* Situated in the East.	River Glen (Lincolnshire), River Glen (Northumbria), River Glen (Ayrshire), Llanidloes, The Glen (Tweedale).
River Dubglas	*Nennius:* Situated in the region of Linnuis; four battles were fought along this river.	River Douglas (several candidates, including at Loch Lomond and Ilchester), Dawlish. *Linnius:* Lincolnshire, Loch Lomond, Ilchester.
River Bassas		Baschurch (Shropshire), Basingwerk (near Newport), Dunnipace (Firth of Forth).
Cat Coed Celyddon	*Nennius:* Situated in the wood of Caledonia.	Southern Scotland, Ettrick Forest, Carlisle, Hadrian's Wall.
Fort Guinnion		Berwyn Mountains, Hadrian's Wall, Gala Water (Tweedale).
City of the Legion	*Nennius:* Fought in the city itself.	Caerleon, Chester, York, Lincoln, Dumbarton.
River Tribruit		Scottish lowlands, Northumbria.
Mount Agned	Some manuscripts replace this victory with one at Breguoin (or variants on that spelling).	Agned: Edinburgh, Maiden's Castle (Cheshire), Agners (France). Breguoin: High Rochester (Northumbria), Leitwardine (Herefordshire), Berwyn Mountains.
Mount Badon	*The Welsh Annals:* A battle that lasted three days and three nights. *Nennius:* Arthur slew 960 enemies. Linguistic note: 'Badon' pronounced 'Bathon' in original British speech.	Bath, Solsbury Hill (near Bath), The Breidden (near Welshpool), Buttington (near Welshpool), Bouden hill (Linlithgow), Badbury (five possible Badburys, all in the Midlands and South).

A few of these possible sites are expanded upon in Chapter Seven. With the exception of the possibility of the City of the Legion as Chester, where a recorded battle between the Britons and the Saxons took place in 616, we have no independent, reliable and dated confirmation for any of these battles. British sources do not help any further, and *The Anglo-Saxon Chronicle* sheds no light on Saxon defeats. Even with Chester, historians believe it to have taken place at too late a date for an Arthurian battle; we also have other sources about the battle at Chester which don't mention Arthur, and which confirm that it was a catastrophic British defeat.

Even assuming that Nennius' source material was accurate, we do not know for sure who Arthur's opponents at the twelve battles were – some commentators suggest that all were waged against the Saxons, others include Britons, Irish and Picts among his enemies. Tradition suggests that by Arthur's time, the Irish and Pictish threat had disappeared temporarily (due to the Saxons' efforts as hired mercenaries), and that Arthur himself may have united the Britons. This would leave the Saxons as the main enemy of the British warlord, in a campaign that would typify the warfare and politics of lowland Britain for the next few centuries.

There is so little in the way of worthy accounts of this period's history, from the view of the Britons, Saxons, Picts or Irish, that we can say little more. Perhaps this is why Arthur's reputation has been able to flourish so much in the intervening centuries, as people have been able to invent their own history. This truly is very sparse evidence from which to reconstruct any history of the late fifth and early sixth centuries.

The Battle of Badon is important in both the study of Arthur and of Dark Ages history. The reason for its importance is twofold: Gildas describes the battle independently of Arthurian legend, lending more credence to its reality, and of all of the British victories we know of, attributed to Arthur or anyone else, it is generally considered to have had the most widely felt impact. Taking place a decade or two either side of 500, and probably having been fought in the year of Gildas' birth, Badon is mentioned by the cleric as the peak of the Ambrosius-inspired British fight back against Saxon invaders. Gildas describes it as pretty much the last action fought in this war of repulsion (not necessarily the last, but probably the final significant encounter), and tells us that the peace it brought about lasted up to his time of writing, forty-four years after the battle. But Gildas does not mention Arthur at all. If it were not for *The Welsh Annals* and Nennius, there would be no reason to connect Badon with Arthur, but both of these sources agree that Arthur himself was Badon's victor. Nennius tells us that Arthur killed 960 enemies, and the *Annals* inform us that the battle lasted three days and three nights. There is no confirmation of either of these statements in other sources, but Chapter Seven discusses some of the possible scenarios surrounding the Battle of Badon in more detail.

Whoever really did win at Badon, and whether it was so great a victory as is now remembered, or just one of a series of similar battles, it appears to have had an effect as Gildas described. It would seem that the Saxon threat that had existed in the decades since the revolt and establishment of Saxon enclaves had been overcome, and for the moment was nothing more than a temporary threat to the Britons. Archaeological data detects the possibility of Saxon migration away from Britain back to their original homelands and the ninth century writer Rudolf of Fulda gave an account of Saxons arriving back home from Britain around 530. Areas such as the Thames Valley, which seem to have been under Saxon dominance throughout much of the fifth century, suddenly appear to have passed back into British hands. Whether this advantage was widespread across the country or whether it only really affected the South-East, we cannot be sure; as with so many of the partial facts that have been passed down to us, there is no indication of how widespread the outcome of such actions were. But it may be that the British campaign culminating in victory at Badon saw a renaissance in British power, and that the previous Saxon footholds were pushed right back. If Arthur was indeed the hero of Badon, the importance of his victory goes some way to explaining why his name has been remembered so vividly in British folklore.

Yet all good things must come to an end, even in history, and British tradition remembers that Arthur's golden era ended in mortal combat at Camlann. We have no real evidence to support *The Welsh Annals*' date for the Battle of Camlann, other than that recorded in Celtic folklore. This is perhaps surprising given the obsession of the Britons and Welsh with reciting lengthy laments about the eventual defeat of their leaders – Cynddylan, Urien, the warriors of *The Gododdin* and even the later medieval prince Llywelyn the Last stand among this list of worthies. The site of Camlann has been much debated, and several possibilities are advanced in Chapter Seven; Birdoswald fort on Hadrian's Wall, and the Camlan Valley in North Wales are commonly cited as possible locations. Of equal interest to the location is the tradition that Medraut (whose name became Modred in legend) fought against Arthur, where as the *Annals* only note that Arthur and Medraut both fell at the battle. It may be that more information, perhaps a now forgotten lament, did exist about Camlann, but without it we can say little more – it is not even possible to judge where the battle really took place, if indeed it ever did take place. However, if Arthur did once live and breathe, his death must have occurred at some point, and it may well be that the great warrior's career was ended in a bloody, hacking finale at a place known as Camlann in 539 or 515.

Whether Arthur's campaigns – fictional or real – were as significant as tradition suggests, and whether they were concentrated in one geographical area or across the country, he was not the only warlord making inroads in the late fifth and early sixth centuries. A number of Saxon warlords were carving out small footings for themselves – either before, during, or shortly after the Badon campaign. Among their number were Aelle, who landed in Sussex in the late fifth century, and Cerdic who landed in Hampshire around the same time. Both posed significant military threats to the southern Britons, and both seem to have registered important military victories as soon as they arrived, immediately carving out their own kingdoms. In the North, it seems that the Britons fared better against foreign invasion, although the Irish ousted Pictish rivals from the south-west region of modern Scotland, sowing the seeds of dominance in the centuries to come. It is difficult to know how the possible campaigns of Arthur, and before him Ambrosius, affected these foreign warlords or indeed their native British rivals and allies. We no longer have any means of judging whether Arthur and Ambrosius' influence spread far across Britain, or whether their effect was fairly minimal – the documents that might have told us simply no longer exist, if indeed they ever did.

Some accounts of Arthur suggest that his battles may have been fought on the continental mainland; we know of other British leaders fighting there in the late fifth and early sixth centuries, so it is possible. Around about this time – perhaps as a direct result of the Saxon revolt, or perhaps simply as rival British or Saxon warlords conquered their lands – some Britons fled to western France. In Brittany (rather as the modern name suggests), the Britons carved out their own kingdom and fought off the rising power of the Franks, and also that of the Visigoths and continental Saxons. It is possible that some or all of Arthur's campaigns were fought on this new front, as there must have been a number of strong military victories as the Britons established their hold on the land. More consideration to a possible Breton candidate is given in Chapter Seven.

A lot of the gaps in Arthur's possible reign could be filled in if we knew even the slightest biographical detail about him. Beyond the fact that he led the Britons (or some them, at least), and that he seems to have fought in and won a series of battles, we really have very little to go on. And that's assuming, of course, that he ever existed. For more on this tricky little stumbling block, take a look at Chapter Seven.

The fall of the Britons and the rise of the Saxons

The death of our potential Arthur and the generation of peace that followed eventually gave way in the mid-sixth century to renewed Saxon aggression. After Arthur's death, Nennius tells us that the Saxons sent for reinforcements and new kings from Germany, and finally ruled over Britain. Pushing out of their eastern land holdings with ferocious power, Saxon kings won strategically important victories against the Britons at places such as Bedford (571), Dyrham (577), Catterick (600) and Chester (616), and held most of the fertile lowland areas of modern England by the middle of the seventh century. The Saxons even found time to fight amongst themselves. A few British leaders found some success against the Saxons, the most famous being Urien of Rheged in northern England in the late sixth century, and Cadwallon of Gywnedd in the mid-seventh century. But such iconic British leaders were few and far between.

Successes were a rarity, and the early seventh century saw the rapid decline of the Britons; any political unity the British leaders had seems to have fractured at this point, and their ability to repel Saxon and other incursions seems to have waned. This period, which witnessed the decline of British political power, also saw gradual formation of seven major Anglo-Saxon kingdoms in lowland England, based around their earlier holdings: Kent, Sussex, Wessex, Mercia, Northumbria, Essex and East Anglia.

The British kingdoms that had formed in the fifth century rapidly began to lose their land to the rising new Saxon kingdoms. Evidence from the seventh and eighth centuries suggest a move away from Romanised British kingdoms to a heroic culture later recognised as 'Celtic'. Important warlords no longer based themselves in towns, but in fortified hilltop or rural residences, and at this late date (much later than many historians gave credit for), urban life appears to have been pretty thoroughly replaced with a solely rural lifestyle. The traditional viewpoint is that life in the old Roman towns ended in the fifth century, but excavations are increasingly suggesting this to be rare. Having said that, plague arrived in Britain in the 540s, probably not for the first time (sometimes the year of Camlann is described as a plague year), and this may have contributed to the decline of town life.

The British defeat at Dyrham in 577 cut the South-West off from the Midlands and North, and the defeat at Chester in 616 split the Midlands and Wales from the northern British kings. Whether the Britons' decline was as a result of a series of crushing military defeats, whether the defeats came about as the result of economic decline, or whether the fall of a historical Arthur's united kingdom had pushed the Britons back into civil war from which recovery would be near impossible, the driving force in political power swiftly shifted to the Saxon kingdoms. The kings or tyrants listed by Gildas as his sixth century contemporaries are made to sound corrupt, arrogant and ineffectual; Gildas may well have had his own motives in describing his British kings in such a way, but such personal attributes would only have fuelled the Britons' collapse. Yet it should be recognised that the two centuries between 400 and 600 had seen the post-Roman British in control of the majority of Britain, which although no mean feat (many other post-Roman kingdoms were more short-lived), has often been overlooked by historians.

The very success of British resistance, whether led by Arthur, Ambrosius, or some other equally plucky or bloodthirsty warriors, ultimately contributed to the downfall of their beloved culture. By severely limiting Saxon advances for so long, the enclaves carved out by the earliest Saxon settlers became thoroughly 'Saxonised' (or, if you prefer, 'Anglicised'), creating a stronger Saxon cultural presence than had been the case with barbarian invasions on the continental mainland. There, invasions tended to wash over the towns and countryside quite rapidly, mixing earlier Roman culture with a diluted form of Frankish, Gothic and many, many other societies. It is in the Saxon areas of Britain that their foreign culture arrived, was geographically restricted and took root. The majority of Saxon tribes who arrived in Britain had little contact with the Roman world before arriving in Britain, and would have been all the more 'different' for it. The Franks and Goths who settled in modern France, Spain and other parts of mainland Europe were more familiar with Roman society, and could adapt to what they encountered. Consequently much of Roman Britain was to irretrievably become Saxon England. Over time, contact and exchange between the Saxons and their British neighbours started to influence the Britons' way of thinking, and this increased through the late sixth and seventh centuries (British and Saxon kings could be found as allies and equals by this period, something perhaps unthinkable at an earlier date). Certainly, by the eighth century, many of the 'heroic' elements of Saxon culture had crept into that of the Britons, ending their memory of Romano-British life for good.

The areas still ruled by Britons in the fringe areas of the South-West, Wales, Cumbria and lowland Scotland were subdued by the Anglo-Saxons after they achieved dominance in the lowlands of England. A later source noted that the Welsh were held under the thumb of punitive Anglo-Saxon raids so much so that they could not even 'pisseth' without incurring Anglo-Saxon wrath; things had definitely gone downhill for the descendants of Arthur. The Anglo-Saxons went on to fight invading Norse and Danish Vikings in the ninth and tenth centuries, and established for the first time ever what we could now recognise as England. They lost this kingdom to William's Norman army at that most famous date in British history: 1066. A lasting legacy of Anglo-Saxon England was the effort made by their scholars to produce an adequate written historical record meaning that Britain's 'Dark Age' was relegated to the fifth, sixth and seventh centuries rather than continuing to a much later date.

How Arthur would have lived

So far in this chapter we've looked at the probable history of early medieval Britain, and have touched upon how and where the Britons lived. The names of various historical characters have been passed down to us over the centuries, but beyond the occasional reference to a battle won or lost, or an important conversion to Christianity, historical records have told us very little of how these people lived. What did a Dark Ages warlord get up to on his days off from battle?

Perhaps above all else, a British king would have been aware of his lineage: this was the very reason he held the right to rule. Many lists of early medieval kings go to great lengths to list all of their forebears, both real and imagined (many kings traced their ancestry back to either early British deities or Roman emperors, both of which were inherently unlikely). Kings would have been born into a royal family, destined to rule their people, and being able to establish an unbroken lineage back to a man of great repute would have lent instant credibility to any royal blood. We no longer know if the kings who claimed to be a relation of such figures actually believed the family trees, or whether it was just a way of signalling their authority to others. The Pillar of Eliseg in Clwyd was erected in the ninth century in honour of the Welsh prince Eliseg, and listed a long line of his ancestors including Vortigern, for whom there is no direct evidence supporting his existence outside of folklore. The pillar also records that Vortigern was Magnus Maximus' son-in-law, a claim for which again we have no other reliable supporting evidence.

A king's place in society would never be questioned in the fifth and sixth centuries in the way that it might be today. The King and his family sat at the peak of a social pyramid passing down through the King's extended family, through the other nobles of the kingdom, to free men and slaves. There were no elected officials – you were either good to hold office, appointed by a ruler or destined to remain powerless. It seems that early medieval British society abided by a strict class system (the comparable systems of seventh and eighth century Irish law – preserved in later documents – even laid down what colours were permitted to be worn by each class).

We are less certain of the social structure of the earlier fifth century, and cannot even be sure of the fragmentation and size of the areas of government formed in the wake of Roman decline. It is likely that the social structure of Rome continued into the immediate post-Roman period; it is even conceivable that some early British kings (or *tyrants*, as Gildas refers to them) were local magnates under the final Roman government, perhaps coming from the British and continental merchant classes rather than truly royal British blood. Several generations on, in the late sixth century, it is unlikely that anyone remembered the more humble origins of some British kings. Certainly by this later period, most of the lowland British areas ruled by the families of former magnates had fallen under the control of Saxon kings. It is possible that the unlanded British royals were exiled into friendly kingdoms, married into the Saxon nobility (it wasn't all killing, killing, killing), or left for the continent.

Trade and political links with overseas lands continued after the withdrawal of Roman authority. St Germanus certainly visited Britain, as, it seems, did Roman governmental or military officials, in the early to mid-fifth century. After this, evidence of continental contact can be seen by the presence of imported goods ranging from pottery to jewellery, found at high status sites (royalty or nobility) across the south of Britain. Continued trading suggests that political envoys would also have passed between British rulers and their continental equivalents, to maintain good links; occasional references exist in European sources to Britons or Saxons abroad, which supports this idea.

In addition to political decisions and potentially leading his army into battle, a Dark Ages ruler would have invested a fair amount of time into the finer things in life. Poetry suggests that hunting was popular, and other references, including the medieval tale *The Dream of Rhonabwy*, show that the nobility may have indulged in strategy-based board-games. Bards and poets were employed to recite stories and songs deep rooted in British tradition, and wealthy rulers also arranged for stories and songs to be built around their own deeds. The rulers of the northern British kingdom of Rheged were particularly blessed in this way. Feasting was another popular pastime, and a recognised way in which to entertain one's guests – *The Gododdin* makes reference to a year-long event before the warriors rode to their doom.

Religion also played a part in day-to-day life. Christian and pagan traditions were scattered around the country, even though the later Roman Empire had been Christianised. Although some rulers may have explicitly stated their singular belief in one or the other, it's also possible that many people hedged their bets with both old and new religions – certainly the Saxon royal burials at sites such as Sutton Hoo and the recently discovered site at Southend in Essex show that the Saxons were accustomed to burial practices showing traces of both. There is no conclusive evidence that Christianity forcibly ejected pagan traditions in the late Roman period, but divisions existed between the followers of Roman Christianity and those rivals who followed the Pelagian way of life in early fifth century Britain or the Irish Christian church at a slightly later date. The concept of Arthur, and other worthy British kings, as Christians was probably introduced at a later date, and there is little evidence to support the idea that a historical Arthur and his Christian allies crusaded against solely pagan foes.

On a more mundane level, what did the Britons wear and what did they eat? To deal with bellies first, archaeologists have excavated remains of barley, wheat, oats and hazelnuts, along with oyster shells and the butchered bones of pigs, sheep and cattle. We also know that the Britons drank mead (a sweet honey wine), and references are made in British writing to cheese, pig's milk, cow's milk, bread, wine, butter, vegetables, eggs and 'Celtic beer' – a beer that earlier Roman soldiers had been particularly taken with. Other finds during excavation show us that plates, wine glasses, knives, spoons and other kitchen utensils would have been found on the British feasting table in the Dark Ages. Clothing consisted of tunics, accompanied by trousers for men. Fifth century Britons were accused by a continental commentator of 'flaunting their wealth in dazzling robes', so at least some Britons may have been particularly well suited and booted. Some town dwelling Britons may have more closely followed the latest Roman styles, and the level of contact between the later British nobility and the continent may mean that they continued this trend. Lower class clothing was generally made of wool, whereas upper class clothing made more use of silk. Chequered, striped and spotted patterns were popular, as were a variety of colours, although purple and red may have been reserved for the nobility and royalty. Jewellery allowed for extra ornamentation, and rings, pins and brooches were all worn; poetry suggests that warriors may still have worn the golden neck torques fashionable in the pre-Roman era.

Warfare in Arthur's time
Political diplomacy wasn't, of course, every king's cup of tea (or goblet of mead, which is what the warriors really drank just before heading off into battle). The majority of chronicle entries for the fifth and sixth centuries concentrate on the deposing of kings and the expansion of kingdoms through armed conflict. No matter how great a statesman the King or his advisors might have been, the presence of a band of battle hardened, veteran warriors ready to defend their king was the deciding factor in many disputes.

The popular view of Arthurian warriors is that they were heavily armoured cavalrymen: to all intents and purposes, knights. This theory imagines that the medieval vision of Arthur as a knight must have been founded on an earlier memory of him as a well-equipped, armoured warrior fighting from the saddle. In fact, there is actually no evidence in early Welsh folklore to suggest that this was the case, so we should really assume that medieval writers portrayed their hero in the image representative of a warrior king of their own era. Having said this, cavalrymen do appear to have played a major part in warfare in the age of Arthur. Cavalry became increasingly important in the late Roman period, and most of the tribes that fought against the Romans in the fourth and fifth centuries made use of horsemen. In tribal armies and the armies of most Roman successor states, the professional warriors and nobility rode into battle, and were prepared to fight from horseback or dismount to fight on foot if the situation required. The Britons, along with their Pictish and Irish enemies, almost certainly did the same. Many military historians have suggested that the Saxons fought exclusively on foot, but there is almost as much evidence to disprove this as there is to prove it. We should be fairly certain that the Saxon kingdoms made as much use of cavalry as their opponents.

Broadly speaking, the armies that fought in the years of Independent Britain and through to the sixth century would have been based on late Roman military models; it was noted by Gildas that the Britons were given patterns from which to manufacture arms and armour by the Romans. Military units would have consisted of mobile cavalry troops, and infantry raised locally to defend towns and the surrounding region. As British society moved away from its Roman past, becoming more 'heroic', warriors received rewards and gifts for their service, rather than a more formal system of pay. This gave rise to smaller yet more professional armies. One way in which a warlord would reward the warriors who served him was to grant land and bestow gold, weapons, armour and horses. As the warriors of this period were paid with goods as opposed to straight currency, it is reasonable to assume that they would have been fairly well equipped and armed, and capable of fighting on foot or horseback.

The basic weapons that all warriors fought with in this period was the spear (or, if capable of being thrown, the javelin). For defence, a warrior would also carry a shield, circular or oval in shape and around three feet in diameter. Throwing axes, bows, slings and long knives were also carried by smaller numbers of warriors, but only the richest warriors would have worn sturdy chainmail hauberks and metal helmets, or have been able to afford a sword (roughly equating to a Rolls-Royce in comparison to the Morris Minor-like spear).

When it comes to determining the size of Arthurian period armies, many scholars have made wildly varying guesses. An often-quoted reference point is the seventh century Anglo-Saxon *Laws of* [King] *Ine*, which declared that an army consisted of anything over thirty-five men. This should be discounted in military terms – as the title suggests, the *Laws* were a legal text and would almost certainly have erred on the side of caution. To demonstrate this, one only has to consider Britain's 1986 Public Order Act, Section 1 of which defines a 'riot' as consisting of twelve or more people: that number's handbags on the football pitch to you or I, but a riot by law. The *Laws of Ine* should be viewed similarly.

So if we discard the numbers given in the *Laws of Ine*, what other historical information can be used? Poetry and chronicle entries cannot be fully trusted. *The Anglo-Saxon Chronicle* suggests that British casualties in battle against the victorious Saxons often numbered in the thousands (the *Chronicle* rarely lists Saxon defeats); however, propaganda was not an invention of modern mankind, so it is possible that these figures were exaggerated. Similarly, heroic British and Saxon poetry often listed numbers of warriors involved in battle, but these numbers frequently sound like poetic conventions or license: for example, *The Gododdin* mentions a British force of 300 or 363 men (both multiples of the popular 'triad' convention used by that culture). Tradition remembers that the Saxons arrived in three ships, which would have borne no more than a few score warriors; this again sounds like poetic license. Instead, we must look at more reliable sources. The late Roman army's establishment in Britain was reckoned to be around six thousand, so it is highly unlikely that any later British kingdom – whether ruling the majority of the former province or a small breakaway state – would have been able to muster more than this number. Leslie Alcock, author of *Arthur's Britain*, reckoned that the successor kingdoms would have probably raised armies of around a thousand men. Eighth century Irish records show army sizes of around seven hundred men, which accords with Alcock's estimate.

Armies would also have varied in size according to their task. A king or warlord would have had his own personal retinue of men, perhaps numbering a couple of hundred, depending upon factors such as the size, wealth and military reputation of the kingdom. These warriors would have served with their leader at all times, living on his estates and earning a wage early in the period, or being paid in gifts as Britain's Romanised economy finally disintegrated in the fifth century. For raids and minor campaigns, the King would probably have mustered only his own warriors. For larger campaigns – perhaps a full scale invasion of a rival king with the intent to topple the throne – a Dark Ages warlord would have summoned the retinues of his allies and lesser nobles, perhaps swelling the ranks of his army to the thousand men projected by Alcock.

Tactically, we know very little about how the battles between the British kings, their rivals and their enemies were fought. Poetic sources suggest that cavalrymen advanced towards their enemies and hurled javelins, with the emphasis on individual prowess and heroism rather than a considered, cohesive approach. They didn't charge with couched lances. Foot warriors would have fought in swarms of individual fighters or as a cohesive, closely formed unit providing mutual protection for each other with their shields – a formation known as a shield wall. Small unit tactics would probably have depended upon the tactical situation more than individual cultural styles (for example, the Saxons would not always have fought in a shield wall, and the Irish would not always have wildly charged their nearest enemies, as some commentators suggest).

Most battles would probably have taken place along the borders of rival kingdoms. A number of the known battles of the Dark Ages took place at rivers, probably at strategic fords. We also know that the dawn attack was sometimes a favoured tactic, presumably gaining an advantage over an ill-prepared opponent. A few battles are described as having taken place at fortresses; whether these were actual sieges, or battles fought within the region controlled by such forts, we do not know. Certain evidence, such as Nennius' statement that a battle took place within the City of the Legion and the record of Pevensey shore fort falling from a Saxon attack suggest that sieges did occur. We also know that Dark Ages armies were capable of campaigning a long way away from their homes – for example, Cadwallon's army from Gwynedd conquered Northumbria in the mid-seventh century.

Finally, as mentioned elsewhere in this chapter, warfare in the age of Arthur was not a simply conceptual conflict between differing ethnic groups – the Britons did not just fight the Saxons, or the Irish, or Picts. It seems that civil war amongst the Britons was rife – endemic perhaps – and once established, the Saxon kingdoms fought against each other too, as did the Irish and Picts. Alliances were made between warlords based on convenience rather than ethnicity. When Cadwallon invaded Northumbria his army's ranks were swollen by the warriors of his ally Penda, the Saxon king of Mercia; when Cadwallon was killed a couple of years later by Oswald of Northumbria, Oswald had the backing of an Irish army. Consequently, one campaign's enemy could be the next campaign's ally; a common feature of hypotheses about the historical Arthur is that he united the squabbling Britons to fight against the greatest threat of all – Saxon invasion. If this is true, Arthur was indeed a very special, possibly unique, Dark Ages leader.

Gawain Challenges The Green Knight

Chapter Three

Arthur's Medieval Biographers

No single, definitive version of Arthur's legend exists – many different writers from many different times and countries have added their own embellishments to the tale. The most famous parts of Arthurian legend were laid down in their current form in the medieval period (roughly between 1100 and 1500 – around six hundred to a thousand years after the 'real' Arthur was considered to have lived). The most famous contributor to Arthurian legend is undoubtedly Thomas Malory, whose fifteenth century tales are considered by many to be a milestone both in the retelling of Arthur's legend and in the printing and book industries; Malory's work has influenced almost all authors of Arthurian literature who came after him.

However, Thomas Malory was not the first medieval writer to pick up on these wonderful tales about a mysterious king. He followed a rich tradition of Arthurian storytelling that had built up in the centuries before, the father of which is considered to be Geoffrey of Monmouth.

Geoffrey of Monmouth

If Geoffrey of Monmouth had lived in the modern world, he'd have been up there with the biggest names in twenty-first century fiction. Geoffrey, a cleric, was the mastermind behind the Arthur we know in his most popular form today – an ancient king of England, whose deeds could never be matched – and his retelling of Arthur's life was a best seller in the medieval world.

Geoffrey's account of Arthur's life in his book *The History of the Kings of Britain* is the earliest detailed account of Arthur that has survived to this day. Writing in the twelfth century (the *History* being completed around 1138), Geoffrey's self-given pen name, Gaufridus Monemutensis, suggests that he was born and brought up in Monmouthshire, on the south-eastern border of Wales. From 1129 to 1151, he was based in Oxford and appears to have held a post of canon at the college of St George's; in 1151 he became Bishop Elect of St Asaph in North Wales (however, it is unlikely that Geoffrey ever visited his seat, due to conflict between the English and Welsh at that time). Geoffrey continued to rise in ecclesiastical circles, and was ordained as a priest at Westminster in February 1152 and consecrated shortly after at Lambeth. According to Welsh chronicles he died at some point around 1155, but we cannot be certain of the exact date.

During Geoffrey's lifetime, Britain was awash with political intrigue and civil war; Geoffrey himself was one of the bishops who witnessed the Treaty of Westminster between King Stephen and the empress Matilda. Despite the turmoil surrounding this period of British history, it would seem that Geoffrey was very patriotic, and by writing his *History*, he wished to celebrate the former glories of Britain. It has often been stated that Geoffrey also had a political motive for writing: his *History* presented a legitimate reminder for the contemporary Anglo-Norman kings of the lineage of the earlier, pre-Saxon kings, who Geoffrey explains fled to Brittany and France centuries before, making Norman ancestry just as valid as that of the native Welsh and Saxons. A secondary, equally powerful motive behind Geoffrey's writing would be gaining favour with various, important nobles – most surviving copies of Geoffrey's *History* begin with a dedication to Robert, Earl of Gloucester, who was a bastard son of Henry I.

Geoffrey's tale of Arthur introduced many of the stories and ideas that have been the backbone of Arthurian legend ever since; however, his Arthur is not quite the chivalric champion of the later medieval period. Instead he reflects a strange combination of Dark Age warlord and contemporary (twelfth century) king. It is just possible that Geoffrey's Arthur does indeed tell a half-remembered history of a king befitting Arthur's reputation. This notion is strengthened by Geoffrey's dating of his Arthurian events: he placed his Arthur in the sixth century AD, dying in 542. This broadly ties in with other historical sources for the dates of Arthur – give or take a hundred years, which is not so long as it sounds given that Geoffrey's *History* starts seventeen hundred years before Arthur's death. As Geoffrey's narrative was the first popular story of Arthur, but also differed in many ways to the later, more familiar tales, it is worth looking at in close detail here.

The History of the Kings of Britain was conceived, as the title suggests, as a historical text; in Geoffrey's day, the concept of 'fiction' and 'non-fiction' did not matter, and the line between what an author intended as real or made up was extremely blurred. So it should not come as a surprise that Geoffrey's tale began with Albion as an isolated, magical land inhabited by giants. Around 1200 BC, Brutus of Troy arrived on the shores of Albion; Brutus was the great-grandson of Aeneas, a fugitive prince from the fall of Troy. Brutus and his followers fought the giants and conquered the island, renaming it Britain in honour of their leader; henceforth the inhabitants were known as Britons.

The History of the Kings of Britain was underway, and Geoffrey had already rather generously handed the ancient Britons a link to the much respected Classical period in the Mediterranean, placing them on a level with the great civilizations of Greece and Rome, high above the other 'barbarian' tribes of that era. It is worth considering Geoffrey's history in some detail, as it provides the basic building blocks of most later Arthurian legend.

Brutus was named King, and founded his capital city by the River Thames, naming it New Troy (later to be renamed London).

Geoffrey then describes the reigns of around seventy-five other kings, most of them seemingly coming from the depths of his own imagination rather than any historical source. One of Geoffrey's kings is Leir, the inspiration for Shakespeare's *King Lear*; as Geoffrey places Leir in the eighth century BC, we have no way of corroborating Leir's existence from other sources – a problem true of all of Geoffrey's earliest kings and events.

Geoffrey goes on to tackle the Roman period in as positive a light for the Britons as he possibly could. After all, the Britons were not mere naked barbarians, but the descendants of Troy! That the Romans had been in Britain could not be denied – in Geoffrey's day the remains of their buildings, roads and walls stood for all to see. But maintaining as much dignity for the Britons as he could muster, instead of ascribing a full conquest to the might of Rome, Geoffrey claimed that the Britons continued to rule their lands after entering into an agreement with the Roman Empire allowing them to remain tributary rulers, almost equal in status to the Emperor himself.

The part of Geoffrey's *History* that commands our attention most, however, is that outlining the history of Britain after the fall of Roman dominance, which occurred in Geoffrey's *History* roughly in the mid-fifth to mid-sixth centuries AD. The disproportionately large amount of space given over to this short period of time suggests that this was the bit that Geoffrey was most proud of – and the bit he wanted readers to take note of. Why Geoffrey was so interested in this period and allowed it so much importance we cannot really be sure; what is evident, however, is that he was a big fan of the major player: Arthur.

After the armies of Britain were weakened by the Roman Maximianus marching them to a continental campaign in the fourth century AD, Britain fell foul of many barbarian invasions – Picts, Huns, Scots and a host of other loathsome, uncivilized races. These barbarians ravaged the island from coast to coast, and the island was only saved by a Roman legion returning to defeat them all. The Romans then built a great wall dividing the Britons from their enemies in the North (here, Geoffrey attributes Hadrian's Wall to the wrong period of history, although his mistake is based upon the testimony of an earlier British source), and then told the Britons to defend themselves. As soon as the Roman army's back was turned, Geoffrey tells us that the barbarians resumed their raids, and unable to defend themselves as well as their pre-Roman forebears would have, the declining Britons turned to the British kingdom of Brittany (in France) for help. The Breton king's brother, Constantine, arrived and scattered the enemies of the Britons; reinvigorated by their new leader and the military success he brought, the Britons crowned Constantine as their king at the city of Silchester. Constantine reigned in peace for ten years, fathering three sons named Constans, Aurelius Ambrosius, and Uther (the future father of Arthur).

Constantine died at the hands of a Pictish assassin, and the British nobles argued as to who would succeed the Breton. One ambitious noble, Vortigern, suggested that Constantine's eldest son, Constans, should rule, despite him previously becoming a monk. Constans agreed to Vortigern's suggestion, only to serve as Vortigern's puppet. Vortigern swiftly took control of the whole kingdom of Britain, surrounded by a band of Pictish bodyguards, and soon arranged for the assassination of Constans at the hands of these warriors; to cover his own tracks, Vortigern then ordered his assassins to be beheaded for their crime. Surrounded by such intrigue and unrest, Constantine's two other sons, Aurelius Ambrosius and Uther, were rushed away by their guardians to their father's land of Brittany.

Angered at the death of their kinsmen, the Picts raided anew, and Vortigern turned in despair to two Saxon brothers – Hengist and Horsa – and hired them as mercenaries. Landing in Kent, the Saxon brothers brought three shiploads of fierce warriors with them; from Kent, they were immediately pushed into battle against the Picts; success followed, and Vortigern granted the Saxons more land, this time in Lincolnshire. Relieved at the respite granted by the presence of the Saxon warriors, Vortigern readily agreed to Hengist and Horsa calling more of their kinsmen to arms; more warriors flooded into Britain from the Saxon homelands of northern Europe.

Vortigern formed a close relationship with Hengist and Horsa, attending banquets with them. At one such gathering, Vortigern met and fell in love with Hengist's daughter, Rowena, and the wily Saxon warlord offered the Briton her hand in marriage, in exchange for the ownership of Kent. Vortigern agreed, much to the disdain of the other Britons, his sons included. As the strength of the Saxons grew in Britain, the natives appealed to Vortigern, but their protests fell on deaf ears. The Britons then turned to Vortigern's eldest son Prince Vortimer and proclaimed him King. Vortimer fought four battles against the Saxons, and was victorious in every one; many of the Saxons fled back to their homelands on the continent, and Horsa was killed in battle against the British prince. But the Britons' success was short-lived – Vortigern's Saxon wife Rowena poisoned Vortimer, and Vortigern was returned to the throne.

Vortigern organised a summit between the most noble leaders of the Britons and Saxons, to agree a peace treaty. At this event – to become known as the Night of the Long Knives – the treacherous Saxons pulled out hidden daggers at a signal from Hengist and murdered each and every one of the unarmed Britons. All except for Vortigern, who Hengist expected to act as a puppet king on his behalf. Hengist must have been disappointed, as Vortigern proceeded to flee to the hills of Wales.

Once in Wales, Vortigern attempted to build himself a new fortress, whilst the Saxons ransacked London. He selected a site in Snowdonia, but, whenever his men started to build the walls, they fell down. Vortigern was advised that the only solution would be to find a boy who had no father, sacrifice him, and pour his blood onto the ground. Vortigern found his boy in South Wales – Carmarthen to be precise – and the boy Merlin was brought to Snowdonia. Merlin's mother had conceived the child with a spirit, and her child was imbued with magical powers: before Vortigern could have Merlin killed, the boy revealed to the King the true reason for the fortress' falling walls. The walls stood over an underground pool in the mountains, and when the pool was drained, two dragons were found inside, fighting each other. One dragon was red, the other white, and at first, the white dragon held the upper hand. Then, when forced back to the edge of the pool, the red dragon fought with renewed vigour and killed its white opponent. Merlin explained that the red dragon represented the Britons and the white dragon the Saxons – although the Saxons were currently winning (with, you might note, Vortigern's help), the Britons would win in the end.

Merlin warned Vortigern that his end was near, and his words were true, as Constantine's two exiled sons, Aurelius Ambrosius and Uther, returned to depose Vortigern and put Hengist to death. Aurelius Ambrosius, the older of the two, was crowned King, and set about restoring Britain to its former glory.

At this point, Geoffrey explains that Merlin and Aurelius Ambrosius built a monument to the British nobles killed at the treacherous Night of the Long Knives. They despatched Uther to Ireland to bring back giant stones from which Merlin constructed a magic circle. This circle could still be seen in Geoffrey's day, as it can in ours, as it was the stone circle at Stonehenge (this is a great example of Geoffrey's historical blundering, as Stonehenge actually dates back to an earlier time, with several building phases from 2900–1650 BC).

Uther ruled with the title 'Pendragon', and fought against rebellious Britons and the remaining Saxons. One such campaign was against Gorlois, Duke of Cornwall, and led to the conception of Arthur as explained in Chapter Five. Uther reigned for fifteen years after the conception of Arthur, until he was poisoned by the Saxons; at which time Arthur succeeded his father as King.

Up to this point, Geoffrey's history of the post-Roman era makes interesting reading in light of the traditional and more plausible 'real' histories discussed in Chapter Two; however, the one king of Geoffrey's countless number who really stood out was Arthur. Arthur was probably already known to some, certainly in the Celtic world, but Geoffrey made sure that Arthur would stand out head and shoulders above the rest, overseeing the most spectacular and glorious reign of any of Geoffrey's monarchs.

Geoffrey's Arthur, unlike the king of later legend, did not grow up in secret; Geoffrey simply states that Arthur succeeded his father Uther. Uther also had another child, a girl named Anna, but being female she would not have been eligible to take the throne.

Arthur was crowned at Silchester, and despite his tender age, he immediately embarked upon a military campaign against the hated Saxons. Aided by Pictish and Scottish allies, the Saxons put up a strong fight, but Arthur defeated them in three consecutive, bloody battles (three battles, it must be said, that earlier British sources had also attributed to the mighty warlord in a list of twelve Arthurian victories). Arthur's victory was complete when the Saxons surrendered, promising to leave Britain.

In battle, Arthur wielded a sword named Caliburn, which had been forged on the mystical, enchanted Isle of Avalon; he also carried a shield emblazoned with the image of the Virgin Mary. This was a curious mix of an old Celtic religion (named, magical swords are common in pagan folklore) and Christian imagery that repeats itself time and time again in the legend of Arthur.

Of course, throughout Geoffrey's *History*, the Saxons had a poor track record – breaking promises and poisoning British kings left, right and centre. So it should be no surprise that the Saxons broke their treaty with Arthur, and sailed around to the west coast, landing in Devon. Arthur's army faced the determined Saxons at Bath, and won a decisive victory. This victory can be identified as the famous battle of Mount Badon, a near ever-present feature of the historical Arthur's life (as discussed in Chapter Two). After the battle at Bath, the Saxon army dispersed, and after Arthur's ally Cador of Cornwall finished his pursuit of them, the Saxons never again proved a threat during Arthur's reign.

Once he had disposed of his Saxon thorn, Arthur turned his attention to the other enduring threats to the Britons: the Picts and the Scots. Pushing them back to Loch Lomond, Arthur made short work of destroying an alliance of Picts, Scots and Irish after a fifteen-day siege, and was only prevented from wiping every last enemy warrior out by the intervention of their bishops. Victory complete against all enemies of the Britons in their homelands, Arthur set about restoring the stability of Britain's government and churches.

Arthur ruled fairly and generously, and married a woman of Roman blood, named Guinevere. Unused to such a benevolent ruler over the turbulent decades just passed, the Britons quickly warmed to Arthur, who had gained a reputation for strength in battle and righteous judgement in civil affairs. With the island of Britain restored to a gracious calm, Arthur set his sights on foreign lands: he invaded and subdued Ireland (the Irish, remember, had aided the Picts and Saxons in Arthur's earlier campaign), and then proceeded to conquer Iceland for good measure.

Arthur then oversaw twelve years of peace, in which time he attracted the cream of nobility from far away lands to join his court, demanding that they acted in a manner befitting their noble bearing. These noble knights wore the coat of arms of the house of Arthur, and by their actions and Arthur's own deeds, his fame spread throughout the world. Foreign rulers feared upsetting Arthur, lest he invaded their lands, and the most noble knights yearned to join his court. Of course, this is the genesis of the Round Table, although Geoffrey himself did not refer to this now famous piece of furniture. Some foreign kings were right to fear Arthur's might – he extended his sphere of influence by invading and conquering Norway and Denmark.

He then looked to challenge the might of the Roman Empire (which was still contemporary to Geoffrey's Arthur, despite his talk of knights and medieval courtly values), by sending an army into Roman Gaul (modern France). Gaul was governed by a Roman official named Frollo, on behalf of the Emperor; when Arthur's Britons and the Roman army met in battle, Frollo managed to run Arthur's horse through with a lance before the British hero split the Roman's head in two with a mighty blow from his sword Caliburn. The Roman army immediately surrendered, and nine years passed, during which Arthur subdued the rest of Gaul, even holding court in Paris. As in the other kingdoms under his control, Arthur applied the same sense of justice and fair rule to his Gallic subjects. He also appointed a number of his most able nobles to govern areas of Gaul on his behalf; among other appointments, his trusted cup bearer Bedevere (in other works spelt Bedivere) was placed in charge of Normandy, and his seneschal Kay held sway over Anjou.

Returning to Britain, Arthur held court at the City of the Legion, a town of former Roman greatness, identified by Geoffrey as Caerleon on the banks of the River Usk in South Wales. He hosted a tournament for his knights to demonstrate their battle skills, and invited the many leaders who now owed him homage. Geoffrey listed the kings and chieftains who attended this important court, and it is worth reproducing his list here to give some idea of the sheer number of leaders who Geoffrey believed had answered to Arthur:

Gilmaurius, King of Ireland; Malvasius, King of Iceland; Doldavius, King of Gotland; Gunhpar, King of the Orkneys; Loth, King of Norway; Aschil, King of Denmark; Auguselus, King of Scotland; Urian, King of Moray; Cadwallo Laurh, King of the North Welsh; Stater, King of the South Welsh; Cador, King of Cornwall; Holdin, Leader of the Ruteni; Leodegarius, Earl of Holland; Bedevere, Duke of Normandy; Borellus of Cenomania; Kay, Duke of Anjou; Guitard of Poiters; Hoel, Leader of the Armorican Britons; the Archbishop of York; the Archbishop of London; the Archbishop of the City of the Legion (who, we are told, was so pious that he was able to cure illness simply by praying); the twelve Peers of Gaul, led by Gerin of Chartres; Morvid, Earl of Gloucester; Mauron, Earl of Worcester; Anarauth, Earl of Salisbury; Artgualchar, Earl of Warwick; Jugein of Leicester; Cursalem of Caistor; Kynniarc, Duke of Durobernia; Urbgennius of Bath; Jonathel of Dorchester; Boso of Oxford; Donaut map Papo; Cheneus map Coil; Peredur map Peridur; Grifud map Nogord; Regin map Claut; Eddeliui map Oledauc; Kynar map Bangan; Kynmaroc; Gorbonian map Goit; Worloit; Run map Neton; Kymbelin; Edelnauth map Trunat; Cathleus map Kathel; Kynlit map Tieton; and many other great nobles who, Geoffrey happily notes, would be too tedious to list!

Geoffrey noted that no prince of distinction from this side of Spain did not attend Arthur's court and tournament at Caerleon. Some of these names can be identified as historical figures, but not all would have lived at the same time as Geoffrey's proposed reign of Arthur. Even so, the list shows Geoffrey's intent that Arthur be seen as the most powerful king ever known in Britain – perhaps even in Europe. It is interesting to note that some of these kings and noblemen go on to figure in the more highly developed Arthurian legend of the later medieval period, whereas others just faded into obscurity as the stories were retold.

In Geoffrey's mind, Arthur had restored Britain to its true place in the world's order, as the most sophisticated, courteous, and affluent country of all. In just over a decade, Britain had been transformed from a land of chaos and rebellion into a kingdom that all others looked to for inspiration. Arthur, without doubt, was Geoffrey's greatest king of Britain.

It was not just the King and his government who were responsible for the celebrated way of life in Arthur's Britain: his noble men and noble women played their part too. Arthur's knights were spurred on to ever more valiant feats by their women, for whom it became fashionable to only give their love to a warrior who had proved himself in battle three times.

Sadly, the good times were not to last, even in Geoffrey's Arthurian utopia. An envoy arrived at Arthur's court, bringing a message from the Roman Procurator Lucius Hiberius. Lucius Hiberius condemned the King's behaviour, stating that Arthur had not paid the tribute that he was accustomed to receiving from the Britons. As if that were not enough, Arthur had seized Roman land in Gaul, and if the British King did not submit to Lucius Hiberius, a state of war and a Roman reconquest of Arthur's lands would follow.

At pains throughout his *History* to patriotically show that his British kings were as good as any emperor the Romans could offer up, Geoffrey naturally didn't have his Arthur backing down to such a threat. After conferring with his nobles, Arthur defied Lucius Hiberius, stating (quite rightly so in Geoffrey's retelling of events, though not so true in real life) that he himself could rightfully claim to rule Rome. With that, Arthur's army set out from Southampton to campaign against Rome, led by the great King himself who decided to leave his nephew Modred (sometimes described as King Lot's son rather than Arthur's, depending on the author) to rule Britain in his absence, jointly with Queen Guinevere.

Landing on the continental mainland in Gaul at Barfleur, Arthur marched for Paris. On the brief journey over the sea, Arthur had a vision in a dream of a dragon fighting a bear; the dragon was victorious, and Arthur's men interpreted his dream for him. They believed that Arthur was the dragon and the bear was either the Roman Emperor or a fabulous beast that he would defeat in battle. It is interesting to note here, especially given the many theories that Arthur's name was in fact a 'battle name' meaning bear (expounded in Chapter Seven), that Geoffrey's version of events depicts Arthur as the dragon and an opponent as the bear. If Arthur had been associated with the bear in Geoffrey's time, he would surely have substituted a different animal for the dream.

As Arthur waited for more allied kings to join him in Gaul, local people reported that a huge giant was terrorising the region, having arrived from Spain. Helena, niece of the local Duke Hoel, had been snatched by the giant and taken to the top of the Mont Saint Michel. Arthur was told that Gallic knights had tried in vain to fight the giant, but all had either died quickly or had been captured and eaten whilst they were still half alive. Twiddling his thumbs whilst awaiting the rest of his allies, and wishing to inspire confidence in his men for the coming conflict against Rome, Arthur decided to take Bedevere and Kay with him to challenge the giant. The three heroes were too late to save Helena, but Arthur did manage to slay the giant, and Bedevere took the giant's head back to their camp, so that everyone could see the intimidating size of Arthur's defeated opponent.

With his giant-slaying side show out of the way, Arthur continued to march to meet Lucius Hiberius' army in battle. Arthur's nephew Gawain fought a preliminary engagement with six thousand warriors against a Roman force of ten thousand, led by Senator Petreius Cocta. Other preliminary skirmishes followed, and at Saussy the two main armies drew up against one another.

Geoffrey names a number of important British nobles who fought under Arthur's golden dragon banner against the Romans:

Auguselus, King of Scotland; Cador, Duke of Cornwall; Gerin of Chartres; Boso of Oxford; Aschil, King of the Danes; Loth, King of Norway; Hoel, King of the Armorican Britons; Gawain; Kay; Bedevere; Holdin of the Ruteni; Guitard, Duke of the Poitevins; Jugein of Leicester; Jonathel of Dorchester; Cursalem of Caistor; and Urbgennius of Bath.

These men had all attended Arthur's earlier court, and his power was still such that these men would bring their own armies to fight beside his. Yet Geoffrey leaves us in no doubt as to the extent of the Roman army that Arthur faced; Lucius Hiberius' army was equally as cosmopolitan as Arthur's, including Spanish, Parthian, Median and Libyan warriors alongside the armies of the Iturei, Egypt, Bithynia, Phrygia and, of course, the legions of Rome herself.

The battle started badly for the Britons, who fell in great numbers before recovering themselves and pushing the Romans back. Gawain fought hand to hand with Lucius Hiberius, before a Roman counter-attack pushed Gawain back. Arthur was in the thick of battle, once again wielding his sword Caliburn with great prowess. A terrific battle ensued, and eventually the Roman host broke and ran from Arthur's warriors. Lucius Hiberius was struck down in the thick of the fight, by an unknown warrior upholding Arthur's cause.

Lucius Hiberius' body was sent back to the Senate, with a message that tribute should no longer be expected from Britain. Arthur's army stayed on the continent during the winter, subduing an unfriendly tribe called the Allobroges. When summer arrived, Arthur prepared his army to cross the Alps and head directly for Rome and the Emperor Leo. He had defeated the Empire's greatest army and now intended to claim the city as part of his kingdom; by doing so, all of Europe would be ruled by the King of the Britons. He had already started into the mountain passes when news arrived that Modred – the nephew he had left to rule Britain in his absence – had taken the crown for himself. What's more, Arthur's wife Guinevere was now living adulterously with Modred, acting as queen to the traitor. Arthur turned his army around and headed back for Britain, leaving an army of Armorican Britons (Bretons) to govern his newly conquered lands.

Modred had made a pact with Chelric, the leader of the Saxons. In return for the lands north of the Humber and south of Scotland, along with the land that Hengist and Horsa had previously ruled, Modred demanded that Chelric summon more warriors from pagan Germany to his aid. Alongside Modred's men and the Saxons, the usurper called in Scottish, Irish and Pictish warriors, along with any other fighting men he could find who hated Arthur. Arthur arrived back in Britain to be confronted by an army of some eighty thousand armed men, who Arthur drove back from the fort at Richborough where he had landed. Gawain, Arthur's loyal nephew, died in that battle.

The campaign to return Arthur to his throne continued, during which time Guinevere fled to York and became a nun. Arthur cornered Modred's army in Cornwall at the River Camblam (usually identified in Geoffrey's work as the River Camel; the spelling was later to change to 'Camlann'), where the two armies clashed once more. Modred was slain and his army utterly defeated; Geoffrey does not say that Arthur killed Modred in single combat, although this is how later legend remembered the end of the battle. Arthur himself was mortally wounded at Camblam and was carried away to have his wounds tended on the Isle of Avalon, the enchanted island where his sword Caliburn had been forged. As he departed, he handed the crown to his cousin Constantine, son of Cador of Cornwall. This happened in AD 542, and Arthur was never to return.

In his poem *The Life of Merlin*, Geoffrey mentioned Avalon again, describing it as an 'island of apples', and noting that Arthur was tended there by Morgen the enchantress. Geoffrey's *History* does not end with Arthur's journey to Avalon, instead it goes on to describe the reigns of the kings who followed him. Arthur's successors fought against the

Saxons, and one British king named Keredic fought against the Saxons' ally Gormund, King of Africa.

Towards the end of his *History*, Geoffrey mentions the British king Cadwallon, along with the Saxon leaders Penda and Oswald. He correctly cites some historical events associated with their lives, so it would seem that he must have had some fairly reliable information for this part of his *History*, as it is one of the few parts that can be successfully corroborated by other sources. Geoffrey's records end with the death of the last British ruler Cadwallader, in AD 689, by which time the Britons have been pushed back into Wales and Cornwall (and Brittany on the continent), and the Saxons control most of modern England.

Despite Geoffrey's romantic and patriotic, though highly inaccurate, visions of Britain's former greatness and his obviously exaggerated retelling of history, it is possible – likely in fact – that there were elements of truth in his writing. Some of his immediately pre-Roman and Roman history bears some relation to what the Romans recorded independently, although there is no consistency in this. Some of the post-Arthur *History* relates quite closely to the perhaps more historically accurate, relatively contemporary histories; but for the stories of Arthur and his immediate predecessors, we have no other sources to correlate Geoffrey's *History* with. Geoffrey claims that Walter, the Archdeacon of Oxford, had presented him with an ancient book written in the British language which actually listed everything he had included in his own work. If Geoffrey did indeed have such a major source, it has long since been lost. However, this is not to say that it didn't once exist: there are many instances of works known to have been written that no longer exist today, and there must be hundreds of libraries worth of books that were written yet of which we have no idea in the modern world.

Unfortunately, Geoffrey's other work suggests to the modern reader that he was not above creating his own stories and passing them off as historical fact. His *Prophecies of Merlin*, included in the *History* but originally intended as a separate volume, speak of dragons, of lion cubs being transformed into fish and of hedgehogs rebuilding cities. All good stuff, but hardly with historical foundation; he went on to write about Merlin at length in a separate volume, and again his work seemed to have little validation in the real world. Yet much of what Geoffrey writes could have been true to some extent, and certainly some of his *History* suggests a level of research and knowledge. Some modern theories as to the identity of Arthur and the popular view of British history in the

Dark Ages owe much to Geoffrey's work, as you can read in other chapters of this book. And, despite his references to giants and magical acts, Geoffrey's kings, not least Arthur, bear more resemblance to a Dark Ages warlord than they do to a medieval king, again suggesting that he may really have used some historical source material as the basis of his work.

Despite this, Geoffrey's *History* has been plagued by many doubters as to its historical value, with both modern commentators and a number of his contemporaries questioning his sources. In Geoffrey's own day, William of Newburgh even went so far as to say that Geoffrey's *History* was wholly a figment of his imagination. But, despite his doubters, Geoffrey had created a story that caught the imagination of those who really mattered – his captive audience included bards, poets and kings throughout Europe.

The writing was on the wall: tales of Arthur were all the rage in courtly circles by the end of the twelfth century. Geoffrey had plucked (or perhaps invented) a character from the dimly remembered margins of European history and placed him on a pedestal for all to adore, blowing events from his reign out of all proportion – perhaps even inventing them completely. Geoffrey's work complete, other medieval writers started to jump on the bandwagon.

The history of Arthur BG: Before Geoffrey

Although Geoffrey of Monmouth was the first medieval writer to promote Arthur in detail, two Anglo-Norman writers mentioned Arthur in passing at an earlier date. William of Malmesbury included a note on Arthur in his *Deeds of the English Kings*, which was completed in 1125. Without going into great detail as to the deeds of Arthur, William simply notes that the Britons recited oral traditions of Arthur, describing their stories as nonsense he thought of them as fables rather than respectable history. The British traditions to which William alludes are described in detail in the next chapter.

Four years after William completed his *Deeds of the English Kings*, and about a decade before Geoffrey of Monmouth wrote his best seller on the kings of Britain, Henry of Huntingdon listed twelve battles that Arthur had fought and won, in his *History of the English*. Henry's list was taken from an earlier British account of Arthur written a couple of hundred years earlier, called *The History of the Britons*. This *History* was the work of a monk named Nennius, who has been mentioned earlier and is described in more detail in the next chapter.

Wace

Hot on the heels of Geoffrey of Monmouth came the Norman poet Wace. He was a native of the Channel Island of Jersey, and was a prolific writer. In 1155, he published a version of Geoffrey's work, adapted into French verse, and dedicated it to Eleanor, queen of Henry II of England. He was later to write a history of the dukes of Normandy for Henry II himself.

Wace entitled his Arthurian work the *Romance of Brutus*. The basis of this *Romance* was Geoffrey's story from the reign of Constantine onward, although Wace couldn't help himself making the odd change to Geoffrey's work here and there.

Wace made two important changes to Geoffrey's work. He introduced Arthur's famous Round Table to the tale, during Arthur's twelve-year reign of peace; Geoffrey never mentioned any table himself. The idea behind the table was that, being round, there was no head or foot, or indeed any 'ladder' to climb to head the table: all who sat at the table would be equal. The symbolism evoked by the Round Table was entirely in keeping with Geoffrey's description of the nobility and chivalry of Arthur's reign. If the history of the concept of the Round Table could be traced back to a pre-Christian era, it is possible that it could have been considered to have held similar powers to the enchanted stone circles found in the British uplands; sadly, no such connection has yet been discovered. By the time of Malory, writing just over three hundred years after Wace, the Round Table had evolved a history all of its own. Malory believed that Uther Pendragon had given the table to King Leodegrance (Guinevere's father), and that Leodegrance in turn passed the Round Table – along with 100 knights – to Arthur when the King married his daughter. Malory also described the table as being large enough for 150 knights to sit at. Of course, by the time Malory wrote of the Round Table, it had become a vital ingredient to the whole tale, and the Siege Perilous (a famous seat at the table at which only Galahad was able to sit) had become ensconced as part of the Arthurian legend. A medieval version of the Round Table was constructed, as you will read in Chapter Six, and it can still be seen in Winchester to this day.

The second important alteration that Wace made to Geoffrey's work was at the end of Arthur's reign. After the calamitous Battle of Camlann (or Camblam as Geoffrey has it), Geoffrey saw Arthur off in a boat, heading to the Isle of Avalon to have his wounds healed. Wace went one better: he predicted that Arthur would return from Avalon when the time was right, and that the King and his knights had not died but were sleeping. Wace popularised the idea of Arthur as the Once and Future King, although this inclusion may well have been based on traditional British and Breton folklore. The theme was certainly to remain in Arthurian legend from Wace's day onward.

Wace was also influenced in his alterations by folklore concerning Arthur from outside the British Isles: there was a strong Breton tradition for stories of Arthur and his other knights, and Wace tapped into it. He claimed that the story of the Round Table came from the Bretons, and he identified the enchanted Arthurian Forest of Brocéliande as an area of Brittany. The Breton tradition of Arthur is explained further in Chapter Four, as befits the close ties between Dark Ages Brittany and Britain.

Wace seems to have been aware that his work, and that of Geoffrey and others before him, was not strictly an accurate history. He described the adventures of Arthur as having been turned into fable, and noted that the stories were not all true but nor were they all lies. Wace certainly acknowledged the story that he told as being based on actual events, even if he (and those others who wrote of Arthur) was not faithfully reconstructing events in their purest historical context.

In his adaptation of Geoffrey of Monmouth's work, Wace moves Arthur closer to the romance of later French writers, developing him from the hero that Geoffrey considered to have a potentially plausible historical genesis. As such, Wace's *Romance* must have been a great influence on the work of those writers who followed in the romantic tradition, and should not be dismissed as a simple translation of Geoffrey's *History*.

Chrétien de Troyes

Chrétien de Troyes is the best known and probably the most important member of the French school of literature which gave birth to the Arthur of Romance that has influenced so many writers in their wake. As Romance literature, these stories are focused more on love and chivalric adventure than the heroic yet bloody values depicted by the likes of Geoffrey of Monmouth and the later English writer Layamon. The plot device that most characteristically sums up a medieval romance is a concentration on the deeds of one knight. The knight is separated from his court and must face various (and often supernatural) adventures in order to make a triumphant return to court, often marrying his betrothed upon his return. Chrétien's own contributions to this type of literature were an important milestone in the medieval period's understanding of how chivalry should be defined and measured. As such, his influence was important far beyond his excellent contributions to the legends of Arthur.

Little is known of Chrétien's own life. We can guess that he originated from or spent much of his life in the city of Troyes, which is within the Champagne region of modern France. Chrétien lived in the latter half of the twelfth century, and produced five Arthurian romances, written in rhyming verse. The last of these five was unfinished, but all five are usually attributed to the period 1170–1190.

Chrétien's first Arthurian romance was *Erec and Enide*. This tale is rather like the Welsh folktale *Geraint and Enid*, and it would seem that Chrétien's work (both in this romance and others) may well have inspired Welsh writers at the start of the thirteenth century. The Welsh writers of *The Mabinogion* and other stories may well have adapted more traditional Celtic tales for their modern, romance-greedy audiences under the influence of Chrétien. The cautionary tale of *Erec and Enide* demonstrates the friction caused by love and chivalry, which would have been a very fashionable debate at that time. Erec was a knight of Arthur's court, and while in the presence of Guinevere, he was set upon by a vicious little dwarf (dwarves often feature in Arthurian legend – Appendix C details these little chaps along with several other Arthurian creatures). Quite rightly, from Chrétien's point of view, Erec headed off on an adventure to avenge his shame on the dwarf's master; on part of his journey, he arrived at the house of an elderly knight and his daughter named Enide. Erec acted as Enide's champion in a tournament, and won – defeating the knight who was the dwarf's master in the process. Erec returned to Arthur's court with Enide, intending to marry her. The happy couple did indeed wed, but in a state of marital bliss, Erec began to neglect his duties as a knight of Arthur's realm. He was ridiculed by his tenants, which Enide overheard, but Erec himself was unaware. Sensing that his wife was unhappy, Erec pressed her for the reason, and discovered what was being said about him. Angry at such rumour, Erec set out on a challenging journey, forcing Enide to accompany him and prove her love for him in a series of arduous encounters that they faced together. Eventually, with Erec convinced of Enide's devotion for him, and Enide convinced of Erec's ability as a knight, the loving couple were reconciled.

The second of Chrétien's romances is named after its hero, Cligés. *Cligés* is set in Constantinople, and begins with the story of the eponymous hero's father, a Greek prince named Alexandre. Alexandre was so proud a man that he refused to be knighted in Constantinople, knowing that only the renowned Arthur's court in Britain would be a suitable location for such an event. He also expressed his love of Gawain's sister Soredamors. The part of the story focusing on Cligés himself is rather like the story of Tristan and Isolde, which was a popular story in it's own right in the medieval period. Cligés was in love with his aunt Fénice; Fénice decided to escape her unhappy marriage so that she could be with Cligés, and pretended to poison herself. This rouse was successful, and the two lovers were free to be together. Above all else, this tale is Chrétien's most rounded celebration of courtly love.

The Knight of the Cart is Chrétien's third romance, and it is also his best known, introducing Lancelot into the world of Arthurian legend. Sometimes, this poem is entitled simply *Lancelot*, and focuses on the adulterous affair between one of the world's greatest knights and Guinevere. It is also one of the earliest tales to describe the famous court of Camelot at any great length. The love story of Lancelot and Guinevere may first have been introduced by Marie, Countess of Champagne in the late twelfth century, and it is possible that her plot provided Chrétien with his story-line. In this story Guinevere is kidnapped by an evil knight named Meleagant, and Arthur and Kay are beaten to the rescue by an unnamed knight (later to be revealed as Lancelot). The title of the romance is a direct reference to Lancelot, who pursues Meleagant and the kidnapped queen so vigorously that his horse dies and he must complete the journey by climbing into a criminal's cart. It transpires that Lancelot was already the queen's lover, and that because he hesitated before climbing into the cart, Guinevere questions his love of her and suggests that he places honour before love. Lancelot proves his love and their illicit affair continues.

The Knight with the Lion, or *Yvain* as it is sometimes known, is often held up as Chrétien's greatest literary achievement. Yvain marries a lady named Laudine, after slaying her husband. Shortly afterwards, Yvain is persuaded to head off on a quest; Laudine agrees to allow her new husband to leave, on condition that he return within a year. Caught up in knightly comings and goings, Yvain forgets to return within this time period and therefore breaks his vow to his wife. In doing so, he loses her love. Yvain then embarks on a number of adventures to make up for his behaviour to Laudine, and on one such adventure he saves the life of a lion, who accompanies him as a companion from that point on. The lion symbolises Laudine's return of devotion to Yvain, and the pair happily reunite in love.

Chrétien's fifth tale was never completed; he most probably died whilst composing it. *The Story of the Grail*, or *Perceval* as it is better known, begins with Perceval's early life, which was so isolated that he never knew what a knight was. When Perceval finally did meet a knight, he realised that it was a knight's life for him. Trying to become a knight isn't as easy as you may imagine, and Perceval discovered this for himself through a series of early, comical adventures. The story-line then shifts to the quest for the Holy Grail (of which you can read more in the section about the Vulgate Cycle, below). Perceval himself failed in the quest, as his lack of courtly understanding (his childhood isolation evidently handicapped him in this) prevented him from securing it for Arthur; despite this, he does actually witness a mystical procession displaying the Grail. Chrétien then turns to the story of Gauvain's Grail Quest (Gauvain being Chrétien's spelling of Gawain) and then ends, uncompleted.

Chrétien's work was to influence other French writers, and his five poems were to form a solid backbone for Arthurian legend well into Thomas Malory's time, greatly influencing his own great work *The Death of Arthur*.

Layamon

Layamon was a priest from the Severn valley who at some point around the end of the twelfth century or beginning of the thirteenth century translated Wace's *Romance of Brutus* into English. Just as Wace had adapted Geoffrey of Monmouth's *History of the Kings of Britain*, Layamon adapted Wace's work. Influenced by Wace, Layamon kept the text as verse – alliterative verse, in fact. Layamon's poetry was also just about twice as long as Wace's *Romance*, which indicates that, like Wace himself, the English priest's work was no mere translation of an earlier work, but instead took the earlier tale and developed and expanded it further. Geoffrey had written in Latin, and Wace had written in French, and Layamon should be credited with the first Arthurian tales of English literature.

However, Layamon's real contribution to Arthurian legend was to interpret it once again as a heroic history, rather than following Wace's lead by placing an emphasis on chivalry and love. Layamon's Arthur was a man of action – violence ruled in Layamon's recital (which, some might say, makes it a peculiarly English romance).

Hand in hand with his treatment of Arthur's legend as heroic history, Layamon further emphasised his backwards step towards the Celtic

Arthur (as outlined in Chapter Four) by introducing further Celtic ideas into his work. Layamon has Arthur being blessed at birth by folklore elves, and as in Wace's *Romance*, he has Arthur's wounds treated by magic on the Isle of Avalon. Another variation introduced by Layamon was that Arthur's queen Guinevere had conspired with the treacherous Modred to gain the King's throne.

Far too much attention has previously been paid to the idea that Layamon was essentially an Anglo-Saxon, English-speaking writer who elevated a former enemy of the Saxons to an almost messianic plinth. Some commentators have suggested that Arthur's defeat of the Saxons was enthusiastically written to announce that the Anglo-Norman rule of Britain had replaced a Saxon domination which began with pagan cruelty: the Saxons who had punished the earlier Briton's sins were now punished for their sins by the Normans. However, this seems a little far-fetched.

It is also a little far-fetched to feign surprise that Layamon depicted his Saxon 'ancestors' as an enemy to the King of Britain. We know so little of Layamon's own life that he may have been of British, Welsh or, like most of the population at the time, a mixture of British, Saxon and Scandinavian blood. There is no reason to assume that just because he wrote in English, Layamon should have been projecting a noble history of the Anglo-Saxon culture.

In fact, Layamon had most likely been swept along by the hysteria surrounding the legend of Arthur that began with Geoffrey of Monmouth's *History*, and was simply adapting the stories for English-speaking audiences to appreciate.

Christ on a bike: The Vulgate Cycle

That's right, this medieval collection known as a cycle largely defined Arthur's links to Christianity and the Holy Grail. The Vulgate Cycle is a huge, sprawling collection of early thirteenth century romance written in prose by a group of northern French monks. There are five main parts to this cycle, the titles of which indicate the ambitious and wide-ranging subjects covered within: *The History of the Holy Grail*, *Merlin*, *Lancelot*, *The Quest of the Holy Grail*, and *The Death of Arthur*. These stories have had a huge influence on all later Arthurian authors, most notably Thomas Malory, and as such the Vulgate Cycle presented some of the themes we now consider to be key to Arthurian literature, and that are included in Chapter Five of this book.

The stories of the Vulgate Cycle portray Arthur and his court as existing in a curious world where chivalry seems certain to fail. Despite the noblest of intentions, Arthur's reign is doomed from the start: without realising, he incestuously fathers a child named Mordred (a variant on the spelling of Modred) with his sister Morgan Le Fay (known as the largely anonymous Anna in Geoffrey of Monmouth's story, but a far more prominent and less pleasant character in the Vulgate Cycle). When the Holy Grail appears as a vision at Camelot, bringing with it indescribable feelings of joy and adulation, Arthur decides that his knights must find this vessel, to restore his kingdom to its former glory. The stories that detail Arthur's knights' quests for the Holy Grail are sometimes pointless and never fruitful. Even the greatest knights of his court fail: Lancelot is superseded by his son Galahad as the greatest of Arthur's knights, and Lancelot's affair with Guinevere brings about the downfall of Arthur's court. Gawain's quest for the Grail is futile, whereas Galahad, Bors and Perceval all come agonisingly close, but all three ultimately fail to bring it back to Camelot. My own retelling in Chapter Five plays down the Christian aspect of the Grail Quest, in an attempt to update the tale for a modern audience.

The Vulgate Cycle is not the first Arthurian story to mention the Holy Grail – Chrétien de Troyes' final, uncompleted poem does so at an earlier date; but the Vulgate Cycle's tales are the first to go into any great detail about this most treasured of religious artefacts. But what exactly was the Grail?

The Holy Grail was never fully described in the earliest stories surrounding it. Some researchers have described the Grail as a large plate or serving platter, and the medieval writer Wolfram von Eschenbach believed it to be a green stone that had fallen from heaven. But most modern authors believe it to be the silver cup that Joseph of Arimathea used to collect blood from Jesus' wounds as he hung on the cross. This blood later miraculously healed Joseph when he was imprisoned in Judea. Later, Joseph and his son Jospehus took the Grail around the western world, holding Mass; it was said that the Grail eventually arrived in Britain, and was guarded for generations by the Fisher King, who appears in such a role in Arthurian legend. Arthur wished for the Grail to be discovered and brought to Camelot, to cure the ailing kingdom. The Grail Quest also has a great deal in common with early Celtic folklore about magical cauldrons, and it is possible that the Grail became part of Arthurian legend due to its similarity to the Celtic tale *The Spoils of Annwn* (detailed in Chapter Four).

Theories surrounding the truth behind the Holy Grail legend and its origins are complex enough to have a sizeable book devoted to them, let alone to be part of a discussion surrounding a potentially pseudo-historical British warrior king. The conclusions that most people draw about the Grail depend on their religious beliefs, and if the Grail did exist, what really happened to it after the crucifixion of Jesus. Some researchers suggest that stories of the Holy Grail actually have Spanish or Portuguese origins, and that the Grail Castle can still be located there today; others have linked the Grail's final home as Glastonbury in Somerset. Stories exist suggesting that three crusader knights brought the Grail back from Jerusalem, and that the Templars (a religious order of knights) hid and guarded it in a chapel – sometimes identified as Rosslyn Chapel near Edinburgh.

By including the Holy Grail, the Vulgate Cycle forced a new thread into seams of Arthurian literature. Geoffrey of Monmouth's Arthur was simply a great king, strong in battle; Chrétien de Troye's Arthurian tales emphasised courtly behaviour and romance; yet the Vulgate Cycle introduced ideas of Christianity and religion into the world of Arthur and, very quickly, the Grail Quest became a central theme of the legend.

Sir Thomas Malory

If Geoffrey of Monmouth is the grandfather of Arthurian literature, then Sir Thomas Malory is almost certainly 'The Daddy'. Most adaptations of Arthurian legend you can read today are based on Malory's fifteenth century writing; my own version as retold in Chapter Five owes a great deal to him, although Malory included many more tales in his famous *The Death of Arthur* than are present in my own chapter. In so many ways, it is fitting that Malory's writing should remain so well known as his work is itself a composite of the many medieval Arthurian writers before him.

Malory completed his Arthurian contribution in 1469 or 1470, but the most popular date associated with *The Death of Arthur* is 1485, when Caxton printed the text as a book. From that point on, Malory's work achieved a wider circulation than any previous Arthurian tales, and has proved a solid foundation for many modern authors to build on. Malory's work should be considered a culmination of the medieval Arthurian tradition, a definitive compilation and consolidation of earlier work into one unified cycle.

So who was Sir Thomas Malory? In truth, we cannot really be sure which 'Sir Thomas Malory' he was, as there are a couple of possible candidates from the fifteenth century. The most commonly accepted identification is that of G L Kitteredge, an American researcher, who pinpointed a certain Sir Thomas Malory (or Maleore) of Newbold Revell in Warwickshire. Born in the early part of the fifteenth century, this Sir Thomas was a naughty chap, and spent the best part of twenty years in prison. His list of crimes included rape, attempted murder and armed robbery, and he apparently made a couple of dramatic escapes from his gaolers whilst in captivity. When he wasn't on the wrong side of the law, Sir Thomas made a career as a soldier, fighting in the service of Richard Beauchamp, Earl of Warwick. The fifteenth century was a time when there was no shortage of active service for a soldier to find, and as part of the ongoing dispute over the rightful ownership of parts of France, Sir Thomas fought for the English against France at the siege of Calais in 1436.

Not surprisingly, a lot of commentators have found it hard to believe that a knight imprisoned for the sort of crimes that the Warwickshire Sir Thomas had been was capable of writing stories with such a high moral and chivalric content. Some linguistic experts also believe that *The Death of Arthur* was written in a style suggesting a northern English dialect (which counts against the Warwickshire candidate), and another Thomas Malory, of Studley and Hutton in Yorkshire, has been suggested as the possible author. Whichever Thomas Malory wrote the book, it seems likely that he did so when he was in prison – he describes himself as a 'knight-prisoner' – and that he died around 1471.

Although Malory's work closely follows stories written by earlier authors, his work is significantly different to theirs in terms of its structure. Whereas the writers of French Romance, and Geoffrey of Monmouth himself, wrote Arthurian legends as one continuous intertwining event, Malory divided the individual components into distinct books and chapters. From a reader's point of view, this has to be considered one of the landmark events in Arthurian literature, as it allowed clear beginnings and endings to be allocated to the individual stories that had gradually been pushed together to make up the Arthurian cycle. It should be said that Malory was equally important in deconstructing the tales of Arthur as he was for constructing them.

By doing so, Malory made it possible for modern scholars to return to the roots of medieval literature. His 'serialisation' of the legend means that those who choose to read and study his work can consider the legend as a number of individual stories, culled from diverse sources and bound together to make the stories of Arthur all inclusive, rather than an ongoing yet never evolving narrative following a single, linear plot-line.

Malory's publisher, William Caxton, hinted in his preface to the 1485 edition *of The Death of Arthur* as to the sources for Malory's work. He says that Malory used 'certain books of French and reduced it into English'. Although some of these continental sources are now unknown to us, it seems pretty certain that Malory included the Vulgate Cycle and other French romances. He also appears to have been influenced by English contributions such as a fourteenth century alliterative poem that shared its name with his own work.

Malory's version of the legend is the lengthiest of medieval Arthurian literature, yet also the best known and most appreciated by modern readers. Contrary to the title of the piece, *The Death of Arthur* recounts Arthur's reign in its entirety and not just the brutal ending. Malory's tale also spans a different, shorter period of time to Geoffrey of Monmouth's great *History*: *The Death of Arthur* begins with the conception of Arthur, son of Uther Pendragon, and ends with the death of Launcelot du Lake (as Malory names him) and the crowning of Constantine, son of Cador, as Arthur's successor. Arthur's early achievements with the help of Merlin are included, before Malory shifts the story-line to recount the deeds of Arthur's knights: Balin, Pellinore, Gawaine and Ywaine (to use Malory's spellings), Gareth, Tristram, Launcelot, Lamorak and Palomides are all included. Malory then proceeds with the story of the Holy Grail, adapted from the Vulgate cycle, whilst focusing on the Grail exploits of Galahad, Bors and Perceval. Throughout this middle section of *The Death of Arthur*, the King himself takes a backseat, often appearing only at the beginning and end of each tale. The deeds of Launcelot are dealt with in detail, and the epic battle between Arthur and Modred is a high point towards the rather downbeat ending of the book, by which point it seems that anyone who is anyone has died. Bedevere returned Excalibur to the Lady of the Lake on Arthur's behalf, and the King was ushered away to Avalon and buried in a tomb the very next day – possibly sleeping, possibly dead.

Other writers who chipped in
Never underestimate the two most prolific authors of all time: Anon and his chum Et Al. Actually, we do have names for some of the other people who added their own twist to the legend of Arthur, but it must also be remembered that many of the stories were traditional, oral tales recited in front of crowds. As such, many bards would have adapted the medieval versions of Arthur's world to suit either their own preferences or that of their audiences. And the names that have passed down to us as the author of a specific strand of Arthurian legend may not have been

the original storyteller, but instead may have just been the first person to commit that strand to parchment. It should also be remembered that the medieval authors of Arthurian legend wrote in Latin, French or earlier forms of the English language which would not be easily recognised today; so in addition to oral storytellers, we also have the translators of the original texts to rely upon and thank for their contribution to Arthurian literature.

Although seemingly obscure, many of the less common tales of Arthur and his knights were snapped up by Sir Thomas Malory when he came to write his famous *The Death of Arthur*. Robert de Boron, a Burgundian poet, was the first to explicitly depict the Holy Grail as a holy relic associated with the Crucifixion, rather than a magical object. Robert wrote three Arthurian romances at the end of the twelfth or start of the thirteenth century: *The Chronicle of the History of the Grail* (sometimes known as *Joseph of Arimathea*), *Merlin*, and *Perceval*. *Merlin* was the first story to include reference to Arthur pulling a sword from a stone to prove his right to kingship. English romances, both in verse and prose, sprung up from the second half of the thirteenth century onwards, including *Sir Launfal* (written around 1350 by Thomas Chestre), *Ywain and Gawain* (also written in the mid-fourteenth century), and two late fourteenth century tales: *Sir Gawain and the Green Knight* and *The Adventures of Arthur* (charmingly entitled *The Awntyrs of Arthure* in its original form). Such English texts are typically reduced versions of earlier French texts, compacted from the sometimes wandering original tales to give action-packed, clear-cut adventure stories.

It wasn't only the English, French and Welsh who wrote of Arthur and his knights' adventures. As the stories told by Geoffrey of Monmouth, Chrétien de Troyes, and the other early contributors spread around Europe, so poets and writers in these countries developed their own versions of Arthurian legend, often with a personal, regional touch. Hartmann von Aue and Wolfram von Eschenbach, two German writers, contributed *Iwein* and *Parzival* respectively (being adapted from the French tales of *Yvain* and *Perceval*). Other German writers retold the stories of Gawain and Tristan. In Ireland, a translation of the Vulgate Cycle's *Quest Of The Holy Grail* was written in the fourteenth or fifteenth centuries, and Scottish poets adapted the stories of Lancelot and Gawain for their own audiences. Arthurian legend also gained popularity as far afield as Greece (where an early fourteenth century poem tells of an old knight who Lancelot, Gawain and Tristan are not able to defeat);

Scandinavia; Iceland (where Tristan and Perceval traditions were popular); Italy; and even Cyprus, where crusading knights held an Arthurian tournament in 1286.

An interesting footnote to medieval Arthurian literature is that Edward I, perhaps the greatest king of medieval England, justified his invasion of Scotland to Pope Boniface VIII in 1301 by quoting excerpts from Geoffrey of Monmouth's *The History of the Kings of Britain*. To a medieval audience, the stories they heard were not just cautionary tales of romance or even simple entertainment – they were histories solid enough to be used to support political claims. As Geoffrey of Monmouth might well have realised when he was constructing his *History*, he was creating a figurehead and forefather to his Anglo-Norman kings.

Arthur's magnet: other medieval heroes who were sucked into the popular legend

As the stories surrounding Arthur's royal court gained popularity, so folk heroes and semi-historical warriors who had previously been completely unrelated to the legend of Arthur were introduced to his court. Some of the most famous Arthurian heroes featured independently in their own medieval literature before being sucked into the court of Arthur. Others had their own spin-off stories on the back of Arthurian popularity (rather like Tucker from *Grange Hill*, and Angel from *Buffy The Vampire Slayer*).

For example, Gawain is one of the earliest characters associated with Arthur in legend and folklore; his original name was Gwalchmai, which translates as 'Hawk of May'. Gawain plays a crucial role in many early Arthurian tales, from Wales, England and, to a lesser degree, France. He was mentioned by this name in the early tale *Culhwch and Olwen* as Arthur's nephew, and is mentioned in a Welsh triad (you can read more about these in Chapter Four) as one of the 'Three Well-Endowed Men of Ynys Prydein'. Lucky old Gawain (no, not that – this endowment meant that he was a powerful man). In some early tales, Gawain's name and role seem interchangeable with that of Arthur himself, and his deeds exist in the separate English tradition of *Sir Gawain and the Green Knight*, committed to parchment around the year 1400, and retold in Chapter Five. *Sir Gawain and the Green Knight* is one of the most accessible and enjoyable set of verses that has survived from the medieval period, and presents the reader with mixed messages of both Christian and pre-Christian imagery. Through *Sir Gawain and the Green Knight* and other folk tales, this hero should be considered to exist in his own right outside of Arthurian legend.

The famous sorcerer or seer Merlin, who was so instrumental in Arthur's rise to power in most legends, also has origins outside of the Arthurian tales. He appears to have been based on a well-known historical Welsh bard named Myrddin. Myrddin was associated with the court of Rhydderch of Strathclyde in northern England and south-west Scotland, in the late sixth century. As well as having several poems attributed to him, Myrddin is remembered as The Wild Man of the Woods, whose mind gave out after the bloody Battle of Arderydd in 573, forcing him to live in the Caledonian woods away from other men. Significantly, given his later role as a seer, Myrddin (as The Wild Man of the Woods) was said to make prophecies and befriend woodland animals (Geoffrey of Monmouth was probably aware of these folktales when he came to write his own version of Merlin's prophecies). This Myrddin may also be remembered as Lailoken, another Wild Man of the Woods in Scottish literature, and as Sweeney the Wild Man in Ireland. In the ninth century, Welsh legend remembered another British prophet, later incorporated into Geoffrey of Monmouth's *History* as 'the boy without a father' who prophesies to Vortigern; sometimes the child is called Ambrosius, but he is also often named as Merlin. It is likely that these two characters from Celtic tales became the composite, single Merlin of Arthurian fame.

Other characters, such as Lancelot, Perceval (or Peredur as he was known in Welsh legend), and Tristan also have separate existences outside of Arthurian legend.

The Black Witch Falls To Arthur's Blade

Chapter Four

Arthur of the Celts

Medieval authors such as Geoffrey of Monmouth and Thomas Malory were not the first people to write about Arthur; the tales Geoffrey committed to paper had, he claimed, originally been written in an ancient book given to him by the Archdeacon of Oxford. If this is true, the ancient book was almost certainly composed by earlier Welsh, Breton or British authors. This is because Arthur had indeed left his mark in the imagination of his native Celtic lands before Geoffrey's time, in both history and literature (and he would continue to do so throughout the medieval period).

Wales, Cornwall and the Celtic world are famous for their rich tradition of oral history. Given Arthur's pre-eminent position in Celtic legend and folklore, it is unsurprising that his name crops up on a regular basis in such stories. But does the Arthur of folklore bear any similarities to a historical king, or is his name just a byword for the attitude and power of Dark Ages and medieval kingship?

The Arthur of the Welsh, Cornish, Irish and Bretons was a very different man to the chivalric, righteous ruler of medieval England and France that he had become by Malory's time. In fact, piecing together the allusions to Arthur in Celtic tales probably brings us closer to the truth of the historical Arthur, if indeed he ever existed.

But who were the Celts? The word is liberally cast around in the modern day, usually referring to Scottish and Irish heritage, but the true definition of Celtic belonging is far more complicated that that. Originally, Celtic culture spread from central Europe into the West during the first millennium BC. In the mid-twentieth century, most historians believed that the arrival of the Celts in a new region must have meant they had invaded the area, perhaps influenced by the turbulent nature of their own era. Now, in more peaceful decades, most scholars believe that it was their culture – not their people – that spread, and that the peoples of ancient Britain were not Celtic by blood line, but instead by their cultural patterns. Essentially, we now think that the Celts were one of the first exponents of globalisation. In the period before the Roman invasion of Britain, and throughout the Roman period, Celtic culture flourished in Britain and mixed with Roman culture too. By the Dark Ages, Britain was one of the few places in Europe that continued to be strongly influenced by older Celtic ideals. As ideas of nationalism spread towards the end of the Dark Ages and the beginning of the medieval period, the peoples of modern Wales, Cornwall, Scotland, Brittany and Ireland all believed that they shared a common 'Celtic' past, and this idea grew and has passed down to the modern era.

Such strong feelings of cultural identity meant that Dark Ages and medieval Celtic art – both literary and imagery – developed on the fringes of mainstream European movements, and Celtic works have retained a strong, independent feel even to the modern reader. The ideals and concepts important in Celtic literature and legend were distinct from those of the Anglo-Saxons, Normans, and later English and French writers. The themes and content sometimes feel more barbaric than their European contemporaries, and hark back to a period of heroic culture and endemic warfare. And from this background, the first recorded stories of Arthur – as both a legendary and theoretically historical icon – were seen to emerge.

The nature of the sources
Many of the Welsh stories involving Arthur existed long before they were written down. Celtic legend – not just in Wales, but in Ireland and Scotland too – had a long and proud tradition of oral history well before written documents became commonplace. So many of the stories about Arthur, although written down in the medieval period, probably represent much earlier tales. And this, of course, presents problems when we come to dating our early Arthurian source material.

The date at which a story was written down does not mean that it really dates from that period. Most of our early Arthurian sources have survived in twelfth and thirteenth century manuscripts – a time by which other European writers had made Arthur a 'star' and his fame had become widespread. Yet the written Celtic histories and folk tales mostly record earlier oral traditions, which were in existence well before the Celts started to commit their stories to manuscripts. This means that such tales were open to corruption, interpolation and misinterpretation between their date of origin and their final appearance on the page of a book. For works such as the battle poem *The Gododdin*, there may have been a period of up to six hundred years between its origination and appearance as a written text – and that leaves a lot of time for mistakes to creep in.

This leaves us with a dilemma – how much of what has survived accurately reflects the Arthur of the Celts in his pre-Geoffrey of Monmouth form? Geoffrey claimed to have used an 'ancient book' as his source for Arthur and the rest of his *History*, so unless he was lying, we can be sure that Arthur existed in some form before Geoffrey's best seller. In fact, the study of language used in Celtic Arthurian sources shows that some of the stories written down in the medieval period did have their origin in the Dark Ages. Many other Celtic tales of Arthur, although their written language does not strongly prove the case, show ideas and snippets of 'lost' tales to again suggest that they appeared much earlier than the date of their written version.

So we can be certain that the concept of Arthur as a warrior and/or a king existed in the tales of the Celtic peoples in the centuries before Geoffrey of Monmouth kick-started Arthur's widespread fame throughout Europe.

The other major problem when trying to use early sources as historical evidence is the way in which the writers of such pieces transparently switch between plain history and clear fantasy. Magical acts, characters from earlier (or later) history, and other incidents that would never pass for 'history' in the modern world enter the equation. Even the authors of these early texts can be semi-legendary: for example, the famous Taliesin, a northern British bard from the kingdom of Rheged, took on magical qualities in later stories about his life, and many poems were attributed to him with little evidence to support his authorship. Although noted as 'history', few of the contemporary sources available to us now can be considered reliable enough to pass as documents that a modern historian could depend on. Despite this, these sources probably contain semi-historical events and partial truths, and if nothing else, at least serve to show us how the Celts perceived themselves and their past. And, of course, if we were to completely ignore such documents on the grounds of them being potentially flawed, we would have no written sources whatsoever of how the Welsh and their cultural kin recorded their past.

Gildas

Gildas is considered to be one of our key sources for the history of immediately post-Roman Britain; despite this, his work was not written with the intention of providing a linear history in the true sense of the word. Instead, Gildas was a man on a mission – a mission to remind the Britons of their foolishness and apathy. His work is known by the catchy title of *On the Ruin of Britain*. Through information that Gildas supplied, we know that he wrote in the forty-fourth year of his life, and that he was born in the year of the Battle of Badon. Estimates as to when this actually took place vary between about 450 and 540, although *The Welsh Annals* record that Gildas died in 572 (however, the accuracy of this remains questionable).

Gildas' text is the only near contemporary source for the time of the historical Arthur, although its content is such that, if other sources still existed, it is unlikely that historians would continue to turn to Gildas for information. As part of his fire and brimstone chastisement, Gildas invokes the Britons' previous history and current affairs, although we do not know how much his commentary is blurred from the truth by religious zealousness. In places, we know he has muddled his dates, but for the end of Roman Britain and the following decades, he might well shed light on otherwise forgotten events. Whatever the truth, Gildas is the only Briton whose written historical testimony has survived from this period. Stories of St Patrick (a Briton taken into slavery by Irish raiders) are near contemporary, but they tell us little of the period's history.

On the Ruin of Britain consists of three constituent parts: a historical prelude, a complaint against the contemporary British kings and a complaint against the contemporary British Church. For the purposes of the study of Arthur, the historical section is the most important, although Gildas' description of his contemporary kings is also instructive.

Gildas' historical section is certainly not a detailed, flowing narrative history of the kind we are used to today; instead, he appears to have selected a number of calamities that he could describe as the result of the sinning and wicked behaviour of the Britons. According to him, when the Romans left, the Picts and the Scots (Irish) invaded Britain, and the weak and enfeebled Britons appealed to the Roman Aëtius for help. Aëtius evidently had better things to do (such as trying to hold on to his continental empire), and so the Britons, led by a 'proud tyrant' (presumably Vortigern) hired Saxon mercenaries. This succeeded, but then the Saxons revolted and drove the Britons into the western regions of Britain, destroying cities and civilized life as they advanced. The Britons were caught between the advancing Saxons and the Irish Sea, and then came their salvation, in the form of Ambrosius Aurelianus, a descendant of the last of the Romans in Britain. Ambrosius rallied the Britons and Gildas describes the ebb and flow of the campaign, culminating in a British victory at Badon Hill – a battle later to become synonymous with Arthur's name. Yet Gildas does not name Arthur, implying (but not clearly stating) that Ambrosius was the victor. Gildas' depiction of Britain was as a plague-ridden, corrupt and rapidly declining region, with its cities crumbling and the land torn apart by warfare and famine. This sounds particularly apocalyptic and slanted to emphasise Gildas' following complaints, yet until recent decades, Gildas' vision provided the blueprint for early post-Roman British history. Chapter Two's history attempts to rectify this popular idea, although it is noticeable that some of Gildas' story appears to be true (for example, a period of Saxon decline that suggests that the British victory at Badon really was as significant as Gildas suggests).

After setting the scene of devastation, Gildas then goes on to complain about the British kings of his time, whose forerunners' sins directly caused the fall of Britain. Gildas points out that the British kings were nothing more than tyrants (recent debate has suggested that the term 'tyrant' should not be thought of in its modern meaning, and instead simply meant they were local rulers with little influence outside their regions). He then goes on to name five such tyrants: Constantinus, 'tyrant whelp of the filthy lioness of Dumnonia'; Aurelius Caninus, a 'lion whelp'; Vortipor, the 'tyrant of the Demetae'; Cuneglasus, meaning 'tawny butcher' according to Gildas, but more likely translating as 'Blue Hound'; and Maglocunus, the 'dragon of the island'. Geographically, most of these rulers can be linked to Wales or the south-west of England, and Maglocunus can be identified with some certainty as Maelgwn of Gwynedd (who probably died in 549 from plague). Gildas' rulers are petty men, and probably no match for their Saxon opponents. From the unification of Britain that Gildas' reference to a 'proud tyrant' suggests, through the intervening hundred or so years to his time of writing, the British power base had fragmented into a handful of smaller, weaker kingdoms.

Having criticised these rulers for their lazy government, Gildas then turns his wrath on the British Church, spitting bile and suggesting that the priests are nothing more than treacherous fools and 'shameless grabbers'. Again, Gildas slams the Britons for their apathetic attitude and shameful lifestyle.

Yet amongst his ranting and chiding, Gildas does not once mention Arthur, which is genuinely surprising if the warlord ever really existed. Not least because Gildas does mention the battle which later became synonymous with the warlord Arthur's greatest victory: Badon.

Gildas wrote other documents too, but skirts around further historical commentary in his other texts (which are mostly fragments of letters). The famous Anglo-Saxon historian Bede drew heavily on Gildas' work when he came to write his *Ecclesiastical History of the English Peoples* in the eighth century, and some similarities can be drawn between Gildas' narrative and the later *Anglo-Saxon Chronicle*. Like Gildas, neither of these two sources mentioned Arthur, but then again, they were written by the descendants of Arthur's enemies.

The Welsh Annals

Preserved in a medieval book dating to the twelfth century is a collection of Welsh texts with a far earlier origin. Amongst the forty or so documents inside the book, one stands out head and shoulders above the rest in our search for Arthur: *The Welsh Annals*. Annals were used in the ancient world to keep track of time and as a reminder of important events: Dark Ages annals were mostly used to record the births and deaths of saints, kings and historic events of great significance. In broad terms, this document is rather like a British equivalent of the *Anglo-Saxon Chronicle*, and reads as a time line of history. Tucked away into *The Welsh Annals* are two crucial references:

Year 72: The Battle of Badon, in which Arthur carried the cross of our Lord Jesus Christ for three days and three nights on his shoulders, and the Britons were the victors.
Year 93: The conflict at Camlann in which Arthur and Medraut [Modred] perished; and there was pestilence in Britain and Ireland.

The years given in the *Annals* do not refer to our modern dating calendar, but would appear instead to start with Year 1 as AD 445 (although some people place the start date as 443 or 448). This would mean that the Year 72 date was AD 518 (sometimes 521, sometimes

516), and the Year 93 date was 539 (sometimes 542, as recorded in Geoffrey of Monmouth's *History* and sometimes 537). Excellent – evidence of Arthur… with dates thrown in for good measure, give or take a year or two. But hang on.

The version of the *Annals* we still have available (in the British Museum's Harleian collection) was written around 1100, and as the last entry in the *Annals'* time line is the death of the Welsh king Rhodri ap Hywel Dda in or around 957, this version can only have been written after 957. That means that the *Annals* as we have them today were written about 400 years after the date given for the Battle of Badon and the death of Arthur at Camlann. This is hardly contemporary evidence – it is akin to my writing a history of the Gunpowder Plot (which took place in 1605).

By the tenth century, when our present version of *The Welsh Annals* was completed, Arthur was known as a character in Celtic folklore – take a look at some of the other texts included in this chapter. It is possible that *The Welsh Annals'* dates were constructed to 'prove' that Arthur really did live, rather than condemning him to life as a dateless legend. Without any surviving earlier sources proving his existence, the *Annals'* writer may have taken an educated guess at the actual years of a real Arthur's life, based on surviving oral tradition.

Having said this, it is possible that the *Annals* were started at an earlier date, and that only a later copy updated in the middle of the tenth century has survived. The *Annals* show the influence of earlier Irish sources (and possibly even long-forgotten northern British annals), especially when providing some of the earlier entries, so it is possible that this document builds on earlier traditions. Supporting this theory is the fact that the *Annals'* dates do not really match Gildas' chronology (Gildas places Badon probably closer to the year 500, a good twenty years earlier than *The Welsh Annals* depict it). If *The Welsh Annals'* author was simply trying to create a history for Arthur, why fly in the face of contrary evidence that was written closer to the time?

The question of Modred's role (Medraut in the *Annals*) is an interesting one. The *Annals* do not state that he fought against Arthur, yet this became an essential ingredient of later Arthurian legend. Geoffrey of Monmouth's *History* shows evidence that he was familiar with *The Welsh Annals* and with the work of Nennius, as he managed to incorporate themes from these sources into his work. Yet we know little else of Modred or his historical counterpart Medraut from any early, reliable source. Could it be that other documents existed in Geoffrey's time, telling us more about Modred, Camlann, and Arthur that are now lost? Again, this may suggest that the Annals built on earlier British oral history, or, again, it could be that Geoffrey simply filled in the gaps as he pleased, making Modred and Arthur enemies.

Despite the promise they offer at face value, *The Welsh Annals* do not provide us with solid evidence for the existence of Arthur. They were written at far too late a date to be of real value, and it cannot be proved that any of their content came from an earlier period. What they do show the modern researcher is that Arthur's deeds were considered to be significant enough by the author of the *Annals* to have been included in a list primarily consisting of basic dates for saints and kings. Whether the author believed Arthur to have been a real-life person, or whether he was creating a historical context for a clearly legendary figure we cannot now know. We do not even know if this Arthur was considered to be a king or just a warrior. However, what we can see is that Arthur was right up there with the kings and religious heroes of the Britons and Welsh in the later Dark Ages.

Nennius and *The History of the Britons*

Another part of the surviving manuscript that holds within it *The Welsh Annals* is *The History of the Britons*. In the prologue of the latter, the author identifies himself as Nennius, a ninth century British monk who probably lived in Wales and may have committed his *History* to writing in 829 or 830. The earliest surviving copy we have today was compiled around 1100 – which is still an early (pre-Geoffrey of Monmouth) date for Arthurian reference material.

A lot of debate has taken place over the past few decades in an attempt to confirm or deny that Nennius really was actually the author (or, more correctly, the editor) of *The History of the Britons*. Professor Leslie Alcock decided to term the manuscript containing this work *The British Historical Miscellany*, and others have referred to it by its library reference code: *British Museum Harleian MS 3859*, to avoid any presumption as to the author's identity. The current consensus is that he probably wasn't, but no one can quite be sure; such a debate just goes to show how little we actually know about the early Arthurian sources that have survived through time. As the jury is still out, I would prefer to give Nennius the benefit of my doubt, so will continue to refer to *The History of the Britons* as being Nennius' own synthesis.

Nennius (or the as yet unidentified editor) claimed to have made a huge heap of all of the extracts of earlier British history that he could gather, and proceeded to write them down in a more cohesive narrative. By doing so, the editor suggested that the Britons would perhaps learn from their predecessors' stupidity and folly. His narrative clearly contains fictional, magical elements, which he may well have believed to have been true; yet within *The History of the Britons*, it would appear that some well-remembered or half-remembered history is present too. Exactly how accurate *The History*'s recollections are is debatable; modern theories suggest that it is useful as a source for the ninth century, but less so for the earlier (Arthurian) period.

Arthur features in Nennius' compilation with a foot in each camp, historical and legendary. *The History* claims that the Saxons were a plague inflicted upon the Britons for their earlier sins (in much the same way as Gildas wrote), and that the British leader Vortigern was betrayed by his Saxon ally Hengist. With Hengist's betrayal, Saxon holdings in Britain grew, and Hengist's son Octha established the Saxon kingdom of Kent. And then the Saxons were held back by the victories of a war leader named Arthur, who fought for the British kings. Nennius does not name Arthur as a king himself, and instead described him as a 'Leader of Battles' – *dux bellorum* in Latin.

Nennius lists Arthur's battles as follows, and tells us that they were all victories for his army; we may assume from the context in which the battle list is given that his enemies were Saxons, but we cannot be sure. The first battle was fought at the River Glein (which Nennius describes as being in the east). This was followed by four battles all along a river named the Dubglas, which *The History* tells us was in the region of Linnuis. The next battle, Arthur's sixth, was on yet another river, this time the Bassas. The seventh battle moved away from rivers and was set in the wood of Caledonia, at Cat Coed Celyddon. The stronghold of Guinnion was the site of the eighth battle, and *The History* informs us that at this battle, Arthur carried the image of the Virgin Mary upon his shoulders (or shield, depending upon the interpretation you choose to accept). Guinnion saw a great slaughter of Arthur's pagan enemies. Following this victory, another battle was fought in the City of the Legion, and the tenth saw him back on a riverbank, this time the River Tribruit. Arthur's eleventh battle was on the mountain known as Agned, but the final and most famous of all battles that Arthur fought (according to *The History*) was that on Mount Badon. Here, *The History* claims that

Arthur slew 960 enemies. Badon is, of course, mentioned by Gildas, but Arthur is not mentioned by name in the earlier monk's work. After Arthur's time, Nennius informs us that the Saxons sent for reinforcements and new kings from Germany, and finally ruled over Britain. *The History* does not say what became of Arthur, nor does it mention his other famous battle – the one at Camlann, where tradition (and *The Welsh Annals*) record that he died.

It seems that *The History of the Britons*' list of Arthur's victories may have been taken from a now forgotten British war poem remembering Arthur's great triumphs (the place names of Badon, Celyddon and Guinnion all rhyme, and this would also explain why his defeat at Camlann does not feature in *The History*). Many researchers have attempted to pinpoint where these battles took place, in the hope that the list would point to the geographical focus of Arthur's campaigns; some of the better theories are discussed in Chapters Two and Seven. The only two that would appear to have any security in their prediction are the wood of Caledonia (which can probably be found in southern Scotland) and the City of the Legion, which most scholars would agree must be one of the Roman cities of Caerleon, York, Chester or Lincoln. None of these cities (except for York, at a push) would be ideally suited as sites of a battle in a campaign that also included warfare in southern Scotland, so it is difficult to judge the truth behind the list, and indeed the time frame over which the campaign was fought. Perhaps most importantly, *The History* shows us that the tradition of Arthur as a historical battle leader was already growing in popularity by the time *The History of the Britons* was heaped together.

The History, however, tells us that the stories surrounding Arthur at this time were more than mere battle tales. Later in the same manuscript – technically not as part of *The History*, but instead as a work in its own right named *The Marvels of Britain* – Arthur is featured again. *The Marvels* is a collection of local folklore, and two of the items included mention Arthur. The first is a mass of stones at Buellt (Builth Wells in South Wales), the uppermost of which is marked with the print of a dog's paw. The paw print belonged to Cabal or Cafall, the dog of 'the soldier Arthur', and the animal set its paw onto the rock during Arthur's hunt for the boar named Trwyth – which is also mentioned in *Culhwch and Olwen*. The stone cannot be moved from the site – if removed, it will magically reappear in its place atop the other stones the very next day. The second mention of Arthur in *The Marvels* refers to the grave of his son, Amr, at a site named Erging. It is stated that Arthur killed Amr and buried him here in an enchanted grave which changed in dimension from time to time. The compiler of *The Marvels* claimed to have measured the grave on more than one occasion and verified the truth of this unlikely story!

It is interesting that Arthur is referred to as 'the soldier' in *The Marvels*. This title reinforces the idea mentioned in *The History* that Arthur fought for the British kings, but was not one himself. The mention of the magical boar Trwyth, which cross-checks with the connection in *Culhwch and Olwen* is also interesting, as this almost certainly points to another early tale of Arthur which found its way into both *Culhwch and Olwen* and *The Marvels*. And the story that goes with the grave of Amr is interesting in that it links Arthur to the death of a close relative – Amr may be his son, but perhaps the later stories of Arthur fighting against and slaying his nephew Modred may have been borrowed from just such a folk tale.

A late twelfth or early thirteenth century copy of *The History of the Britons* has some additional marginal notes known as the Sawley Glosses, and they contain some different traditions about Arthur not found in other copies of Nennius' original manuscript. The Sawley Glosses refer to Arthur as 'son of Uthr' and note that Arthur's name translated into Latin as 'horrible bear' or 'iron hammer'. The Sawley Glosses then move on to say that Arthur visited Jerusalem, and that he there made a cross of the same dimensions as the Blessed Cross which he had consecrated and kept a prayer vigil over for three days. This cross granted him victory over his pagan enemies, and (just to make doubly sure of this) he also carried an image of the Holy Mary. These marginal notes re-emphasise Arthur's Christian sentiments, and give a little background to the statements made elsewhere in *The History* about Arthur's religious battle icons. Whether the margin notes draw on additional tradition not recorded in writing in any other surviving source, or whether they were a medieval invention brought about by Arthur's new found twelfth century fame, we cannot be sure. Yet someone took the trouble to include them.

The problems surrounding the use of *The History of the Britons* as a valid historical source are plentiful – the date of the work and possible corruption of its text, the identity of its real author and the reality of the 'heap of material' from which the History was collated are all problematic. Yet alongside the work of Gildas and *The Welsh Annals*,

The History of the Britons is the only source from a period so much as remotely approaching Arthur's lifetime that a modern scholar could even begin to describe as a historical source. Every other Celtic source that names Arthur was written down as either hagiography or a work of literature. And no other source devotes so much space in its record of Arthur's deeds as *The History*'s list of twelve Arthurian battles.

Tales of the bards and poets

Not only did the Britons and their Celtic counterparts attempt to record their own history – perhaps better considered as pseudo-history – but they also boasted one of the world's greatest traditions of oral folklore and legend. Naturally, as their latter day saviour, Arthur featured in a number of Celtic tales, but not always in the guise of a heroic warrior and king.

Some of the most significant and best remembered tales are detailed in their own sections later in this chapter (*The Spoils of Annwn, Culhwch and Olwen, The Gododdin*), but many more excerpts of Celtic literature make reference to Arthur and his followers. Beyond the tales where Arthur plays a central role in the story, there exist several more passing references to him.

One of the later yet most complete stories in its own right is *The Dream of Rhonabwy*, which was probably written down between 1149 and 1159. The fictional character Rhonabwy set out on a mission for Madog ap Maredudd, who was the ruler of Powys in the mid-twelfth century. Rhonabwy fell asleep and in a vision or dream found himself magically transported back to the world of Arthur, the Dark Ages warlord. It was the eve of the Battle of Badon, and Arthur was in his camp, playing a chess- or draughts-like board game (with the excellent name *gwyddbwyll* – I can't see it replacing *Monopoly* these days) with another warlord, named Owain ab Urien. Arthur does not pull his concentration away from the game, even though Owain's ravens and Arthur's warriors are fighting and killing each other in the camp. Both leaders sit by, placidly playing their game, until a third party intervenes and calls a truce.

The Dream of Rhonabwy is a very curious piece. Unless the later dream section of the story was lifted from another source, we can be sure that the tale was first set down in the mid-twelfth century, when Madog ap Maredudd is known to have lived. This in itself is a rare opportunity to accurately date an Arthurian tale. The story appears to show an inverted world – Arthur is a weak leader, the Battle of Camlann, we are told, occurs before Badon, and Arthur is uncaring about his men's deaths, and bettered by a lesser warlord, Owain. Owain's inclusion in the piece is interesting in itself – he was a late sixth century northern British leader, otherwise unconnected to the Welsh borders. Perhaps the tale remembers some long-forgotten feud between Arthur and another warlord of Owain's high authority, or perhaps, as others have suggested, it is a beautifully composed example of medieval Welsh parody.

In other examples of Celtic literature, Arthur plays a far more familiar role. So many of these tales have only survived in medieval manuscripts, but many of them probably hark from an earlier date, and again may provide glimpses of truth about a real-life Arthur, beloved warlord of the Celts.

The Stanzas of the Graves is a work of verse in the Black Book of Carmarthen, which is difficult to date precisely. It recalls the sites of graves of heroic figures from the past, and along with Gwalchmai (an early form of Gawain), Owain son of Urien, and a reference to Camlann, it is noted that a grave for Arthur is 'the world's wonder' – meaning it's location is no longer remembered. At some point, probably in the later medieval period but possibly from a much earlier date, Welsh folklore and literature started to claim that Arthur would return as a saviour of the nation, rather like a few other national heroes. Similar stories also emerged in Cornwall, but there is no solid evidence to tell us how early these stories were in circulation in Wales or Cornwall.

One of the other poems alongside *The Stanzas of the Graves* in the Black Book of Carmarthen, is the otherwise untitled piece *Pa Gur* (from the opening line of the poem, which translates as: 'What man is the gate keeper?'). Usually dated to the eleventh century, *Pa Gur* is an incomplete work, as a leaf of the book is now missing. What we do know is that the piece relates a conversation between Arthur and Glewlwyd, the gatekeeper; it later develops into a list of the deeds of Arthur's men. The plot device seems to be that Arthur is explaining who he is to his own gatekeeper, who does not recognise him; in doing so, Arthur outlines who his followers are and what their greatest deeds were. This plot device may have been common in the Dark Ages and medieval Celtic literature – *Culhwch and Olwen* has a similar device as part of the story, as does the Irish *Battle of Mag Tuired*. At a slightly later date, Shakespeare's *Macbeth* may carry an echo of Celtic literature, including as it does a comic episode involving a gatekeeper. *Pa Gur* may well have been rendered a humorous piece – the idea that Arthur's own gatekeeper (or any other gatekeeper) did not recognise him has an air of parody about it. Through his account of the deeds of his men and himself, Arthur is portrayed in this poem as a figure of legendary action, undertaking superhuman tasks, battling enchanted and life-like enemies (Arthur's companion Cei slays witches and the Cat of Palug, and there are several references to battles). A number of the deeds listed in this poem have similarities to the achievements of Arthur's men in other works, and it is possible that this poem may have been an attempt to bring together the memory of many diverse strands of earlier Arthurian folklore that may otherwise have been lost. The irony of this would be that at least one folio of the poem no longer exists, and we do not know what lost gems may have been waiting on the next page.

The Dialogue of Arthur and the Eagle survives in a fourteenth century manuscript, although it is probable that this poem is a work of twelfth century origin. It consists of a conversation between Arthur, who describes himself as a bard in this poem, and a great bird. The setting is Cornwall, and Arthur is also referred to as 'Chief of the Battalions of Cornwall' and as a 'bear of men' (this title is interesting given that one possible meaning of the name 'Arthur' is 'bear', as discussed later in this book). Despite the probable date of this poem, Arthur is not the king of later literature, but is instead still very obviously a great warlord and leader in battle – the traditional Celtic status of Arthur before the medieval period.

Geraint Son of Erbin also shows Arthur in his role as a warlord. Purporting to tell the tale of the Battle of Llongborth (probably Portchester in Hampshire), *Geraint Son of Erbin* dates at least as far back as the ninth century, and is perhaps even older. This makes it an early addition to Arthurian literature, and importantly demonstrates that Arthur was considered to be a worthy battle hero at that time. Geraint was a Dumnonian prince (a kingdom in modern Devon and Cornwall), and the poem records the defeat of his army, probably by the south coast Saxons. Geraint himself features in later Arthurian literature as the knight Erec, and is addressed as a great warrior in this poem. Yet alongside this great warlord fought Arthur's 'brave men' (sometimes translated as Arthur in person), and Arthur himself is referred to as an emperor, a rare title to be associated with him.

The Dialogue of Gwenhwyfar and Arthur is set to the background of the traditional Welsh abduction of Guinevere by Melwas (as outlined in the *Life of St Gildas* elsewhere in this chapter). Although our surviving versions of the poem are rather late – dating to the sixteenth century at the earliest – it is important to see that this event does not exist purely from a single source, and was instead an important enough tale to figure in multiple retellings of Arthurian folklore.

Arthur makes an appearance, and is referred to, in a number of other medieval Welsh poems. However, by the medieval period, Arthur was strongly established as a heroic, chivalric king even in Welsh literature, and his occurrence in later poems sees him hardly distinguishable from the English and French tales written about him in the same era.

A Welsh translation of Geoffrey of Monmouth's Latin *The History of the Kings of Britain* diverts slightly from the original work in several places, probably to account for native Welsh traditions that the translator would not allow to be overlooked. This includes a change to the end of the battle of Camlann, where the Welsh version notes that Geoffrey does not tell the complete tale of the battle (although, agonisingly, the Welsh writer does not elaborate).

Standing aside from the more routine poetry of the Celtic world were the short verses now known as triads. Celtic folklore (and poetic tradition) was fond of presenting things as threes, or as multiples of three – the 300, or 363, warriors in the poem *The Gododdin* is a good example; the idea that three elements made for a good poet is another (knowledge of history, poetic art and old verse). The triads similarly recited things in threes, and were probably devised as short 'memos' by oral historians, poets and bards, learned off by heart to allow a broad knowledge of Celtic tradition. The earliest written triads that survive today were written in the thirteenth to fifteenth century – several centuries after Arthur 'made it big' in mainstream medieval storytelling; however, it is almost certain that many of the triads, being devised as reminders before writing became widespread, are far older than this. Arthur appears, or is referred to, in the following triads:

> Three tribal thrones of the Island of Britain (Arthur is Chief Prince in St David's, Celliwig, and Pen Rhionydd)
> Three generous men of the Island of Britain (Arthur is noted as being more generous than the three men mentioned)
> Three well-endowed men of the Island of Britain (Llachau, son of Arthur, is included)
> Three chieftains of Arthur's court
> Three frivolous bards of the Island of Britain (Arthur is named as one – although he is seldom referred to as a bard in other literature)

Three favourites of Arthur's court – or battle horsemen

Three red reapers of the Island of Britain (Arthur is named as greater than all three)

Three powerful swineherds of the Island of Britain (one, named Drustan, kept his animals safe even when Arthur, Cei and Bedwyr attempted to steal them)

Three fortunate concealments of the Island of Britain (the head of Bran the Blessed, buried in London, kept Britain safe from Saxon invasion, until… see the next entry)

The three unfortunate disclosures (Arthur dug up Bran's head, claiming that his own strength would defend Britain – obviously when Arthur died, the Saxons could then flood in unopposed)

Three exalted prisoners of the Island of Britain (Arthur was held in an enchanted prison, a greater imprisonment than the three others mentioned)

Three harmful blows of the Island of Britain (one being recorded as initiating combat at Camlann – the battle where Arthur died)

Three unrestrained ravagings of the Island of Britain (Modred arrived at Arthur's court, ate all of his food and drank his drink, and struck Gwenhwyfar [Guinivere])

Arthur's three great queens

Arthur's three mistresses

Three unrestricted guests of Arthur's court

Three peers of Arthur's court

Three who could not be expelled from Arthur's court

Three faithless wives of the Island of Britain (Gwenhwyfar was more faithless than the three named, as she shamed Arthur)

Three futile battles of the Island of Britain (Camlann is named)

Three skilful bards at Arthur's court

Three splendid maidens of Arthur's court

These triads may retain some echo of history in them; perhaps a number of the people named in relation to Arthur were actually his contemporaries. Some of the deeds attributed to Arthur – such as stealing animals from rivals (rustling seems to have been a ritual activity and 'sport' in the Dark Ages), being a 'red reaper' (a great warrior), and employing skilled bards – have a ring of historical truth about them. That Arthur appears in so many of the triads shows that he was, by the time the triads came to be written down, a significant and pivotal character in Welsh literature and bardic tradition – the deeds of others were often compared to and belittled by his own. It is likely that Arthur featured in the earlier, orally recited triads, although we cannot now know if Arthur was always present, or if he displaced other heroes in Welsh literature only during the medieval period, when his popularity had spread throughout Europe. Certainly, a number of the triads appear to reflect stories made popular through French and English tales, not native Welsh ones. The triads were a device for aiding the memory of poets and bards from an early date, and it seems probable that the titles and deeds bestowed upon Arthur reflect his significant role in the early literature and folklore of the Welsh, although not realistically any historical truth.

The status of Arthur in this mixed bag of folklore and tradition is somewhat varied and seldom easy to identify. It can be assumed that Arthur was considered to be a warrior – albeit not always the great victor of medieval chivalric tales – and also a noble. His status as a king is less certain in a great body of Celtic stories, and his morals and values are often called into question. This might be a result of Arthur's growing popularity in medieval England, which could have upset Welsh patriots and caused them to abandon and discredit their former national hero. Alternatively these Welsh tales may reflect the personality of a more realistic, life-like leader of Dark Ages warriors, who was more complex than a one-dimensional chivalric king, living instead as a greedy noble of the type whom Gildas chided as being 'tyrants'.

The Spoils of Annwn

The Spoils of Annwn appears in The Book of Taliesin, and is attributed to this great northern British poet. Doubt remains as to whether Taliesin really did write all of the poems attributed to him, as he quickly became a figure of legend himself, having many deeds and a great deal of writing attributed to him no matter how unlikely this may have been. Taliesin seems to have lived in the late sixth century, so, if The Spoils of Annwn really was written by this great bard, and if Arthur was not introduced into the story at a later date, this would be just about the earliest surviving reference to Arthur.

In The Spoils of Annwn, Arthur, the bard Taliesin and Arthur's warband set out on an expedition to the Otherworld, with the intent of bringing back a magic cauldron named 'the Head of Annwn'. This cauldron, it was said, was a champion's cauldron, and the food of a coward would never heat or boil in such a magical receptacle. The expedition was a disaster – of the three shiploads of Arthur's warriors who set out to the Otherworld, only seven returned.

The location of the mysterious Otherworld has been debated by many researchers: it has been interpreted as Hell (which, of course, is only relevant if the story is read with Christian sentiment), the Fairy Fortress (an enchanted stronghold of the elven faerie world), and the Fortress of Glass (which may be interpreted as Avalon – where Arthur departs from with his mortal wounds). However, another possibility is Ireland; Arthur would, of course, need to sail across the Irish Sea to reach Ireland, and *The Spoils of Annwn* shares some common traits with one of Arthur and Culhwch's tasks in Ireland in *Culhwch and Olwen*. Curiously enough, Nennius' *The History of the Britons* relates a tale about a Spanish warrior band attacking Ireland, who come across a glass tower in the sea and lose 29 of their 30 ships when they attack it. This could perhaps be the Isle of Man or the Scilly Isles, or part of Ireland itself, and may well share a common folk legend with the Otherworld's identification as the Fortress of Glass.

If written by Taliesin, *The Spoils of Annwn* dates to the late sixth century, making it a very early reference to Arthur. It also places him in a supernatural environment, showing how early Arthur's name began to start detaching from any of his historical deeds. The story at the centre of *The Spoils of Annwn* is probably even older than the sixth century, perhaps even predating the Roman invasion of Britain. We can guess at this because the story mirrors a type of adventure remembered in much older Celtic myth (and in medieval romance in its holier guise of the Grail Quest): a quest for a cauldron. If this is the case, it may well be that Arthur appeared as a substitute for an earlier hero whom we no longer remember. *The History of the Britons'* tale of the Spanish warrior band attacking the tower of glass goes some way to support this theory.

The Spoils of Annwn is a curious piece in that it shows Arthur being defeated as a warrior; other early tales sometimes show him to be outsmarted, or ridiculed by a saint, but seldom do we hear of Arthur's band of warriors being so utterly defeated in early literature.

Culhwch and Olwen
Culhwch and Olwen was probably written in Wales in the early twelfth century, shortly before Geoffrey of Monmouth placed Arthur on a pedestal in his *History of the Kings of Britain*. Although this is the date at which this Welsh legend was first written down, it is very probable that

it remembers one or more much earlier tales. *Culhwch and Olwen* survives today in two different manuscripts: the White Book of Rhydderch (dated to approximately 1350), and the Red Book of Hergest (dated roughly between 1385 and 1410). As one of the many strands of Welsh literature, *Culhwch and Olwen* is one of the most complete and lengthy early stories, and as such it deserves to be treated separately from the other tales told by the bards and poets.

It seems as though the writer of *Culhwch and Olwen* was trying to gather together many traditional Welsh tales, listing many heroic characters and locations and weaving them into one cohesive story. In places, the story seems more like a list of important Welsh heroes and what they were famous for doing. However, extensive lists such as these were a common feature of medieval Welsh literature, so the writer may just have followed standard convention.

In essence, the original Welsh tale is as follows. A chieftain named Cilydd ap Celyddon Ledig and his wife Goleuddydd had a child, but Goleuddydd had gone mad during her pregnancy and would not enter any buildings. Wandering away, she gave birth to her child in a pig sty; naturally enough, being a mad lady, she decided to name her newborn child Culhwch, which translates as 'pig sty'.

Goleuddydd died shortly after her son's birth, and Culhwch was brought up by his father. Culhwch was of noble blood, being a cousin to Arthur, and grew into an honourable youth, so when his father remarried and Culhwch's stepmother summoned him to court, he naturally attended. The reason for his summons was in an attempt to get Culhwch to marry his stepmother's daughter, which Culhwch refused to do. His new stepmother then placed a curse on him, proclaiming that he would never have a wife until he won the heart of Olwen, the daughter of the fearsome giant Ysbaddaden. Culhwch's father Cilydd suggested to his son that he should visit the court of the boy's cousin, the great Arthur, and enlist his help in winning Olwen's heart. Recognising good advice when he heard it, Culhwch set off to visit his renowned cousin.

Upon his arrival at Arthur's court, Culhwch had to persuade the gatekeeper to let him in (dialogue with a difficult gatekeeper featured several times in Welsh literature at this time, and perhaps stood as a parody of the attitude and role of the gatekeeper). This accomplished, Culhwch gained an audience with Arthur and explained the curse placed upon him by his stepmother. Culhwch reminded Arthur that they were cousins, and that he was determined to win the heart of Olwen, the giant's daughter. In doing so, Culhwch flatters Arthur with an acknowledgement of Arthur's power and prowess, listing the names of all of Arthur's warriors (of whom *Culhwch and Olwen* tells us there were more than 250) and asking for their help in his quest.

Arthur listened to Culhwch's story, and swore that he would help his cousin to complete his task, giving everything he could, all except his most treasured possessions. These possessions were: his ship (not named in this tale but known elsewhere as *Prydwen*), his armour, Caledfwlch his sword, Rhongomyniad his spear, Wynebgwrthucher his shield, Carnwennan his dagger, and last (but presumably not least) his wife Gwenhwyfar (Guinevere).

As Arthur had agreed to assist his cousin, he despatched six of his warriors to help find Ysbaddaden: he sent Bedwyr (later famed as Bedivere), Cai (later to become Kay), Gwalchmai (an early form of Gawain), Cynddylig, Gwrhyr, and Menw. For many months, the companions had no success in locating Olwen's giant father Ysbaddaden, but eventually they met a shepherd named Custennin. Custennin knew Ysbaddaden well – the giant had slain 23 of his sons. Despite this, Custennin's wife knew Olwen and was on friendly terms with her, and she invited the giant's daughter to her cottage. When Olwen arrived, and was revealed to be stunningly beautiful, she was introduced to Culhwch. Olwen explained that she could only marry with the blessing of her father, and that she would never get this as Ysbaddaden was destined to die when his daughter married.

Yet Culhwch went to Ysbaddaden three times, asking for the giant's blessing to marry Olwen. The cruel giant attempted to kill him on each occasion, yet each time Culhwch managed to cheat death. On the third occasion, Ysbaddaden set Culhwch a series of forty impossible tasks, each of which needed to be completed before his daughter's hand would be offered in marriage.

With the help of Arthur and his warriors, Culhwch set about each of the forty impossible tasks; *Culhwch and Olwen* details just over ten of them, yet Culhwch (or at times, Arthur or one of his men) attempted them all. The main task described involves hunting the magical boar Trwyth, a tale that was associated with Arthur as early as Nennius' *The History of the Britons* in the ninth century. It has been suggested that this tale may dimly remember a conflict fought between the historical Arthur and another warlord whose battle name was 'The Boar'. Another of

Arthur's own actions is to slay the Very Black Witch with his knife, after a botched attempt to do so by some of his warriors. Another of the tasks set by Ysbaddaden, rather like that told in *The Spoils of Annwn*, concerned the search for a magical cauldron from Ireland in which the wedding feast was to be cooked. It may well be that *Culhwch and Olwen* and *The Spoils of Annwn* were later adapted to associate the legend of Arthur with a separate legend of the Holy Grail. In *Culhwch and Olwen*, to obtain the cauldron Arthur has to fight Diwrnach the Irishman and the armies of Ireland; in this mission, Arthur is more successful than in the disaster remembered in *The Spoils of Annwn*. With the help of his cousin Arthur and Arthur's warriors, among whom stood Cai and Bedwyr, Culhwch finally succeeded in all forty tasks. Despite his cruelty, Ysbaddaden stayed true to his word and allowed Culhwch to marry his daughter; Goreu, one of Arthur's followers, chopped off the giant's head and took over his fortress, fulfilling the prophecy of the giant's death. Arthur's obligation to his cousin completed, he and his men left, and Culhwch and Olwen became man and wife.

In this tale, Arthur's role is much more like that of English and French medieval stories (outlined in Chapter Three): although he takes part in some of the tasks, most of the action falls to his warriors, chiefly Cai and Bedwyr. This may reflect Welsh medieval writers picking up on popular English or French tales, or perhaps suggests that *Culhwch and Olwen* collected together many now forgotten stories about other heroes (who were to become part of Arthur's legendary court) and reorganised them to fit into an Arthurian narrative. If the latter is the is the case, there are three strands to the story solely remembering Arthur: a list of his possessions, a list of fabled tasks he undertook, and the lengthy list of warriors remembered as having been part of his court. By identifying these, we can perhaps see something of the earliest legendary tales of Arthur shining through the centuries.

The Gododdin

Frequently described as 'the oldest Scottish poem', *The Gododdin*'s true historical origin lies in the waning seventh century British kingdoms of the North: geographically the poem may be Scottish, but culturally it is very much British literature.

The Gododdin is a lament; it tells the story of a group of British warriors who ride to their deaths against Saxon foes. We presume that it is based on a historical event. Having prepared in the great hall of King Mynyddog

Mwynfawr of the northern British kingdom of Gododdin, based around modern Edinburgh, feasting and drinking mead to celebrate the glorious battle ahead of them, the richly armoured and bejewelled horsemen ride out to meet their Saxon enemies. The location of the battle is no longer known, but most scholars believe it to have been the old Roman site at Catterick, North Yorkshire (still an army base to this day). It would appear that the battle took place around the year 600, although there is no other source to corroborate this.

Although the British warriors were defeated – pretty much wiped out in fact – the poet tells us that they fought bravely, and commends many individuals for their deeds. Among the glorious British dead is the beautifully named Gwawrddur, who, we are told, 'glutted black ravens on the wall of the fort, although he was no Arthur'.

So what does this strange little excerpt mean? Basically, despite the fact that Gwawrddur killed many enemies (feeding the ravens was a Dark Ages poetic term for such unadulterated slaughter), he wasn't as great a warrior as Arthur. This implies that, when the poem was recited for an audience, they would be aware of Arthur as a great warrior. Therefore, his name must have been synonymous with victory in battle at the time the poem developed, and Arthur must have been known in the northern British kingdoms (if not those to the South too). Otherwise, there would have been little point in comparing another warrior's skills to his. What the poem doesn't tell us is whether Arthur was alive at the time, or if he was but a distant memory from the past.

The problem with this line in *The Gododdin*, and with the poem in general, is that the written version of it survives in two versions, both in the late thirteenth century *Book of Aneirin*. One version is longer and appears to be organised in better order, yet the second version appears to be older. This suggests that extra text could have been interpolated at any time between the date of the battle (600) and the late thirteenth century, although the style of language used suggests that it was present in the tenth or eleventh centuries at the very latest. The poem itself is almost certainly much older than this date, and probably dates back to the period immediately after the battle featured in the poem; until committed to writing, the poem would have been part of the Britons' rich oral history. Although often attributed to the famous bard Aneirin, we cannot be certain that he really was the author, but a seventh century date for the poem does make sense.

If we take *The Gododdin* at face value, it tells us that the Britons – the northern Britons at least – considered Arthur to be a famous warrior by whom others' deeds in battle could be judged. That they did so at a date early enough for it to be recorded about a warrior in a poem constructed shortly after a major battle fought around the year 600 must also be recognised, although this depends greatly upon exactly when the poem was written down in a manuscript.

The *Lives* of the saints

The *Lives* of the saints are not a single collection of hagiography, but instead *Lives* is a term used for a style of Celtic ecclesiastical storytelling, perhaps broadly based on historical events. Many of the *Lives* were probably first written down before Geoffrey of Monmouth wrote his famous *History* – the book that launched Arthur's deeds into the mainstream of European literature – and they paint a slightly skewed picture of Arthur when compared to the more famous English and French romances that followed.

Arthur features in the stories of many of the early Welsh Saints, stories of saints with such a broad date range that they cannot all possibly be true. Despite this, the authors of several *Lives* of the saints saw fit to work Arthur into their chosen saint's lifetime.

In the *Life of St Illtud*, Arthur is noted as Illtud's cousin. Illtud himself was a great warrior in his day, and decided to visit his cousin to observe the household of a champion so well renowned as Arthur. Illtud set sail from Brittany, and was impressed with Arthur's host of warriors and the generosity of the King. He is also remembered as one of Arthur's warriors.

St Carannog was a native of the Welsh region of Ceredigion, but often ventured further afield. The *Life of St Carannog* tells how, on one such trip to the Severn Estuary, the saint met Arthur, who ruled the region (perhaps along with another king named Cadwy). Arthur was attempting to hunt down a dragon that had laid waste to part of his kingdom, and Carannog helped Arthur to find the dragon. When Carannog came face to face with the fiery beast, it meekly bowed its head before him, acknowledging his power as a servant of God. He then ordered the dragon to depart, causing no harm to Arthur's kingdom in the future. In return, Arthur granted Carannog new land, upon which the saint built a church and monastery.

The *Life of St Euflamm* sees Arthur in combat against a dragon, rather like the story of St Carannog's worthy deeds. This tale is set in Brittany, where, we are told, Arthur went to seek out monsters to slay. Arthur, armed with a club and lion-skin covered shield, fought against a mighty dragon for a whole day, and although gaining the upper hand, he could not deliver a killer blow. Dragon slaying being thirsty work, Arthur went in search of water before resuming the fight, and unable to find any, was assisted by Euflamm, who prayed for water to be granted by God. Miraculously, water sprang from a rock and Arthur was refreshed; he also begged the saint to give him blessings, which Euflamm did. In the end, Euflamm himself vanquished the dragon through the power of prayer, saving Arthur – the champion of Christ – the trouble of doing so himself.

However, not all saintly *Lives* are so complimentary of Arthur. For example, in the *Life of St Padarn*, the saint is in his church when Arthur, described as a tyrant, enters. As mentioned before, it is possible that the term 'tyrant' simply described a king (perhaps a minor king) in the Dark Ages. Arthur takes a fancy to the tunic that Padarn is wearing – a garment apparently given to the holy man in Jerusalem – and demands it from him. Padarn refuses, and Arthur leaves in a blazing fury. When he returns, having decided that the tunic must and will be his, Padarn suggests that the earth should swallow him up, and lo and behold it does, right up to Arthur's chin. This quite rightly causes Arthur to reflect upon the situation, and he apologises to God and Padarn, asking for forgiveness for his anger and greed. This is granted, and Arthur takes Padarn as his patron, leaving as a better man than he arrived as.

In the *Life of St Cadog*, Arthur intervenes in a feud between two rival kings, but is not portrayed in a flattering light. One of the kings, Brychan, had his daughter kidnapped by a force of 300 men belonging to his rival, a king named Gwynllyw. A battle ensued on the border between the two kingdoms, and Gwynllyw's men were badly mauled, losing 200 of their number. Gwynllyw escaped, with Brychan's daughter still in his clutches, and came across Arthur, Cei and Bedwyr, sitting at the crest of a hill, playing dice games. Arthur was tempted to kill Gwynllyw and rape the girl, but Cei and Bedwyr reminded him that it was their duty to aid those in distress (a probable reference to the flourishing French idea of chivalry in Arthur's court). Arthur questions Gwynllyw as to the nature of the dispute, and then asks upon whose land they are currently standing. When Gwynllyw tells Arthur that they are in his kingdom, Arthur, Cei and Bedwyr lend their support to his cause, defeating Brychan and allowing Gwynllyw to steal his rival's daughter to marry – Cadog being their first born son. This story is rather curious inasmuch as Arthur attempts to intervene in the name of justice, yet ends up assisting the wrong party.

Arthur reappears later in the *Life of St Cadog*. A man arrived at Cadog's monastery seeking sanctuary, as he had killed three of Arthur's warriors. The fugitive stayed with Cadog for seven years, until Arthur eventually hunted him down, and told Cadog that sanctuary could not be given for such a lengthy period of time. In a parley, it was decided that Arthur was owed one hundred cows as compensation for his warriors' deaths; in a haughty fashion, Arthur decreed that the cows should be red at the front and white at the back, otherwise he would not accept them; Cadog managed to find one hundred such beasts with divine intervention, and handed them over to Arthur at a ford in a river. As Arthur's warriors waded in to round the cows up, the animals turned into bundles of fern and washed away. Arthur was forced to admit defeat by the saint, and agreed that sanctuary could be given for a further seven months and seven days.

The *Life of St Gildas* (that's right, the grumpy chap from earlier in this chapter was made a saint) is also rather damning of Arthur. His *Life* explains that he was a contemporary of Arthur, who is described as the King of the whole of Britain. Although Gildas was loyal to his king, his brothers (23 in all) fought against Arthur, refusing to accept him as their king. Huail, Gildas' eldest brother, would frequently better the King in battle, but on one occasion was pursued to the Isle of Man, where Arthur slew him. Upon hearing this news, Gildas travelled back to Britain from Ireland (where he had been studying), and forgave Arthur for the murder of Huail. Another Welsh tradition remembers the outcome slightly differently to Gildas' *Life*, suggesting that the saint never forgave Arthur, and instead threw away all written references to Arthur's great deeds, thus explaining his absence from any historical text.

Another section of Gildas' *Life* explained that the city of Glastonbury was besieged by Arthur. He did this as one of its inhabitants, King Melwas, had raped Gwenhwyfar (Guinevere) and taken her to Glastonbury as a hostage. Arthur commanded the entire armies of both Cornwall and Devon, and only when the abbot of Glastonbury intervened (with the help of Gildas) was the situation diffused. This episode, combined with the death of Huail, shows Arthur to have been considered a rather aggressive and warlike figure, and is depicted in an unfavourable light in Gildas' hagiography.

The key features of Arthur's central roles and cameos in the *Lives* of the saints are significant, regardless of the historical authenticity of the stories themselves. Firstly, Arthur is a complex character, with many more dimensions than his later medieval, chivalric embodiment; in several of the *Lives*, Arthur lives instead as a greedy noble rather like the historical type whom Gildas criticised as being 'tyrants'. Perhaps Arthur is even used as being representative of the attitude taken by British kings in the Dark Ages, using his name and fame, but without possessing any personal traits evident in the real-life, historical Arthur's psyche. He is often at odds with the holy men, and is invariably outsmarted by them – this incarnation of Arthur is not the sharpest tool in the box. The Arthur who appears in the *Lives* is a warrior and a leader of men, but does not always appear to be a king; he certainly takes part in noble pastimes, but his true status is often not dwelt upon. Perhaps the authors of the *Lives* expected their audience to know Arthur's status, or perhaps he was deliberately kept as a shadowy figure to avoid overpowering the true heroes of the *Lives* – the saints themselves. Whatever the reasons behind Arthur's depiction, the *Lives* of the saints once again emphasise that Arthur had become an expected ingredient of almost any Celtic oral tradition. Despite the obvious discrepancies in dating and perhaps in his true role, an audience would have known his name and recognised what he stood for – a symbol of the power of a warrior. Perhaps the Arthur as depicted in the *Lives* of the saints comes far closer to the true personality of a historical Arthur than is found anywhere else – if Gildas spoke the truth of a typical Dark Ages leader, similar traits are well reflected in these hagiographic tales.

The Breton stories
The Breton stories of Arthur bridge a literary gap between the Arthur of medieval English and French writers, and that of the Celtic world. In the fifth and sixth centuries, Brittany – little Britain – became home to a large number of ex-pat Britons, who emigrated from their homelands to establish a new, continental power base. With them came their social and cultural history – and whether at this time or slightly later, Arthur came to feature in their folk tales.

The idea that Arthur was a 'Once and Future King' – that he would return one day – may have originated in the Breton tales, and the *Legend of St Goeznovius* included enough partially remembered history to suggest that Arthur had cleared swathes of land from Saxon dominance in the fifth century. The original stories of Arthur's famous Round Table may also have originated in these lands (the medieval writer Wace claimed to have first heard of the Round Table from Breton folk tales), and a number of twelfth century lays (a lay being a form of song) recited some of the more fabulous stories about Arthur, his deeds and his forthcoming return from the dead.

Whether these Breton tales developed independently of the Arthurian stories recited in the British Isles, or whether they record extra Arthurian material long since lost in British form, we do not know.

Significantly, the Breton Arthur has more in common with the Arthur of medieval romance than he does with the warlord of British Celtic folklore. This may ultimately have provided the stepping stone for turning the hero of the Celtic culture into the hero of an entire Age, allowing Arthurian tales to be accessed by the Anglo-Norman and French poets of the medieval era. Wandering poets and bards translated the Breton stories into language more familiar and suitable for Anglo-Norman and French courts, and without this crossover, Arthur may well have ended up as yet another obscure Celtic hero whose name barely registers in the modern world.

Historical figures who became part of the legend
A fair number of the characters who became so well known in romantic Arthurian legend had their origins in earlier British history, and many originally took their place alongside Arthur in the folk tales of the Celts before being absorbed into the legendary cycle of the all powerful King himself. Just like the figure of Arthur, the later legends that sprang up around the name of a historically attested person were not necessarily based upon factual stories – the storytellers may have simply borrowed the name of a well known historical figure to hang the plot of a folk tale from. They probably became associated with Arthur as his was the 'big name', the most loved of all pseudo-historic Celtic heroes.

Owain, famous in later Arthurian legend as Ywaine (and Ivan and Iwein), definitely existed. He was the son and successor of Urien, King of the northern British kingdom of Rheged, and was celebrated along with his father for holding back Saxon advances in the late sixth century. Owain probably died in 604, and in one of the many poems attributed to Taliesin about the campaigns of Rheged, Owain is described as the slayer of the Saxon king Fflamddwyn (probably Theodric). Owain's father Urien also became a character of Arthurian legend.

Arthur's sorcerer and advisor Merlin appears to have been based on the sixth century bard Myrddin, as previously detailed in this chapter.

Tristan and his uncle King Mark, famed in their own medieval story and then dropped into Arthurian legend, may be identified as the Drustanus and his father Cunomorus (known elsewhere as Marcus) immortalised on an inscribed stone near to Castle Dore in Cornwall. However, we know little else of these two historical characters, and the case for a northern, probably Pictish, Drust (or Drystan) has also been made by some researchers.

Geraint, hero of the Battle of Llongborth mentioned elsewhere in this chapter, evolved into Erec, a medieval knight of Arthurian romance, and Peredur, the British King of York who died in 580, went on to find fame as Perceval in Arthurian legend.

A telling footnote to the integration of historical figures into Arthurian legend is that the majority – if not quite all – of them lived in the late sixth century AD, and have strong connections with northern British kingdoms. Perhaps these people were contemporaries of a real-life Arthur, who fought alongside him, gradually filtering from folklore and oral history into the legends that sprang up around Arthur in later centuries.

A Boy Becomes King

Chapter Five

The Legend of
King Arthur

This is the tale of our once and future king, the noble and worthy Arthur. Many have recited this story before, for a thousand or more years; and many will do so long after our time.

This is a modern retelling, and includes some of the greatest tales from the legends of Arthur and his knights. Many more tales were written but have not been included in this recital, as a book far greater in length than this could be devoted purely to retelling the legend. The tales as you read them here are not in their purest form – this recital absorbs and combines many influences from Celtic, medieval and more recent retellings of the legend. The more traditional tales can be read about in Chapters Three and Four.

A land without a king

Centuries ago, within a lifetime of the Romans' flight from Britain's shores but many lifetimes before you sit here now, Britain was a dark land in which to live. Raiding inland far from the border forts that had once kept them out, howling Scots, painted Picts, and fur-clad Saxons terrorised the Britons, whose lazy, bickering dukes were powerless to act. One noble lord – a descendant of the Romans – stood against the barbarian raiders. His name was Ambrosius. Ambrosius put countless Saxon warbands to the sword, and forced the Scots and Picts back to their own lands. When he was cut down by a Saxon assassin, Ambrosius' brother Uther continued to challenge the enemies of the Britons, and finally forced peace upon them all, becoming the High King of all other British kings.

115

Uther Pendragon – the 'Head Dragon' of the island – was a coarse man but a strong king. He not only had to contend with foreign threats, but also with rebellious Britons. With the aid of a sizeable army and an ancient, wise counsellor named Merlin, Uther brought peace across the lands of Britain, except for the island's south-western tip, where the Duke of Cornwall loudly and violently questioned Uther's right to rule.

Uther marched his royal army into the rugged Cornish countryside – a land once inhabited by the giants who dwelt in Britain before mankind arrived – and laid siege to the insubordinate Duke at his castle at Tintagel. Tintagel was a rocky coastal promontory, unassailable from all but one causeway, which the Duke had fortified so strongly that Uther's warriors could not storm the castle. Uther's men camped outside in siege, sustaining themselves with honey-brewed mead, watched all the time by the Duke of Cornwall's garrison.

Uther spent many a day gazing at the fortress of Tintagel, wondering how his army could force an entry. One morning, his eyes fixed upon a face at a window in the fortress. It was the face of the beautiful Igraine, wife to the Duke of Cornwall. Uther's lust overtook his need for victory, and he summoned his wizened counsellor Merlin. Uther demanded that he must take Igraine as his own wife, knowing that Merlin would command the ancient arts of magic to this end. Merlin considered this demand for a short while, and agreed to aid Uther – on one condition. In his impatience, Uther agreed to any demand that Merlin might make of him, hardly dwelling on the old man's prediction that a child would certainly be borne of their first meeting, and that the child would have to be surrendered to Merlin at birth. Uther waved Merlin away, his mind focused solely on his approaching encounter with Igraine.

At dusk, Merlin returned to Uther, and urged him to drink a freshly prepared potion – a magic potion that would alter Uther's appearance to mirror that of the rebellious Duke. At that moment, either by luck or by Merlin's planning, the Duke of Cornwall decided to surge forth from his castle in an attempt to break Uther's siege. Uther, in the guise of the Duke, entered the castle, and lay that night with Igraine, who believed him to be her husband. At the same time, the Duke's sally failed miserably, and he died a bloody death on the spear points of Uther's army. Uther's warriors pushed the remnants of the Cornish army back into Tintagel castle, following them so doggedly that the castle fell by morning. With Tintagel in the hands of Uther's men, the

King confessed his true identity to Igraine, and, as if to confirm his story, the potion wore off as he spoke, restoring Uther's own likeness to his body. She was shown the stricken body of her husband, and the subjugation of Cornwall was completed when Uther forcibly took Igraine's hand in marriage.

Nine months later, just as Merlin had foreseen, a child was born to the new queen. Igraine's first and only act as a mother was to name the child Arthur. Before Uther had arrived to see his son, Merlin took the child and carried him into the wild hills of Wales.

Shortly after the flight of Merlin and the baby Arthur, Uther fell ill. The greatest physicians in the land tended the King, but without the immeasurable guidance of Merlin, no one could do anything but sit and watch Uther slowly die. News spread far and wide that the King lay in a weakened state, and rumours that the Saxons, Irish and Picts were mustering in strength proved correct. In a hoarse whisper, Uther gave his final command – to send his royal army to defeat the barbarians. Supported by the might of Uther's army, the British lords who held the borderlands inflicted a string of defeats upon their foes, yet each time total victory drew near, the barbarians would disappear into their highland and fenland strongholds. When the royal army marched onward to confront the next barbarian tribe, those who had recently been defeated would return and raid deeper into Uther's lands. The Britons became nervous – the King was ill, and his lords were unable to guarantee safety for his people – and called for their king to save them.

One morning, without warning, Merlin returned to Uther's side, bringing news of the battles and the pleas of his subjects. He also brought with him a potion that allowed Uther to rise from his bed and don his golden armour. Still much weakened, Uther was helped onto his warhorse and accompanied by his closest followers to confront his enemies. By now, the Scots, Picts and Saxons had conspired to become one great army, and had pushed far into Uther's lands. He met this combined terror at St Albans, and defeated all three enemies in the bloodiest battle of his generation. Already weakened by his illness, and outnumbered by the barbarian masses, Uther received a fatal blow in the battle, and died three days after his triumphant return to London.

The death of Uther, who had cemented unity amongst the Britons, was a prelude to greater disaster. The British nobles, no longer having to fight the barbarians who Uther had decisively defeated in his last act of kingship, renewed their petty bickering. Dukes who had ridden side by side under Uther's red dragon banner now fought for ownership of land and cattle. The mightiest lords argued as to who should take on the mantle of kingship. They had all forgotten or ignored the fact that Uther had fathered a son in the baby Arthur. For more than a decade, Briton fought Briton, and Uther was never replaced.

But what of Arthur, heir to Uther's throne? Merlin had taken Arthur to a lowly yet honest knight, Ector, who lived deep in the Welsh hills, at the western edge of Uther's kingdom, far away from the power struggle. Merlin foresaw great things for Arthur – even before he was conceived – and wished for him to grow up untainted by the pettiness of court life. Merlin had known Ector for many years, since Ector was a boy in fact, and he was entrusted with the boy's life by the wise old sage. Ector had a son, Kay, who was only a few years older than Arthur, and Ector brought them both up as his sons. Though he was a relatively poor knight, Ector brought both children up well, teaching them how an honourable knight should act. He taught them the folly of the power struggles around them, and drilled them well as squires, in preparation for knighthood. Ector trusted Merlin completely, and never once enquired about Arthur's background.

Merlin, for his part, visited Ector, Kay and Arthur every once in a while, and shrewdly questioned Ector about Arthur's progress. After one visit in the fifteenth year of Arthur's life, happy with what Ector had reported, Merlin rode south to consult the Archbishop of London.

The sword in the stone
The Britons needed a king, and a strong king at that. The Archbishop of London was a man of great faith, and was held in high esteem by all, no matter what their own grievances were. As a just man, he wished to see a rightful heir on the throne, and he knew that Merlin would want this too. For that reason, he listened to Merlin's carefully orated idea. Merlin's proposal to the Archbishop initially made the religious man question the strength of mind and of body that a mere fifteen year old boy could possess. But Merlin, wily old sage that he was, kept talking and convinced the Archbishop that Uther's rightful heir, the child Arthur, could be relied upon.

Both the Archbishop and Merlin finally agreed that Arthur would be a suitable heir to Uther, yet both men also knew that many British nobles would oppose his coronation. Merlin had already thought this dilemma through and instructed the Archbishop to summon all British nobles to London at Christmas, and to inform them that the strongest among them would be crowned then. Merlin's definition of strength differed greatly to that of an average British duke – Merlin was used to exercising his brain, while the cream of British nobility were used to flexing their muscles. Ector had brought Arthur and his own son Kay up to exercise both muscle and mind. Merlin's work done, he disappeared on other business.

Christmas came, and despite the snow covered roads, a great number of British dukes descended upon London, readying themselves for a tournament and the chance to be crowned High King. As British tradition demanded, all comers attended a Christmas Mass on Christmas Eve, held at London's great cathedral. The Archbishop gave a sermon in honour and celebration of the future king. As the congregation filed out of the cathedral at the end of the service, they saw a wonder to surpass any other. Standing prominently in the cathedral's grounds was a great square stone. It had not been there before the Mass, yet now it stood for all to see, and atop the stone was a steel anvil, and deep into that anvil a brilliant, shining sword had been driven.

As the Britons gathered around the stone in amazement, they saw that the stone carried an inscription:

'Who So Pulleth Out The Sword From This Stone And Anvil Is The Rightful And True Born High King Of The Britons'

As soon as his was heard, a great clamour went up among the thronging crowd, and the foremost dukes pushed their way to the front, intent on wrenching the sword from its resting place. Many tried, but not one – not even the most accomplished warriors – could even so much as move the sword. Disenchanted, and humiliated by their individual failures, the dukes began to argue amongst themselves as to who should be crowned. Acting on the advice of Merlin, the Archbishop quickly announced that the tournament would be held on New Year's Day, and that the dukes should save their strength and anger for that. Ector and Kay, whose lowly rank had prevented them from attempting to remove the sword, retired to prepare for the tournament, and Arthur readied himself to act as their squire.

Between Christmas and New Year's Day, the outlying area around London was filled with the sights and sounds that preceded a great tournament. Swords and armour were polished, horses were fed and exercised, knights practised their skill at arms and made idle boasts, squires made sure that their masters were well equipped, and above all else, there was excited chatter about the tournament and who would be crowned King thereafter.

Snow fell heavily, and as church bells rung in the new year and the start of the tournament, knights and peasants alike flocked back to the city. With so much to do in the build up, and having never attended such a grand tournament before, it was not surprising that Arthur forgot one crucial item. As he helped Kay into his armour shortly before his first joust, the pair of them realised that Kay did not have his sword. As any good squire would, Arthur rushed off to find such a weapon for his knight to flourish.

With so little time in which to find a sword and return to Kay, Arthur panicked. He wasn't likely to find a sword for sale at a blacksmith's – the number of knights buying new weapons especially for the coming tournament had seen to that – and he did not know where he had placed Kay's own sword. And then he remembered the sword in the stone that he'd seen after Christmas Mass. It was worth a try.

The cathedral grounds were empty when Arthur rode up; everyone was on their way to the tournament. Without stopping to think of the implications, Arthur jumped from his horse, strode up to the shimmering sword still lodged in the anvil on the stone and with no effort at all, drew it. Arthur had drawn the sword. The sword of the rightful King.

Without stopping to think about what he had just done – he had other things on his mind, like getting a sword to Kay in time – Arthur remounted his horse and rode as fast as he could. When he reached Kay, Arthur thrust the brilliant sword into his older brother's hand. Kay marvelled at the quality of the blade, and asked Arthur where he had found such a weapon; Arthur told him, and Kay could do nothing but stare at the sword in his hand. And then he turned to his father, Ector, and announced himself to be the rightful heir to the throne, as he held the sword from the stone.

Ector surveyed the scene: his eldest son stammered and held the sword aloft, while Arthur stood close by, regaining his breath after his maniacal quest for a weapon. Ector asked Kay if he had drawn the sword himself, and his son could not lie to his father, instead announcing that Arthur had returned with the sword. To some degree, Ector was not surprised; he knew Merlin well, and had always expected to be surprised by the child. But he hadn't quite expected this.

Ector led both boys back to the cathedral grounds, and asked Arthur to replace the sword into the anvil. He then asked Kay to remove the sword, but try as he might Kay could not manage to do so. Ector then asked Arthur to remove the sword, and the younger boy did so without the slightest effort. With that, both Ector and Kay fell to their knees and then kissed the hand of the rightful King of Britain.

This event had not gone unnoticed, for the Archbishop had stood watching the trio by the stone. He advanced to meet them, and Ector told him what had happened. He also told the Archbishop that Merlin had brought Arthur to him as a baby, and entrusted him to his care. In turn, the Archbishop told Ector, Kay and Arthur what Merlin had revealed to him: Arthur was the son of Uther Pendragon, and was indeed the rightful heir to the throne. Arthur stood silently, amazed and concerned by all he had just heard.

The Archbishop sent word to the tournament that the new King of the Britons had been found, and a vast array of Britons flocked to the cathedral, from the noblest dukes to the common folk of London. They all wished to see their new king.

The thronging masses were astonished to see a wide-eyed boy pushed before them and announced as King Arthur. The Archbishop's words were drowned out by the angry crowd, and in desperation the holy man told Arthur to replace the sword and draw it from the anvil once more. As Arthur did so, the crowd fell silent. They knew what the boy's success meant. The boy Arthur was indeed destined to become King, yet this was all too much for some proud British dukes to bare. Arthur had to draw the sword three more times before the majority of the nobility believed what they were witnessing, and even then a number rode angrily away, declaring the morning's events to be a simple trick.

Yet other dukes who were present accepted what they saw; the Archbishop was an honourable man, and the story of wise old Merlin's involvement had quickly spread through the crowd. Arthur was knighted by Ulfius and Brastias, two of the most celebrated British dukes of the time, and preparations were made for him to be crowned.

The healing of Britain

On a cold, bright January morning, Arthur was crowned King of the Britons by the Archbishop of London. During his coronation at the cathedral, Arthur swore an oath to commoner and noble alike that he would be a just king until his dying day. Few in the assembled crowd would imagine how eventful a reign was to follow, the most glorious reign in the history of Britain.

Arthur's first task was to listen to the outstanding grievances that needed a royal mind to judge. Merlin, who had arrived to see Arthur's coronation, helped the young King to make sensible decisions, and Arthur correctly punished offenders and compensated their victims. Arthur's first actions as King were well received, and it seemed that those nobles who were present greatly appreciated having a king once more; before Arthur, they had squabbled between themselves, and very few matters were ever resolved without resorting to combat.

Arthur then appointed a number of royal dignitaries, once again with the shrewd judgement of Merlin. Arthur's almost-brother, Kay, was appointed Steward, Ulfius became Chamberlain and Brastias was given the task of defending the borderlands from Pictish, Scottish and Saxon raiders. Arthur knew of the problems caused by these tribes in the past and was determined to keep them under firm control, giving Brastias a large royal army to aid him in this task.

As his first day as King drew to a close, Arthur asked Merlin what he should do next; things had moved fast for Arthur, and he was painfully aware of his lack of regal knowledge. Merlin simply advised Arthur to head to the royal court of Camelot and take up his royal residence there. Arthur's retinue, along with the red dragon banner of his father Uther, headed to Camelot from London, and Kay set about organising a great banquet for the new royal household.

Kay's organisational skills were put to the test, as many of Britain's finest dukes gathered at Camelot to pay their respects to the new King. Among the throng were six noted kings, Lot of Orkney and Urien of Gore being the two finest; a number of other minor kings had gathered to meet Arthur, their new High King, so the young man was not surprised to know that such esteemed warlords were camped beyond his castle's walls. Yet Merlin was less ambivalent – he pointed out to the naive Arthur that the six kings had arrived with large retinues, and that instead of setting up richly decorated tournament tents, the kings had set up canvas tents – tents used when an army went to war. Sure enough, the six kings addressed Arthur, and declared that he was a mere boy and not fit to rule. Their warriors laid siege to Camelot, and within days, Britain had lurched from regal festivity to the outbreak of war.

Arthur met with Merlin to discuss what he could do; the slaughter of British kinsmen was the last thing he wished for, and he suggested that he could offer the rebelling kings rich gifts. Merlin explained that this would be a futile action against an army intent on removing him from the throne. The only defence open to Arthur, Merlin decreed, was attack.

Arthur rode into battle against the six rebel kings, under the dragon banner of Uther Pendragon, and defeated them. Arthur excelled in battle – even though this was his first battle – and further gained the respect of the knights and dukes who fought for him. All six of Arthur's enemy leaders fled, and regrouped, bringing with them five more rebel kings. Once more Arthur led his loyal knights into battle, this time on the banks of the River Humber, and once more his martial skill, and the bravery of both him and his men, won the day. Yet he could not have done so without the intervention of the loyal King Ban of Benwick, a colony of Britons on mainland Europe, who sent a large number of battle hardened warriors to help his new High King. With the defeat of the rebel kings, and the sworn loyalty of those who survived his first real battle, Arthur and his trusted advisor Merlin continued with their healing of the wounds of Britain.

Following on from this, in a series of battles culminating with a great victory at Badon Hill near Bath, Arthur's armies defeated the Saxons, the Scots and the Picts. He gained the loyalty of these peoples' own kings, and as the High King, Arthur rebuilt the structured government that Britain had lacked during its years of strife. As Arthur's power grew, and as his benevolent influence was seen by others to work, more and more British dukes rallied behind him, pledging the support of themselves and their allies. The boy King and his wily counsellor had regained the unity lost by the Britons so long before.

Excalibur

Even with the defeat and sworn allegiance of the Saxons, Picts and Irish, Arthur still had much work to do to restore peace and justice to a land long used to anarchy. Yet each and every week saw more famed and skilled knights arriving at Camelot to swear allegiance to Arthur. Among their number were Gawain, one of the most renowned knights in all of Britain, and Modred, both of whom were sons of Arthur's half sister and King Lot of the Orkneys. Many other knights also arrived, famous and not so famous, yet all were ready to serve their just High King.

One morning, word came to Arthur that a knight had set up camp in a nearby forest, and was claiming to be on the trail of a miraculous beast. Offering to joust with any other passing knight, this stranger had bettered several of Arthur's retinue. Later that same morning, Arthur rode out to meet this troublesome knight, accompanied by Merlin.

The King and his counsellor entered the forest, and spotted a brightly decorated tent standing by the edge of a lake. Arthur rode towards the camp, and blew a horn hanging from a tree at the edge of the clearing. Upon hearing this sound, a huge knight came rushing at the King, levelling a lance at his chest. The knight declared that he was hunting a magical beast, and had been doing so for the previous year, and that the beast had recently arrived in the region of Camelot. To prevent any other from taking this quest from him, he was jousting with any knight who passed by. His intent declared, the knight turned his horse round, backed off to prepare to charge at Arthur, and then kicked his horse into a gallop. Arthur did the same, and the pair crashed into each other's spears, shattered pieces flying everywhere. Unseated, Arthur struggled to his feet, and the giant knight lunged towards him with a sword. The duel went on for a lengthy time – hours – until suddenly, Arthur's sword snapped in two whilst parrying a tremendous blow from his opponent. At that point, the huge knight fell to the floor, and promptly started to snore.

Merlin stepped forward and told Arthur that the meaningless fight had gone on long enough, and he felt it was time to cast Arthur's opponent into a deep sleep. This fearsome knight, Merlin explained, was named Pellinore, and he would be of great service to Arthur, as would be his future son. Pellinore, Merlin said, was chasing a strange creature known as The Questing Beast, with the head of a serpent and the body of a leopard; Merlin believed the creature would never be captured, and that the pursuit was driving Pellinore slightly mad. Nevertheless, he was a strong and principled knight, and Arthur would be well served by him.

After the duel, Arthur stood with his sword broken in two – the sword he had drawn from the stone was no more. He told Merlin his concern that his symbol of authority had been shattered. Merlin advised him to walk to the edge of the lake that stood close by. Arthur did so, and as he approached the shoreline, the water in the middle of the lake began to ripple. There was no wind in the air, so it seemed unnatural. As Arthur watched, a gleaming metal point emerged from beneath the lake's surface, and very gracefully, a gloriously finished sword emerged, clasped gently but firmly by a feminine hand. As the sword and arm stood proud, the lake suddenly went very calm. Merlin whispered to Arthur to fetch his new sword, and indicated a small rowing boat close by. Arthur pushed the boat out into the water, and rowed cautiously toward the sword. As he approached, he stared down into the water, and vividly saw the shape of a beautiful maiden, clad in white robes. He clasped the sword's hilt, and with this the maiden smiled at him, and the arm and body gracefully retracted, sinking into the depths of the lake. Unsure of what to do next, Arthur turned to Merlin, who beckoned him back to the shore.

As the astonished and confused Arthur clambered out of the small boat, Merlin told him that he had just met the Lady of the Lake, the mistress of all water, and a powerful enchantress who wished to honour Arthur's kingship. Turning to the gleaming, well crafted blade in Arthur's hand, Merlin explained that this sword was named Excalibur, and that it would bring the King many victories and provide him with strength and power in the eyes of others.

Arthur, Guinevere and the Round Table

As Arthur's power grew and peace spread throughout Britain, word spread that the High King would intervene and resolve disputes between the other kings and dukes in a fair manner. On one such occasion, Merlin delivered a message to Arthur that a friend of his father Uther, named Leodegrance, was embroiled in a dispute with his rival Ryons, and that he had sent a plea for Arthur to settle the growing conflict. Merlin advised Arthur that Ryons was at fault for the dispute; he was a duke with a cruel reputation, and wore a cloak stitched together from the beards of his defeated enemies.

By the time Arthur and his retinue arrived in Leodegrance's land, Ryons had marched with his army to besiege his rival's castle. Arthur's retinue charged Ryons' warriors, and with the help of Leodegrance's men, who sallied from the castle, Ryons was defeated. Leodegrance admitted Arthur into his castle, and threw a splendid feast in honour of his king's help. At the feast, Arthur could not take his eyes away from Leodegrance's daughter, Guinevere. Without doubt, she was the most beautiful maiden Arthur had ever seen, not only stunning in looks, but with a sharp mind and charming manner. As Arthur rode back to Camelot, he could think of nothing but Guinevere's smiling face and the sound of her laugh.

In the days that followed, Arthur continued to think only of Guinevere. He consulted Merlin, who agreed that a wife and queen would be good not only for Arthur, but also for the bloodline of Britain. Merlin explained to his young king that marriage could lead to a rightful heir to Arthur's throne, ensuring that Britain would not fall back into chaos when Arthur eventually passed on. Merlin's other advice to Arthur was that the decision could be Arthur and Guinevere's alone; the counsellor could not predict all of Arthur's life for him. Guinevere, Merlin pointed out, was a beautiful woman and a strong-headed woman, but whether she would make a suitable queen for the High King of Britain, he did not know. Her father, however, had been a loyal supporter of Arthur's father, and Merlin predicted that the wedding would have a profound effect on Arthur's kingdom.

Arthur, in love and impatient, immediately rode back to Leodegrance's castle, and asked for Guinevere's hand in marriage. Leodegrance happily agreed – the honour of becoming father-in-law to the High King filled him with joy – and Guinevere was thrilled with the thought of becoming Arthur's queen.

The royal wedding was arranged and took place in the chapel at Camelot. A vast crowd of spectators arrived to watch the new yet well-loved King wed his bride. The most powerful British dukes all took their place in the chapel to witness the first royal wedding since Uther had taken Igraine as his wife. A grand ceremony took place, and afterwards, a colourful procession led by Arthur and Guinevere headed towards the feasting hall, accompanied by dukes, knights, ladies, maidens, bards, acrobats, jesters and musicians. Bride and groom were very obviously smitten with each other, and Arthur became even more overjoyed when Leodegrance presented his wedding gift to the couple.

Leodegrance led Arthur into the great hall of Camelot, and threw his arms wide open, gesturing at the gift. In front of Arthur, filling a huge amount of the expansive hall, was an oaken round table, beautifully crafted from very ancient wood, with 150 chairs seated around it, more than enough to accommodate Arthur's greatest knights. Leodegrance explained that this, the Round Table of Albion, had been given to him as a wedding gift by Arthur's own father Uther. Its shape meant that no knight who took his place at a seat could be considered any closer to the head of the table than any other seated knight, and this symbolised democracy, piety and equality between the High King, his dukes and lesser kings, and his knights. Arthur saw the value of this, as it appealed to his just ideas of ruling, and after consulting with Merlin, announced on his wedding night that he would form the Order of the Round Table.

The Order would be made up of the 150 most chivalrous and renowned knights in Britain, each of whom would swear to abide by Arthur's rule and, in his absence, act with the same judgement and honour as he would do himself. This, Arthur realised and Merlin reassured, would bring more unity to the land, and make Arthur's realm a splendid place to live, not only for the dukes, but for ordinary people too, who would benefit from honest local rulers.

The knights who had gathered to pay their respects to Arthur and Guinivere all pledged their oath the next morning, and over the following months, many more knights and dukes became members of the Order. Leodegrance even offered the services of his own men. Among the first to sit at the Round Table were Ector, Kay, Pellinore, Ulfius, Brastias, Gawain and Lucas. Prosperity and fairness did indeed spread around Britain, as the Order was true to its word, and the kingdom flourished under the just rule of Arthur and the beautiful Guinevere.

Gawain and the Green Knight

Of all the adventures that began in the great hall of Camelot, perhaps the most unnerving was an early deed of Gawain's. Gawain rightfully had a reputation throughout Britain as a great knight of repute, and quickly rose to act as the High King's champion on many occasions. It was on the first New Year's Day after Arthur married Guinevere that Gawain was first called upon in this role.

Heavy snow lay around Camelot, and the entire court of Arthur's household had gathered in the great hall for a feast to celebrate the beginning of the new year. The warm glow of the fireplace was most welcome, and knights and maidens had gathered around to hear Merlin narrate a story of Britain's earliest High Kings, who had lived many centuries before the Romans arrived.

Suddenly, the door of the hall flew open, and crashed to the ground. A flurry of snow swirled in through the doorway, and through it rode a giant of a man on a huge warhorse. He dwarfed all of Arthur's knights, and was clad all in green clothing and armour. He wore a cloak of green fur, a belt decorated with precious green jewels, had ivy carefully tied into his tressed hair and beard – both of which were green – and his skin even held a strange green hue. His horse was harnessed with green leather, and was covered in moss, and as he slid gracefully from his saddle, he unsheathed a massive two-handed axe, which gleamed with a shimmer of the same colour. The Green Knight demanded to meet the lord of the castle, booming his challenge out in an extraordinarily deep voice.

Arthur strode forward and attempted to welcome the aggressive stranger to his household, as was the custom of the Britons. He introduced himself, at which point the Green Knight retorted that he had heard of Arthur's weak rule, and that the King's knights were beardless and sickly. He called upon Arthur's men to prove their valour – he pausing to point his axe at various knights seated in the hall – by one of them accepting a challenge from him. Gawain rashly stepped forward and accepted the challenge without hearing what it was; he was unable to sit back while this giant insulted the High King.

The Green Knight scoffed at Gawain, and beckoned him. As Gawain advanced, the Green Knight explained that he would kneel before Arthur's warrior and ask to be beheaded. In return, Gawain would have to accept a similar blow from the Green Knight in twelve months' time, at an unknown place named the Green Chapel. Gawain readily accepted, not wishing to dishonour Arthur, and confident that no man, not even one as large as the green apparition that stood before him, could withstand an axe stroke from Gawain.

Gawain took the green axe, swung it to test its weight and balance, and asked the Green Knight to kneel before him. The huge green man did so, and Gawain swung quickly and heavily at his unprotected neck. The Green Knight's head fell from his shoulders and rolled across the floor. Gawain turned in triumph to the assembled throng, awaiting their applause. But it did not come; instead a look of fear and disbelief could be seen on everyone's face. Gawain turned around, and saw the body of the Green Knight rising to its feet. It calmly took the axe from his trembling hands, and strolled across the hall collect the head. The body then remounted, turned the horse about and cantered from Camelot, with the dismembered head reminding Gawain to find the Green Chapel in twelve months' time. Gawain's face looked almost as green as his adversary's.

In the weeks and months that followed, snow gave way to spring, and spring to summer. As autumn arrived, Gawain knew that he must leave to search for the Green Chapel – the whereabouts of which no one at Camelot knew – and once he found it, await his destiny. Absolutely terrified, but showing this to no one, Gawain donned his best armour and set out on his quest. Gawain wandered the countryside, asking all whom he met if they knew of the Green Knight. None did. Winter set in, and as heavy snow fell once more, Gawain found himself in North Wales on Christmas Eve. The North Welsh wilderness was an unhappy place to spend a winter, and he had not seen a living soul for many a day; then he crested a hill, and saw a castle below him. He rode down in high spirits, hoping to call upon the duke's goodwill at Christmas for a warm meal and flagon of mead. The gatekeeper allowed Gawain in, and lead him to a hall where he set eyes upon a comely woman and a broad-shouldered man. They bade him sit, and were as courteous as any other host that Gawain could have wished to meet. The man, a local duke named Bercilak, discussed Gawain's presence in Wales, and Gawain explained to him about the Green Knight and his quest for the Green Chapel. To his surprise and relief – having but a week remaining to locate the chapel or disgrace Arthur by his absence – Bercilak told him that the chapel was barely an hour's ride, and that Gawain should remain as his guest until his New Year's Day appointment.

Christmas was enjoyed by all, and Gawain even managed to forget his fear for a short while. On New Year's Eve, Bercilak went hunting at dawn. Gawain stayed behind, contemplating his forthcoming beheading. Never an easy thing to do, even for a brave knight in Arthur's service. As the hunt headed off, the door to Gawain's bed chamber creaked open, and Bercilak's glamorous wife appeared. She crept towards Gawain's bed, and tried to slip in beside him. Beautiful as she was, as an honest man, Gawain would not let her between the sheets, but she managed to plant a kiss firmly on his lips. And with this, she left.

Later in the morning, before Bercilak had finished, the lady of the castle cornered Gawain once more, and kissed him again. He pushed her away, despite the feelings of lust he had for her. He explained that if she were not married, he would gladly be in her service, but that he could not dishonour his generous host, her husband. She kissed him once more, thanking him for his gentle words of devotion and thoughts for her husband, and passed to Gawain her belt of green lace as a keepsake. Bercilak returned from the hunt, and Gawain said nothing of the kisses or the belt. He did not wish to upset his host, nor cause trouble for Bercilak's wife, so he acted as though nothing had happened. Bercilak's wife did not mention the morning's event, and greeted her husband lovingly.

On New Year's Day, Gawain awoke to see a howling blizzard outside. Nevertheless, he bade Bercilak and his wife farewell and thanked them for their hospitality. He wore the lady's belt under his armour, so besotted with her was he. He followed Bercilak's directions and rode through the snow to the Green Chapel. He dismounted and stepped unsteadily out of the snow and into the chapel.

Gawain waited inside for no more than a minute before the Green Knight rode up on his horse, dismounted gracefully and stepped into the chapel, bringing with him a swirl of snow. His head was back in place, as though it had never been lopped off. Gawain greeted him fearfully and knelt to receive his return blow. The Green Knight complimented him on keeping his promise, and told him that he was a credit to Arthur's court. And then he swung his axe.

Gawain heard the blade rush through the air, and although he tried not to, he flinched away from the blow. The Green Knight chided him, and reminded him that he had not flinched from Gawain's blow. Gawain steadied himself and knelt again, trembling with fear. The axe swept through the air once more and this time he did not move an inch. The blade bit into his neck and stopped. Blood dripped onto the snow on the chapel's floor, and Gawain realised that the blow was a flesh wound that barely broke the skin on the back of his neck.

As he started to rise uncertainly to his feet, Gawain was pushed back down by the Green Knight, who was preparing to strike again. Gawain shouted out in fear and begged him to stop, crying that he had only struck once at the Green Knight a year before. The Green Knight held the axe high above his head and boomed out that Gawain was a dishonest man who kept secrets from those who helped him; he then lowered his axe, and his face changed from that of anger to one of sadness. And then Gawain saw that the Green Knight was a heavily discoloured Bercilak.

Gawain rapidly untied the green lace belt that Bercilak's wife had given him as a memento of unrequitable love. Reddened with shame, he explained to Bercilak what had happened, and that he would never have chosen to deceive or cheat his gracious host, but that he also did not wish for Bercilak's wife to be in danger. That, he said, was why he had kept quiet. And then he waited for the axe to swing down on him once again.

Instead, Bercilak put the axe down, and told him to keep the belt as a reminder of the dangers of feminine charm. He explained that he had asked his wife to perform the task, and that he himself was an enchanted friend of Merlin's, who had requested Bercilak's help in testing the mettle of Arthur's knights. Merlin wished to make sure that the knights who served Arthur were as honest and trustworthy as their High King. Merlin, Bercilak reported, would be happy with what had happened. And with that, he despatched Gawain back to Camelot, the court he had represented so chivalrously on Arthur's behalf.

The coming of Lancelot

In the early days of the Round Table, Arthur's greatest knight was without doubt Gawain. Gawain was a ferocious knight, and lived for adventure; he was renowned both within the walls of Camelot and throughout the lands beyond. Yet even Gawain was eventually to be overshadowed by another knight, a knight who arrived from the overseas lands of Benwick. His name was Lancelot of the Lake.

Lancelot of the Lake was the son of King Ban of Benwick, who had given military aid to Arthur at the Battle of Bedegraine Forest. When Arthur learned whose son knelt before him, he eagerly enquired as to Ban's health. Lancelot bluntly replied that his father was dead.

Lancelot explained that when Ban had marched to aid Arthur at Bedegraine Forest, a rival had laid siege to Benwick. When Ban returned, he fought his enemies, but eventually had to abandon his castle. Leaving in secret at the break of morning, Ban, his wife and the young Lancelot crept along the edge of a nearby lake, and turned to watch the King's castle fall, burning to the ground. Ban died of a broken heart there and then, and as his mother grieved, Lancelot saw the waters of the lake part. A beautiful maiden rose from it and beckoned him.

The Lady of the Lake led Lancelot into the water, and raised him in her enchanted castle below. She taught Lancelot the skills he would need to become a valiant knight, and when he came of age, she sent him to serve Arthur as a Knight of the Round Table. And she had taught him well.

Arthur gladly received Lancelot into the service of the Round Table – Excalibur had been one great gift bestowed upon him by the Lady of the Lake, and the King recognised that this fine and handsome knight would be another. In honour of Lancelot's arrival, a tournament was held, during which the newcomer proved himself to be the most skilled horseman and knight in Arthur's court. As the tournament's victor, Lancelot was rewarded with a gift from Guinevere – one of a set of nine diamonds found by Arthur on one of his earliest quests. From that year onwards, The Diamond Tourney was held annually, with the victor being awarded another of the diamonds by Guinevere's fair hand. His eyes fixing upon the queen's beautiful face as he was awarded the first diamond, Lancelot vowed to win each of the following annual tournaments, so that he would receive his prize and pledge his honour to her each year. This he did.

From his arrival, until a final act that ultimately led to his king's downfall, Lancelot was to prove to be the greatest knight to serve Arthur's Round Table. He undertook many brave adventures, and gave great service to his king, replacing Gawain as the High King's favourite champion. He took a fortress of his own in northern Britain, after ousting a brutal tyrant from within, and renamed it the Castle of the Joyous Gard. He fell in love with a queen – of which you shall read more later – but also attracted the attention of many other maidens. One such maiden was named Elaine of Astolat – the Lady of Shallot – who starved herself to death when Lancelot spurned her advances. Another Elaine, Elaine of Carbonek, also fell in love with Lancelot. An enchantress tricked Lancelot into sleeping with Elaine, and from this union a child named Galahad was born; Galahad, like his father, would serve Arthur well.

The tale of Ywaine and Cynon

Another knight who arrived at Camelot to serve the mighty Arthur was Ywaine. He was the son of Urien of Gore – a former enemy of Arthur – and Arthur's half-sister Morgan Le Fay. Ywaine showed no animosity to Arthur, instead wishing to make up for his father's opposition by devoting himself to the High King.

Ywaine served Arthur and Guinevere quietly yet effectively without ever forcing himself into the limelight. This was to change, however, with the arrival of yet another young knight at Arthur's court. The newcomer's name was Cynon, and upon his arrival at Camelot, in keeping with custom, he was asked to recount the story of some remarkable event in which he had been involved. Cynon explained that he had only one such story, as he was a very inexperienced knight, and the story began as he went out riding one day. He arrived in a lush dale, thriving with wildlife and seemingly untouched by man. Birds sang in the trees, boars rustled through the undergrowth alongside herds of deer, and salmon leapt in a stream that ran through the valley. Continuing to ride further into the dale, Cynon spotted a great castle and rode towards it. The castle, he claimed, made Camelot look like a peasant's cottage – a comment that made the assembled crowd murmur with displeasure, not least Ywaine. Arthur hushed the crowd, and Cynon continued with his story. Entering the castle, Cynon met 24 maidens, all wearing astonishingly beautiful matching robes; each of the maidens, according to Cynon, outshone Guinevere. Again, a murmur went around the court of Camelot, and Ywaine began to object to the newcomer's lack of respect. Again, Arthur cut short these complaints and asked Cynon to continue. The maidens, Cynon recounted, looked after his horse, cleaned his weapons and armour into a brilliant sheen, and fed him a meal of the finest mead and game he had ever had. The next morning, Cynon left, and rode back through the dale. Then he found himself in a glade; in the centre of it was the tallest fir tree he'd ever seen, and underneath that sat a fountain. Cynon approached the fountain, and filled a pitcher that sat beside it. Carelessly, he poured the water away, onto the marble surround of the water feature. At that moment, the sound of clattering hooves could be heard, and as he turned to face the direction they came from, a horseman appeared from the forest, clad from head to foot in black armour, and riding a large black warhorse. Cynon attempted to parry the horseman's lance, but was flung from his mount and lay stunned on the floor. The black-clad warrior circled him, mocking Cynon's prowess, and chiding him that he was not ready for adventure. As Cynon lapsed into unconsciousness, he heard the sound of hooves fading away, and when he came to, he was by himself once more, and travelled home as quickly as possible.

The assembled court of Camelot fell silent as Cynon told of his encounter with the fearsome warrior, but when his tale finished, the adventure was the subject of a long discussion and created much excitement. Cynon was seated in the feasting hall and fed well. Ywaine, however, sat quietly, mulling over what he had heard. The next morning, Ywaine was seen leaving the gates of Camelot, fully armoured. He was heading off to take up the adventure that Cynon had not completed, hoping that he was better prepared to meet the warrior at the fountain than his predecessor had been.

Ywaine searched long and hard for the beautiful dale and castle of 24 maidens, and eventually, after weeks of searching, he found it. The countryside was as idyllic as Cynon had described on his journey to the castle. But before he found the castle, Ywaine found the glade with the fir tree and fountain. He poured water from the fountain onto the marble surrounding it, and, as expected, the black-clad warrior appeared from the undergrowth and charged at him. Ywaine was ready and waiting, and hacked at his opponent with his sword. The warrior dropped his lance, and slumped in his saddle, but his charging horse kept on moving, and ran from the glade at a canter. Ywaine gave chase, following the bloody trail left by the wounded horseman; the trail led to the castle of the maidens – which Ywaine regrettably noted was indeed as grand as

Cynon had described. Continuing on the trail of the defeated horseman, Ywaine entered a tower within the castle, where he was accosted by one of the 24 maidens whom Cynon had described. Again, Ywaine noted that Cynon's description of their beauty was indeed true.

The maiden introduced herself as a lady-in-waiting to the Lady of the Fountain. The black-clad warrior, she explained, was the Lord of the Fountain, and the ruler of the wonderful dale and castle. As the maiden spoke, a woeful wail echoed through the tower, and a chapel bell began to toll. The Lord of the Fountain had died, and Ywaine was his slayer. Taken before the mourning Lady of the Fountain, Ywaine was stunned by her bountiful beauty, which was greater than that of her ladies-in-waiting, and he immediately offered his sword and his service to her. Stricken with the loss of her husband, the Lady of the Fountain dismissed Ywaine out of hand, desperately explaining that the death of her husband meant that no one would now defend her glorious castle, dale or marble fountain. Ywaine vowed to stay, defending the castle and dale for the Lady of the Fountain, and he took on the guise of the black-clad warrior to do so. Within a year, he won the heart of the Lady of the Fountain, and Ywaine himself became the new Lord of the Fountain, protecting his new castle and realm.

At Camelot, Ywaine's absence over the year was noted. Cynon, himself now a more experienced knight, decided to set out to avenge Ywaine's presumed death at the hand of the warrior at the fountain. With him went some of Arthur's foremost knights – including Kay, Bors, Gawain, Agravain and Pellinore. They arrived at the fountain and poured the water. The sound of hooves was heard, and the warrior appeared through the undergrowth. Not one of Arthur's knights recognised the well-disguised Ywaine, and by the love of the Lady of the Fountain, Ywaine was spurred on to unhorse first Cynon, then Bors, then Kay, Agravaine, Pellinore and several others. Gawain launched himself at the fierce horseman, but even he was unhorsed. Holding his sword to Gawain's throat, the black-clad warrior removed his helmet to reveal his true identity to his defeated opponents. Each and every one of the knights was surprised and overjoyed to see that Ywaine remained alive – and marvelled at the skill he had developed over the previous year.

Ywaine led the knights to his castle, and set a mighty feast before them; the food, they all noted, was as wonderful as Cynon had reported when he first arrived at Camelot. Gawain asked if Ywaine would return to Camelot with them. Ywaine replied that he could not, as his duty now lay at the castle, but that he would forever be an ally of his High King, Arthur.

Merlin's fate

Throughout the years of Arthur's reign, and in the years of Uther's reign before him, Merlin had proved a sterling and wise counsellor to the High Kings. No living person rightfully knew his age, nor of his history before the Romans fled from Britain; that he was ancient and wise was common knowledge. That he was in love was not.

The target of Merlin's affection was none other than the Lady of the Lake, or to use her given name, Nimue. Long before she had offered Excalibur to Arthur, or coaxed Lancelot through the skills of knighthood, the enchantress who lived under the water had become a confidante of Merlin's. Her fledgling powers of sorcery and potions quickly flourished under the old sage's guidance, and with each and every skill she learned, she craved more. Nimue began to crave power also, and realised that the opportunities opened by her exquisite feminine charms allowed her to twist Merlin around her finger, and over countless decades, during which time neither of them seemed to age, Merlin's admiration of his acolyte turned into love.

Merlin constantly begged Nimue to become his wife throughout the years of Uther's reign, and during the early years of Arthur's. Nimue always refused his advances, promising him that one day she would agree to marry him, and that in the meantime, she must learn more from him. Each time he was spurned, Merlin acted like a jealous, besotted old fool, but each time he returned to Nimue and taught her new magical arts. He was a secretive man, and no one ever knew of his desire for the Lady of the Lake, not even Arthur, who came to consider himself a good friend of his counsellor.

As Nimue grew more knowledgeable and powerful, she began a plot to become the most powerful and wisest seer in Britain; to do this, she knew that she would have to rid herself of the smitten old man who currently filled this post. The opportunity arose one day as she rode through a deep, rarely explored forest with Merlin at her side (Nimue could, of course, live above the water's surface too). The pair of riders spotted a collapsed cave entrance, and as they approached it, Nimue suggested to Merlin that they should look inside. Merlin replied that he could certainly move the rocks, but that once opened, no one would ever be able to reopen the entrance, if the rocks should fall once more. Even so, eager to please his companion, Merlin uttered a few magical chants, and the rocks covering the cave's entrance rumbled out of the way.

Nimue whispered to Merlin that if he entered the cave, and was to emerge carrying any hidden treasure from within as a present for her, she would reward him with a kiss. Without thinking, Merlin rushed into the cave on this promise, and as he did so, he heard the sound of the rocks rumbling once more. And then all was dark.

Outside, Nimue mockingly called to him, reminding Merlin that he himself had proclaimed that the cave would never be reopened, and that her own sorcery was even more powerful than his own. With this, she rode away to fulfil her ambition of being the greatest seer in Arthur's Britain, and Merlin was left with little more to do than scream for help at the top of his voice, in a cave in a forest hardly frequented by mankind.

Merlin's absence was noted by Arthur at Camelot. The High King sent his knights to search the land for his much-loved counsellor. Gawain explored deep into the forest, and his well-trained warhorse heard the barely audible sound of Merlin's muffled cries. The horse made Gawain aware of the sound, and the knight dismounted and shouted through the collapsed entrance to the cave. When he realised that Merlin was inside, muscle-bound Gawain tried to shift the rocks to rescue the old man. Yet not one rock budged. In a resigned voice, Merlin explained his predicament, and asked Gawain to give a message to the court at Camelot. He foresaw that a great misfortune would befall Camelot, and that a great rift would divide the Order of the Round Table. He proclaimed that only the Holy Grail would prevent Britain from plunging into a dark age of doom. And with that, Merlin fell silent, and neither Gawain, nor those who visited afterwards to try to rescue Merlin, ever heard another word from inside.

The tale of Perceval and the Black Knight

Of the many riders who arrived at Camelot to serve the High King in Arthur's long reign, one stood out as being very different to the rest. He was not splendidly armed or armoured, did not ride a gallant warhorse and did not present himself with the courtly manners or customs that the assembled entourage of Camelot expected. Looking like a farm boy, riding a thin, gangly nag, and sliding unsteadily from its back and crossing the courtyard, the boy approached Camelot's brash Steward, Kay. The newcomer had a belt made of string, and straw falling from his hair. Kay questioned the boy as to where he had ridden from, to which he received the reply that the boy's mother had sent him to join the Order of the Round Table and to serve Arthur. His name, he announced in a most unassuming manner, was Perceval.

Kay laughed openly at the boy and told him that no simple farm boy should make such an arrogant claim. As he did so, two of Camelot's dwarves, who served Arthur's knights, looked at the boy and began to shout out that Perceval, the best knight destined to serve Arthur's court, had arrived at last. Kay turned to them, and seeing that neither dwarf appeared to be jesting, hit them both with the flat of his sword until they fled the courtyard, as he felt they were mocking Kay himself. The boy, in turn, announced to Kay that he had never met such a rude man in all his life, and that he had been raised to be far more chivalrous than Kay appeared to be. When he was accepted as a knight of Arthur's court, Perceval promised, he would punish Kay on the dwarves' behalf.

Kay continued to laugh at Perceval. He hadn't met such a yokel in many a year, and certainly never one who wished to join the Order of the Round Table. Kay told Perceval that he would need a sword, lance and armour before he could carry out his promise, and directed him to fight the Black Knight, who unhorsed riders for fun on the meadow outside Camelot. The Black Knight, Kay knew, was a brilliant fighter, and the thought of the country upstart being humiliated appealed to Kay's cruel streak. Perceval quickly remounted his nag, and urged it out of Camelot as quickly as it would carry him. Which was very slowly indeed.

As Perceval approached the Black Knight, he was hailed by the acclaimed warrior. The Black Knight asked if Perceval was another one from the castle, here to give him sport. Perceval replied that he had been sent by Kay to win the Black Knight's armour and weapons. The Black Knight scoffed, flourished his lance in the air, and charged at Perceval. As he couched his lance at Perceval, the gangly nag that the boy rode reared up on its hind legs and trampled the Black Knight beneath its hooves. Perceval dismounted, picked up the fallen warrior with one hand, an act that should have required the strength of ten men, and started to pluck his formerly feared foe's armour from him.

Meanwhile, Kay was wondering what humiliation might have befallen the farm boy. He decided to ride down to the meadow, hoping to mock the bruises that Perceval would have sustained to both his body and ego. Kay was a brilliant warrior himself by this point, but still approached the Black Knight's encampment with trepidation, such was the man's reputation. As he entered the camp, a black-clad warrior charged towards him; fumbling for his lance, Kay prepared himself for defeat, and rightly so, as the charging horseman's lance threw him from his saddle. The blow was delivered with such tremendous force from both horse and rider that it broke Kay's arm. From the ground, he looked on in wonder as the horseman, on a gangly but now speedy nag pulled up short of him and took his helmet off. Perceval sat wearing the Black Knight's armour, and his place in the Order of the Round Table was assured.

As Perceval was introduced to his king, Merlin explained to all that Perceval was in fact the son of Pellinore, the knight who had broken Arthur's first sword. What he lacked in courtly grace, he more than made up for in loyalty, honour and strength. The other knights at Arthur's court took it upon themselves to teach Perceval his courtly manners, and he proved to be a popular and gallant member of the Order. Kay, jealous as he was, forever gave Perceval a wide berth, just in case his earlier mocking came back to haunt him once again.

The Quest for the Holy Grail

Arthur had gathered the Order of the Round Table in its entirety for a great feast on a cold winter evening. When each and every esteemed knight had taken his seat at the table, the newest members of the Order were introduced. Among their number was Lancelot's son, Galahad, whose destiny it was to sit at a seat formerly never occupied, and known as the Siege Perilous. It was a seat that Merlin had once foretold could only be taken by the world's greatest and most chaste knight. Galahad was the only knight ever able to take the seat.

As the Order sat awaiting their feast, the sound of thunder rumbled outside. A few knights went to watch the storm that was brewing, but returned quickly, saying that all was still outside. As they retook their seats, the sound of thunder grew louder and echoed around the hall of Camelot – so loudly that it seemed that the walls might collapse. The great hall went very dark, and then the thunder stopped suddenly and the hall was filled with a blinding light. As the knights shielded their eyes, a simmering vision appeared over the centre of the Round Table. A white cloth suspended itself in the air, and underneath it was enshrouded the shape of a great vessel – everyone who observed it sensed that it was a great golden cup. As this hung in the air, the Round Table creaked under the weight of the most fragrant meal ever seen in Britain, which magically appeared in front of the assembled knights. The veiled cup began to float up and away, borne out of the hall by an invisible force. And then it disappeared, and calm returned to Camelot's great hall.

As the vision disappeared, Arthur and his knights sat motionless. Galahad announced to the stunned audience that this was a vision of the Holy Grail, the holiest and most precious object in the whole world. Arthur remembered Merlin's last words from his cavernous prison, that finding the Holy Grail would prevent the fall of Britain. Without Merlin to advise him further, Arthur became obsessed, the vision constantly playing on his mind. He rallied his 150 knights of the Round Table, and sent them out to find the Grail and return it to him to use for the good of the British people.

Forsaking the duties to their own lands and people, every knight of Arthur's court set out on his own personal quest for the Grail. No one knew where to look, or how long it would take. Many knights never returned, risking all to please their High King and dying in the process. Britain fell into decline without the judicial presence of Arthur's men, and fearsome barbarians began to raid once more.

Gawain quested long and hard, undertaking many adventures across the chaotic realm, but had no success. One night, he had a vivid dream involving 150 bulls out at pasture; all but three were pure black, and those three were pure white. One by one, the black bulls became sickly and starved, and many died; the three white bulls remained untouched. A perceptive old hermit interpreted Gawain's dream for him, explaining that only three of Arthur's knights would find the Grail, and that the black bulls represented the other knights of the Round Table, who would fall ill, lose heart, or die in their quest for the Grail. Gawain, the hermit assured him, was one of the black bulls. In despair, Gawain gave up the quest and returned to Camelot. Upon his return, he found several other knights who had also given up, many of whom told stories of the deaths of their fellow knights at the hand of all manner of mysterious beasts, cruel knights and unnatural pestilence. Arthur himself was very concerned, as he had never witnessed his assembled knights – the greatest in Britain – suffer such defeat and disgrace. Nevertheless, the quest continued, as Arthur wished to fulfil Merlin's prophecy.

Arthur's other greatest knight, Lancelot, also failed in his quest. Throughout his journey, he was hounded by foul luck, losing his sword and his horse whilst asleep, and becoming separated from Perceval, who he had initially set out alongside. With nothing to do but continue his search for the Grail on foot, Lancelot carried on. Eventually, he met a mounted warrior whose shield bore a red cross on a white background; the horseman approached, lifted off his helmet, and Lancelot saw it was his son, Galahad. The shield, he said, he had found in an old abbey, and anyone who had carried it before had befallen bad luck. However, he had also found out from an enchanted knight clad in silver armour that the bearer of the shield would be led to the resting place of the Grail, and that he knew he should carry it. Father and son continued the quest together, Lancelot finding a new mount, and then boarding a ship with Galahad, to broaden their search overseas.

During a violent sea storm, Lancelot fell ill with sea sickness. He had many visions and heard many strange voices, one of which was beckoning Galahad away, telling him that he would never see his father again. When Lancelot recovered from his swoon, he found that he was no longer on the ship, but instead on dry land, in a very unfamiliar desert region. As the sun set, he arrived at a dark and tall castle, the gate of which was guarded by two lions; the lions allowed Lancelot to pass without attack, and the knight entered the castle. It appeared to be deserted, but as he entered the castle's hall a blinding light stunned him and a thunderous voice boomed out that he must flee, as he was forbidden from viewing the Grail. He had entered the Grail Castle, the final resting place of the holy chalice. Brave Lancelot, greatly disorientated and in pain from the dazzling light and thunderous roar, staggered into the hall, determined to fulfil Arthur's request for the capture of the Grail. A radiant brilliance was emitted from the chalice, which sat on a table, covered by a red cloth. As Lancelot attempted to lift the cloth, he felt a great pain surge through him, and fell once more into a swoon. The most accomplished knight of Arthur's court lay stunned within grasp of the Grail.

When Lancelot came round, he was being attended to in bed by the Fisher King, the guardian of the Grail. The Fisher King was a kindly soul, entrusted with the safe-keeping of the Grail; he meant Lancelot no harm. The Fisher King explained to him that Lancelot would never be able to take the Grail, as great a knight and noble man as he was, he was not pure and chaste enough to do so. Only a man without guilt, and pure of heart, would be able to lift the Grail, and Lancelot was not such a man. Lancelot was nursed back to health by the Fisher King, and sent on his way back to Camelot. The Fisher King's parting words to Lancelot were that he had achieved much more than any of Arthur's other knights so far, getting so close to the Grail as he had. For Lancelot, the quest for the Grail was over.

Galahad had continued with his search, travelling as he wished yet still bearing the shield that would eventually lead him to the Grail. On the ship with his father he too had suffered strange visions and heard enchanted voices, including that of the silver-clad knight he had met when he acquired his shield. Following the advice he heard, he abandoned his father after a final embrace, landed in a strange, foreign desert, and continued the quest alone. He sensed that he was close to the end of his search, and that the shield would lead him truthfully. As he travelled through the dusty region, he met Perceval and Bors, both of whom had undertaken many brave adventures to arrive in this place. The three knights rode together, and eventually they saw the same tall, dark castle that Lancelot had entered before them.

The three knights passed by the lions who guarded the gate, and were met inside by the Fisher King. He greeted them courteously, and explained to them that he was only permitted to allow the purest and most chivalrous man in the world to touch the Grail. He immediately ruled Perceval out – his upbringing outside of Camelot meant that he could not address the Fisher King in the correct courtly fashion; Bors too, failed to prove himself suitably pure and chivalric, despite excelling at both. Galahad stepped forward and the Fisher King nodded his approval. He led the three knights into the hall of the Grail Castle. The dazzling light was brilliant but not painful, and the Fisher King, explaining that his work was complete and that Galahad would succeed him, faded away. As Perceval and Bors looked on, Galahad strode towards the enshrouded chalice and removed the cloth. He lifted the Grail, and the room was swathed in white light. As Galahad grasped the Grail, both he and the chalice began to rise from the ground and levitate in the air. The rolling sound of thunder that had been present when the Grail first appeared at Camelot sounded once more, and both man and chalice rose into the air and disappeared. Perceval and Bors looked on astonished, as the purest man in the world assumed guardianship of the Grail, and magically moved with it to a new, secret location. Neither were to be seen again in Arthur's reign.

Profoundly affected by the event he had witnessed, Perceval immediately fled and became a monk, dying shortly afterwards, happy and fulfilled at having seen the Grail, but heartbroken that he had failed his king when the Grail was so close by. Bors was able to return to Camelot to tell the downtrodden survivors of the Grail Quest what had happened.

The Grail had been found, but the Order of the Round Table had failed to bring it to Arthur. Merlin's prophecy thus foretold doom. Certainly, while the knights were away on their quest, Britain had slipped into chaos, and law and order had dissolved. Few worthy men remained alive after the gruelling demands of the quest, and Arthur faced a struggle to regain stability in his kingdom. Yet his troubles were only just beginning.

Lancelot's and Guinevere's betrayal

Lancelot, returning from the Grail Quest and mulling over his failure, knew one of the chief reasons for the lack of purity that prevented him from lifting the Grail. For several years, unknown to all – especially Arthur – Lancelot had been enthralled in an adulterous affair with Guincvere, Arthur's queen. Ever since she awarded him the prize of the first Diamond Tourney, he had harboured secret desires for her, and one day he had been unable to withhold his passion any longer and declared his love to Guinevere in a private garden. The queen was flattered and worried at the same time – Arthur was by this time always busy with affairs of state rather than affairs of the heart, and here was a handsome young knight declaring his love for her. Yet she dearly loved Arthur, despite his many distractions, and knew full well that a queen should always be loyal to her king. She resisted Lancelot's charms, remaining devoted to Arthur, and tried to avoid the younger knight whenever she could, to keep temptation far from her thoughts.

Yet once, when Arthur was campaigning far from home, Guinevere was kidnapped by a jealous knight named Meleagant, whose retinue had brutally slaughtered Guinevere's escort. Lancelot, not requested by Arthur on his campaign nor, to prevent suspicion, by Guinevere for her escort, armed himself and gave chase. His horse shot from underneath him by one of Meleagant's bowmen, Lancelot commandeered a peasant's horse-drawn cart to give chase. Catching Meleagant at his castle, Lancelot put him to the sword, along with his henchmen, and returned Guinevere to Camelot.

The cart was a totally undignified way for a knight of Lancelot's standing to travel, and by doing so, his actions made it clear to Guinevere exactly how deeply he loved her. Unfortunately, Arthur's eagle-eyed, mischievous nephew Modred also noticed the significance of Lancelot's actions. Completely swept away by Lancelot's gallant rescue, Guinevere began a passionate yet treasonous secret affair with Arthur's chief knight. Modred, who had developed a taste for the discomfort of others, kept an eye on them.

Lancelot's return from the Grail Quest saw the resumption of the affair, and at this point, Modred – who had been one of the first to give up the quest – revealed Lancelot and Guinevere's affair to Arthur. His brother, Agravaine, backed up Modred's claim. Irrefutable evidence was laid out before Arthur, and in a fury, he called for Gawain to tie Guinevere to a stake and burn her, and to banish Lancelot from Camelot for evermore. Gawain attempted to talk Arthur out of his fury, suggesting that the queen and Lancelot should first give their side of the story, but Modred egged Arthur on with lurid tales of the affair.

Modred and Agravaine dragged the queen to a stake, and were in the process of setting a fire beneath it when Lancelot, along with his close friends Lionel and Bors, rushed into the courtyard, fully armed and armoured. A vicious, swirling fight ensued within Camelot's walls, with some knights supporting their king, whilst others – unable to stand by and watch their beloved queen murdered – sided with Lancelot. Several worthy knights were felled in the battle; Lancelot slew both Gareth and Gaheris, and the arrogant Agravaine. Lancelot's supporters managed to snatch the queen from the flames that welled up around her, and rushed out of the royal castle heading towards Lancelot's stronghold of the Castle of the Joyous Gard, and then onto the continent, to his homeland of Benwick.

Arthur, still supported by a number of loyal followers including the long-serving Gawain, Kay, Lucas and Bedievere, had no option but to declare war on Lancelot. In effect, Lancelot had kidnapped Arthur's queen, and had in any case committed treason through the loving affair he had shared with her. Modred, self-righteous and angry, urged Arthur to pursue Lancelot into Benwick and give battle; Arthur's more staid knights urged caution. Yet Arthur's mind was made up when Modred promised to act as his regent, ruling Britain for Arthur during the King's continental campaign. The High King, upset yet grateful to Modred for unveiling the queen's affair, agreed to this, and marched to war. The Order of the Round Table had broken, and Britain was sliding further into the decline foretold by the long-departed Merlin.

Arthur crossed to the continent with his red dragon banner, and marched his large army to Benwick. Lancelot had ensconced himself in the region's strongest castle, and Arthur laid siege to it. Former comrades at the Round Table fought against each other; Gawain, wishing to avenge the deaths of his brothers at Lancelot's hand, undertook some very brave deeds. But Lancelot's castle showed no signs of falling, and Arthur's queen was inside with him.

Then, news came from Camelot. Modred had taken the throne for himself, and had invited the Saxons, Picts and Irish back into the realm to batter the population into submission to him. Split between taking vengeance on his queen and her lover, and protecting the people of his realm, Arthur had to choose the latter. Despite his recent rage, he was still a just man, and wished for no more than Britain to be safe. He ordered his army back to Britain, but left his broken heart in the siege-works of Benwick.

The last battle

The cruel streak in Modred was shown to all as he governed in Arthur's place. He introduced barbarian warriors to fight those Britons loyal to Arthur, and even took an axe to the Round Table, making it an oblong with a prominent seat for himself at its head. Grizzly Saxons, savage Picts and intoxicated Irish chieftains sat at it with him, feasting from Arthur's rich cellars. When Modred heard of Arthur's imminent return, he mustered his barbaric horde and marched from Camelot to Dover, where he intended to oppose Arthur's landing.

As the ships carrying Arthur's army sailed into view, Modred's howling hordes, and a number of treacherous Britons, drew themselves up ready for battle. First from Arthur's ship was Gawain – his role as Arthur's greatest knight restored now that Lancelot had betrayed the High King. In the vanguard of the battle, Gawain hacked scores of Modred's army aside, and behind him came Arthur's red dragon banner. In the face of such a furious assault, Modred's huge army retreated; they were fighting for money and spoils, not for the love of their king or country, and that made Arthur's knights superior in every way except for sheer numbers. As Modred's army faded away, Gawain charged at a group of Irish warriors who were still fighting, and clashed with a tattooed Irish champion who was a giant of a man. To Arthur's horror, Gawain was felled at the same moment as he delivered a killer blow to the Irishman.

Arthur's army was called to heel, to prevent similar tragedies occurring so late in the day. He gathered the few surviving knights of the Order of the Round Table to his tent – there were very few left, the Grail Quest, skirmish around Guinevere's stake, the campaign in Benwick, and now the Battle of Dover had taken their toll on his loyal following. Arthur declared that he would pursue Modred's army, defeat them again, and continue to pursue and defeat them until he had regained control of his realm and restored the peace and prosperity that he had introduced so long ago at the start of his reign. Kay, Bedivere, and Lucas the Butler – three of his staunchest knights, who had joined their king right at the start of his reign – applauded his decision.

Arthur's scouts followed Modred's retreating horde, and hunted them down to Cornwall. Arthur's army followed up, and at Camlann, on the River Camel, the two armies drew up once again. Both sides were cautious – the Battle of Dover had been a bloodthirsty affair – and Arthur agreed to meet Modred's chieftains in a parley. Kay advised against the meeting – just like Arthur, he knew how treacherous Modred was – but Arthur agreed to the meeting, hoping that Modred would surrender without a fight.

Arthur and his finest nobles rode to meet Modred and his fur-clad barbarian chieftains midway between the armies. Modred wished only to sneer at the rightful High King, rather than appeal for peace, and his ferocious mercenary chiefs laughed along with him. As the warriors faced each other, one of Modred's men drew a sword – an adder had struck at his ankle – and he killed it with a reflex blow. Even so, Kay, ready for subterfuge and impetuous as ever, thought that the warrior was an assassin, and struck him down. A skirmish erupted, and the armies began to move towards each other, war horns blowing and banners flapping in the wind. The sky darkened and rain started to fall; thunder rumbled and lightning flashed in the sky – until then, it had been a clear day. Ravens circled above, waiting to pick the flesh of the dead. The Battle of Camlann had begun.

Never had such a bloody battle been fought on British soil. Dover, though grim, did not compare. Arthur's army was smaller than Modred's but the fight swung this way and that. Rain poured down, and Arthur, in a blind rage at the fate of his kingdom, saw Lucas fall dead and Kay beheaded by a Saxon axe. The battle lasted for hours; Arthur stood in the thick of it, his red dragon banner planted firmly on Cornish soil. As the day wore on, the number of combatants gradually decreased – Britons fell dead fighting for either king, and barbarian warriors, their pockets full of Modred's pay, slipped away when the battle turned against them.

The rain tailed off, and Arthur surveyed the scene around him. He stood alone at the top of a pile of bodies, and close by sat the loyal Bedivere, exhausted by battle fury. Across the field of dead the High

King spotted his usurper, and strode toward Modred. Summoning all of his remaining energy, Arthur held Excalibur high above his head, ready to send a blow crashing into Modred's skull. But Modred was quicker; he had fought all day long too, but was younger and more dextrous. He lofted his blood-caked spear and plunged it deep into Arthur's chest. Blood spilled everywhere, mixing with the blood of hundreds of other men on the ground.

Arthur, his strength leaving his body, pulled himself up the spear shaft, and in pure rage he lopped Modred's head from his shoulders with a single blow, as the usurper desperately twisted the spear into Arthur's body once more. Modred fell dead, and in a swoon of exhaustion and pain, Arthur fell on top of him.

To Avalon and beyond

Arthur, his life rapidly draining from his body, was carried from the battlefield by Bedivere, who had witnessed his king's final deed. After he had put some distance between the battlefield and themselves, and when he could no longer hear the cries of ravens feasting on the battle corpses, Bedivere laid Arthur down to attend to him. The High King's heavy, pained voice made one final demand of Bedivere.

He told Bedivere that Excalibur must be unbuckled from the King's waist, and thrown into a nearby lake. Bedivere, ever loyal, agreed to do so, yet hoping above all else that Arthur would recover from his wound, and knowing that Excalibur was a symbol of the High King's authority, he hid the sword rather than throwing it into the lake. To discard Excalibur, he thought, would be an act of treason. Bedivere returned to Arthur, and the High King weakly asked what happened when the sword hit the water. Bedivere's answer was the answer that any man would have given, saying that the sword sunk below the surface; he had not been present when Arthur received Excalibur from the Lady of the Lake, and could not have expected her intervention. Arthur, growing angry despite his draining strength, told Bedivere to return and complete his instruction. Once more, Bedivere could not bring himself to do so, and returned with the same answer to Arthur's question. For a third time, Arthur sent Bedivere to throw Excalibur to its watery grave, and this time, through sheer love of his king, Bedivere did so. As the blade neared the water, a feminine arm broke the lake's surface, gracefully caught the sword's hilt, flourished the blade three times, and retracted under the surface, taking Excalibur back into the watery realm of the Lady of the Lake.

Astonished by what he had seen, and saddened by this symbolic ending of Arthur's kingship, Bedivere returned to his king and told the full story. Arthur nodded in grim satisfaction, briefly breaking into a smile, and then asked Bedivere if he could be carried to the shoreline. Carrying his king in his arms, Bedivere placed Arthur as he had wished, and watched as a black barge glided effortlessly across the water's surface.

On board the barge were three black-clad maidens, who disembarked and silently loaded the King onto the barge's deck. The sun began to set, casting a red sky over the scene, and the black barge disappeared into the west. A mist swirled around, and the barge faded into it. Although long gone, Bedivere heard Arthur's voice, whispering to him that nobody should mourn the King, for he was departing to the enchanted Isle of Avalon, where his wounds would be magically healed by the Lady of the Lake. He would then be ready to return when Britain was in grave danger and the Britons needed him more than ever. From that day to this, Arthur has not returned.

Guinevere saw her days out as a nun, greatly mourning the sins she had committed and her contribution to the fall of Arthur's kingdom. Lancelot returned to his own tower, the Castle of the Joyous Gard in northern Britain, and lived in solitude, ashamed that his actions had led to Arthur's downfall. When Lancelot heard of Guinevere's death, he escorted her funeral procession to Glastonbury, where she received a worthy burial. Bedivere, Arthur's last remaining loyal follower, died of old age, as did Lancelot, and with them ended the tale of Arthur's rule. Perhaps one day he shall return, and our once and future king sleeps, patiently awaiting his final summons by the British people.

Merlin, Britain's Wisest Counsellor

Chapter Six

All Mod Cons: Arthur in the Modern World

The success of Arthurian legend, and the popularity of the stories to this day, should not wholly be attributed to the medieval writers who created or embellished the complex tales of life at the Round Table. Many great medieval heroes have been relegated to supporting roles on English literature courses; for instance, Roland, Sigurd and Gamelyn are hardly household names these days, but they were all hot news for medieval storytellers. Instead, credit must also be given to the writers, poets and movie directors of the post-medieval period, who have breathed enough modern life into the Arthurian legend to make it entertaining and relevant to people today.

This doesn't belittle the work of Malory, Geoffrey of Monmouth or the countless other medieval authors who devoted substantial portions of their lives to writing about Arthur – we should just acknowledge that without relevance to a modern audience, legends and folklore simply falter and disappear. The majority of people who talk to me about Arthur speak in terms of Rosemary Sutcliff's and Bernard Cornwell's novels, and movies such as *Excalibur* or *Monty Python and the Holy Grail*, not Wace's *Roman de Brut* or the story of *Culhwch and Olwen*.

Before the nineteenth century

In the same year that Caxton published Thomas Malory's *The Death of Arthur* (1485), a new king hacked his bloody way to the throne with victory at the Battle of Bosworth. Henry Tudor – to become Henry VII when crowned – defeated his rival Richard III, mustering his army under the banner of the red dragon, a symbol which proudly displayed his claim on Welsh ancestry. Henry claimed to be the descendant of Geoffrey of Monmouth's final British (or Welsh) king before the ascent of the English – Cadwallader – and therefore a descendant of Arthur himself. Henry VIII followed Henry VII, and he also displayed an interest in the life of the legendary Arthur.

Henry VII had named his first son Arthur, and if Arthur had not died so young in 1502, it would have been interesting to know if he would have been crowned Arthur I or Arthur II, such was the level of interest in his namesake at that time. Henry VIII also named a son Arthur, although sadly this child lived for barely two months. At an earlier date, the son of Richard I's brother Geoffrey was also named Arthur… this led one chronicler to refer to him as 'the hope of his people'. This Arthur was not very lucky, either – embroiled in civil war, he was put to death at the age of sixteen by King John. While on the subject of royal Arthurs, it is interesting to note that both Prince Charles and his son Prince William have Arthur as one of their middle names – any of which they are allowed to use when crowned.

Although the Tudors are perhaps the best known line of monarchs to align themselves with Arthur's dynastic blood, they were not the first to do so. Henry II, who ruled 1154–1189 and who grew up as the medieval stories of Arthur began to flourish, would have been aware that a poet depicted Tristan in Henry's coat of arms. Another story was circulated claiming that Henry had discovered the location of Arthur's grave shortly before his death. There is a little truth in this: Henry had encouraged the monks of Glastonbury to search for Arthur's grave, and during his successor's reign (Richard I, 1189–1199), they did uncover someone – you can read more about this in Chapter Seven. Edward I (1272–1307) placed these remains on display before reinterring them in an impressive tomb. Arthurian relics were to be found in the hands of other royals – John (1199–1216) possessed a number of items, and Richard I gave a sword he claimed to be Excalibur to a Sicilian friend on the Third Crusade of 1191.

Of all the Plantagenets, Edward III (1327–1377) was perhaps the most intrigued by Arthur. He visited Glastonbury in outlandish Arthurian garb (and this was in the days before the Festival), and founded the Order of the Garter – he even toyed with the idea of refounding the Order of the Round Table. Edward may have been responsible for the construction of the famous Winchester Round Table (which can still be seen today, hanging in the grand surroundings of Winchester's Great Hall), although a late thirteenth century date seems more likely. This massive table was repainted in Henry VIII's reign, depicting Arthur in Tudor clothing and with a face not unlike that of Henry himself.

Chaucer's *Canterbury Tales*, written in the latter half of the fourteenth century, made reference to Gawain, but did not dwell upon Arthurian literature or characters. Given the interests of England's other great playwright, William Shakespeare, it is perhaps surprising that he did not dwell on Arthur, either. Shakespeare wrote a play based on another character known mostly from Geoffrey of Monmouth's *History* – King Lear – but his great, if heroically flawed, Dark Ages warrior king was to be Macbeth, not Arthur. During the sixteenth century (and up until the late nineteenth century, when educational standards opened the stories of Arthur to a wider audience), Arthurian legend was still seen essentially as the folklore of the upper classes, and perhaps would not have attracted the kind of audience that Shakespeare wrote for. Or perhaps the tales were far too well known for him to adapt for the stage – it is difficult to tell for sure. Yet for whatever reason, Shakespeare never included the tales of Arthur in his series of history plays.

Other post-medieval writers pondered over the tales they had heard of Arthur. The sixteenth century antiquarian John Leland believed that Arthur had been a real-life leader, and that the presence of wholly legendary events in the stories of Arthur did not prevent him from having been a real king. In 1542, Leland also recorded that South Cadbury hill fort was Arthur's Camelot (or 'Camalat' as he styled it). Another antiquarian, William Camden, also recorded local folk stories about Arthur, placing him in the West Country (his nationwide survey *Britannia* came out in 1586). During Elizabeth I's reign (1558–1603), others took up the possibilities created by Arthur with vigour. Elizabeth's astrologer John Dee introduced the idea that Arthur himself may have colonised the New World, and Edmund Spenser's *The Faerie Queene* (1590) included Arthur, Merlin, Tristan and Uther. Spenser even brought Arthur more directly into the bloodline of the Tudors.

The death of Elizabeth I either signalled the end of England's general interest in chivalry and Arthurian romance, or just happened to coincide with it. Henry Purcell and John Dryden worked together to produce an opera entitled *King Arthur* in the late seventeenth century, but the accession of William of Orange made sections of the opera seditious, and the plot had to be altered and then finally fizzled out. It was not really until the beginning of the nineteenth century that such ideals became fashionable once again.

The Victorians

The Victorians were not averse to changing history (or, if you're feeling of a kinder disposition, misunderstanding it) to suit their own standards and social niceties. The chivalric aspect of Arthurian legend appealed greatly to the Victorians, and almost without warning, an upsurge in new Arthurian literature and art made the King a household name once again. For the first time, education standards and printing technology allowed Arthur and his knights to become heroes to a much wider audience than ever before; the lower classes adopted the King as a folk hero, and the upper classes saw the King and his court as a symbol of aristocracy. What's more, the fact that Arthur was said to have ruled an empire across much of Europe would not have been lost on the upper classes in this century of modern empire building: here was a king for the modern monarchy to measure up to.

Shortly before the beginning of the nineteenth century, Edward Gibbon wrote a lengthy study of *The Decline and Fall of the Roman Empire* (completed in 1788 and extremely influential in the Victorian period that followed). Gibbon's tome was a standard scholarly work on the years in which Arthur may have lived, yet the majority of nineteenth century writers took more of an interest in the Arthur of legend, not the Arthur of history.

Towards the end of the eighteenth century, a growing trend for British writers and artists to indulge in romantic themes started to appear. Encouraged by a new fashion for all things Gothic, the romantic ideals of the late medieval period began to re-emerge, and scholars started to study long-forgotten medieval texts once more. The more artistically inclined began to mimic the subjects of this era, and in the early years of the nineteenth century, medieval English poetry and chivalric thought were popular once again. In 1802, Joseph Ritson published three editions of Arthurian romance, and in 1804, (the later Sir) Walter Scott edited a version of *Tristram and Iseult* from a Middle English text. In 1816-17, a new edition of Thomas Malory's *The Death of Arthur* was printed, and, as no newer editions were printed between this date and 1858, it seems likely that the 1816-17 edition must have reprinted many times in the intervening forty years.

The revival of interest in historical and medieval literature continued, but Arthurian legend comprised only part of it. Sir Walter Scott, ten years after editing *Tristram and Iseult*, published his historical novel *Waverley* in 1814, and other authors wrote their own medieval-styled or Gothic-themed stories. In 1848 Edward Bulwer-Lytton's *King Arthur* was published; Bulwer-Lytton attempted to produce a poem of epic proportion, drawing upon Norse and classical mythology to help the story along. Although poorly received by many modern commentators, *King Arthur* was pretty popular in its own time, as four editions of the poem were produced in a thirty year period. William Morris contributed the poem collection *The Defence of Guinevere* in 1858, and a respectable number of other writers dabbled with Arthurian poem and prose. Another 1858 book, Thomas Bulfinch's *The Age of Chivalry*, is still a popular read and retells the most popular stories of Arthurian legend in a mixture of prose and poetry.

But the most famous poet of the Victorian period to tackle Arthurian legend – indeed the most famous writer of any form of text on this subject in the nineteenth century – was without a doubt Alfred, Lord Tennyson. Born in Lincolnshire in 1809, Tennyson went on to study at the University of Cambridge, but left without taking his degree in 1831. Amongst his many poems, his great Arthurian masterpiece *The Idylls of the King* stands out above the rest. The *Idylls* was not written as a single epic piece of poetry, instead being created over many years, and it was not completed until the final publication in twelve books in 1888. Tennyson's first poem of the *Idylls* was 'The Lady of Shallott' (a piece about Elaine of Astolat) which was published in 1832, and which was probably based on an Italian romance rather than Thomas Malory's work. A later variation on the same theme, this time using Malory's story for inspiration, saw Tennyson set down 'Lancelot and Elaine', which was to be one of his most successful pieces. Such an ambitious undertaking – to recreate the entire legend of Arthur in an epic poem – helped Tennyson cement his reputation as one of the greatest poets of his age, and he was rewarded for his vision and talent by achieving laureate status in 1850. The greatest of Tennyson's Arthurian pieces is generally considered by critics to be 'The Passing of Arthur', although this is not technically one of the *Idylls*, and more correctly should be considered an end piece.

As many writers did before him and have continued to do ever since, Tennyson bestowed upon Arthur and his followers the virtues and values that were considered important in his own day and age. Arthur himself represented everything that was thought to be virtuous in Victorian society, and social comment and sin were passed through Tennyon's portrayal of Guinevere and also Gawain. Tennyson's work was tremendously popular with readers of the Victorian generation, and although the poet is perhaps better remembered in the modern period for *The Lotos Eaters*, *The Charge of the Light Brigade*, and *Maud*, his Arthurian contribution should never be underestimated.

Mark Twain (whose real name was Samuel Clemens) was doing for Arthur in America what Tennyson was in Britain. Twain's *A Connecticut Yankee at King Arthur's Court* was first published in 1889, and told the story of Hank Morgan, an American factory supervisor, who awakens one morning to find that he has been transported back to sixth century Britain – the Age of Arthur. *A Connecticut Yankee* is an anarchic narrative of Hank's adventures, and satirises much of what the nineteenth century world stood for. Twain's novel is still considered one of the cornerstones of American literature.

The modern image of Arthur as an ageing, ineffectual king was greatly influenced by such Victorian writers. Medieval romances, although portraying Arthur as a sedate ruler and focusing more on the deeds of his knights, never seem to have implied quite the same lack of royal vigour as the Victorian storytellers did. The Victorian Arthur was very much a stay-at-home figure, who sent his knights out to quest on his behalf, quickly playing down his role after the infamous Sword in the Stone incident. Perhaps this interpretation of Arthur could be linked to the waning power of the nineteenth century monarchy when compared to the rising power of Parliament, the role of which was comparable to the Round Table of Camelot.

Not all later Victorian Arthurian literature was new; in the 1890s, the prolific publisher J M Dent produced an edition of Thomas Malory's *The Death of Arthur*, boldly illustrated in stark black and white images and page décor by the then unknown artist Aubrey Beardsley. Published in twelve parts, this work made Beardsley famous almost overnight.

Beardsley was not the only artist to portray Arthurian scenes. The upsurge in popularity of Arthurian literature generated an interest in Arthurian-inspired art from some of the foremost artists of the period including Dante Gabriel Rossetti and Gustave Doré. The Pre-Raphaelite Brotherhood, formed in 1848, breathed new life into medieval romance and their work – which frequently bore the inspiration of medieval and Victorian Arthurian tales – became perhaps the most significant British art movement of the era. The Brotherhood included notables such as

Rossetti, John Ruskin, William Morris, Arthur Hughes and Sir Edward Burne-Jones.

Towards the end of the nineteenth century, education standards for children from all levels of society steadily increased, and this led to a new form of Arthurian legend: tales for children. Sir James Knowles' *King Arthur and His Knights* was published in 1862, and was followed in 1880 by Sidney Lanier's wonderfully titled *The Boys' King Arthur* (the Victorian mind clearly wondered what girls in their right mind would want to read of knights and adventure when they could have dolls and cooking instead!). This trend for children's Arthurian literature continued into the twentieth century, and is still popular today.

Twentieth century fiction

Arthurian writing in the twentieth century can broadly be split into two categories: theories regarding the existence or otherwise of a historical Arthur, and fiction usually based on Arthur's legendary court, but occasionally in a more secure historical setting.

F J Snell's *King Arthur's Country* (1926) was the first comprehensive account of Arthurian sites, but rather than claiming complete and purely historical accuracy, Snell combined the different strands of literature, history and folklore to create an enthralling companion to the locales of Arthurian tales. The main theories surrounding a possible identity for the historical Arthur are dealt with in the next chapter (and believe me, there have been plenty of them bandied about over the years), leaving this section to deal with some of the accomplished modern fiction spawned from our medieval heritage.

Many early to mid-twentieth century books retold the popular stories of Arthur and the Round Table, heavily based on Malory's work. Thomas Bulfinch's earlier *The Age of Chivalry* grew in popularity, and H A Guerber's *Myths and Legends of the Middle Ages* (1919), M I Ebbutt's *The British: Myths and Legends* (1910) and T W Rolleston's *Celtic Myths and Legends* are very typical of this genre. Yet such traditional regurgitation of the legend was not all that was on offer; for the first time in post-Victorian Britain, writers were starting to produce original works with an Arthurian content. Both Thomas Hardy and John Masefield tackled Arthurian themes in their plays, and the 1920s and 1930s saw an upsurge in the popularity of contemporary Arthurian literature once more. Edward Arlington Robinson wrote a trilogy of tragic Arthurian verse: *Merlin* (1917), *Lancelot* (1920), and *Tristram* (1927), and T S Eliot's esteemed 1922 poem *The Waste Land* carried similar themes. Another early to mid-twentieth century author who took up the gauntlet of writing contemporary Arthurian fiction and poetry was Charles Williams, whose 1938 poetry collection *Taliessin Through Logres* and 1944's *The Region of the Summer Stars* conveyed powerful images of Arthurian legend. Williams' friend C S Lewis (well known for his own works of fantasy fiction) produced a guide to Williams' sometimes difficult to penetrate work, and contributed his own legacy to Arthurian literature by resurrecting Merlin in his 1945 novel *That Hideous Strength*. Edward Frankland contributed another intriguing interpretation of the historical background of Arthur in his 1944 novel *Arthur: The Bear of Britain*, which focused on Arthur's twelve famous battles, and his eventual downfall at the hands of Modred and Guinevere.

Yet in the first half of the twentieth century, there can be no doubt that the leading contemporary Arthurian author was T H White. White initially wrote three novels: *The Sword in the Stone* (1938), *The Queen of Air and Darkness* (1939) and *The Ill-Made Knight* (1940). These were republished as an omnibus in 1958, along with a later novel titled *The Candle in the Wind*, as *The Once and Future King*. A fifth book, *The Book of Merlyn*, was posthumously published in 1977, although White wrote it at some point around 1940. White's books broadly follow the story-line set down by Thomas Malory in the fifteenth century, but include dashes of humour, anachronisms such as guns, and a page of Arthur's being named Thomas Malory. This page, incidentally, is sent away by Arthur before his final, fatal battle, so that someone will live to tell the tale.

T H White's place at the top of the Arthurian pile was arguably replaced in 1963 by Rosemary Sutcliff, who attempted to set fiction about Arthur into its correct historical context. Her well-respected historical novel *Sword at Sunset* is based on Nennius' early list of Arthurian battles, and sees the King as a post-Roman warlord fighting against the tide of invading Saxons. She even went to the trouble of visiting possible battle sites (no mean feat when you find out she was in a wheelchair), and discussing the possible realities of such a military campaign with historical warfare experts. Sutcliff also contributed her own retelling of the classic medieval Arthurian legends, and a number of other historical novels based in Roman and post-Roman Britain such as *Dawn Wind* (1961) and *The Lantern Bearers* (1959). Rosemary Sutcliff should always be remembered for her contribution of Arthurian stories for children (and like-minded adults), and the appreciation and love of history that she has given to so many readers.

ALL MOD CONS: ARTHUR IN THE MODERN WORLD

Like Rosemary Sutcliff, Mary Stewart made solid use of early Arthurian sources along with themes from Celtic magic and folklore when researching her own novels. She uses Merlin as the storyteller in her first three novels; *The Crystal Cave* (1970), *The Hollow Hills* (1973) and *The Last Enchantment* (1979). In her fourth novel, 1984's *The Wicked Day*, she shifts the storyteller to Modred, unusually sympathising with his view on the downfall of Arthur.

Marion Bradley's *The Mists of Avalon* (1982) has a strong modernist feel to it, focusing on twentieth century concepts such as modern paganism and feminism. The stories are told from the point of view of women – which is unusual even in modern Arthurian literature – and have strong appeal to modern Mind, Body and Spirit enthusiasts. Such an interpretation of Arthurian legend shows – like Geoffrey of Monmouth in the twelfth century, and Tennyson in the nineteenth century – how the characters of Arthur and his followers, and the stories which are told about them, can be adapted to suit contemporary audiences in a writer's own age.

Bernard Cornwell, more famous for his Napoleonic Rifles officer Sharpe, followed in the footsteps of Rosemary Sutcliff by producing a worthy attempt at recreating a plausible Arthurian history in fictional form. His *Warlord* trilogy, comprising *The Winter King* (1995), *Enemy of God* (1997) and *Excalibur* (1997), attempts to place Arthur and many of the better known characters from Arthurian legend into a possible historical context in the late fifth century. Cornwell works a number of well-known names into the story, such as the legendary Culhwch, Pellinore and Lancelot, alongside historically named characters including Aelle (a Saxon king), Brochvael (a British king) and Cerdic (another Saxon king).

In the last few decades of the twentieth century, a vast amount of Arthur related fiction was published. As well as the authors mentioned above, some of the other more notable contributions have come from Stephen Lawhead, who produced an Arthurian trilogy in the 1980s (emphasising pagan aspects of the legend), Phyllis Ann Karr who wrote the murder mystery *The Idylls of the Queen* (1982), and the great John Steinbeck, who rather surprisingly opted for a rather straightforward reworking of Malory's writing in 1976's *The Acts of King Arthur and His Noble Knights*. Thomas Berger's *Arthur Rex* (1978) was another worthy contribution to the genre, as is the more recent *The Summer Stars* by Alan Fisk (2000), a novel written as the autobiography of the British bard Taliesin.

Perhaps my favourite take on the story of Arthur, and on Celtic and medieval British legend in general, is Joy Chant's *The High Kings* (1987). Chant attempts to retell the stories of a number of British heroes who lived before Arthur's time – in doing so, her fiction is greatly influenced by Geoffrey of Monmouth's fabulous *History*, but also by the tales of the native Welsh and Britons. Chant is on familiar ground as she retells the stories of Magnus Maximus, Vortigern, Ambrosius and Arthur, but begins by telling the stories of earlier folk heroes and legendary warriors. Britain's founding father, the Trojan prince Brutus, and the story of Leir (Shakespeare's King Lear), and several other notable figures are all retold in Chant's beautiful prose. In between the legends, Chant presents short essays on different aspects of early British life, from warfare to ornamentation to marriage, which helps her book flow along most successfully.

Outside of the English language, a number of writers made twentieth century literary contributions in Italian, French and German. Even so, it would seem that English remains the primary language for future developments of Arthurian fiction.

Arthurian legend was first presented in a form suitable for children in the Victorian era. With faint echoes of fairy tales and stronger references to magic, it seems as though Arthurian literature was almost purposely written to enchant young audiences. Indeed, some of the most handsomely rendered versions of the legend of Arthur were originally commissioned as children's books. Rosemary Sutcliff, mentioned earlier in this chapter, wrote books primarily for children, but the stories were so well constructed that adults could enjoy reading them too (it's always constructive to remember that the *Harry Potter* books were not the first kids' books to make this important commercial and literary crossover – Arthurian books have been doing so for years). Ladybird Books introduced young readers (including me) to Arthurian legend in the late 1970s and during the 1980s, producing a series of four books in 1977: *Mysteries of Merlin, The Deeds of the Nameless Knight, Sir Lancelot of the Lake* and *The Knight of the Golden Falcon and other stories*. Desmond Dunkerley wrote all four of these books, which are broadly based on Malory's work; what really makes these titles stand out above the strong competition in the children's Arthurian market is Robert Ayton's beautiful artwork. These Ladybird books enthralled me as a kid, and kick-started my interest in Arthur (I've since realised that the four cover images by Ayton actually comprise one picture if you push them all together). Many other children's books, mostly compilations of stories based on Malory's work, although often diluted down for young ears, can be plucked from the shelves of bookshops.

Dean Wilkinson's *The Legend of Arthur King* (2003) uses the themes of Arthurian legend in the broadest possible way to tell the story of the life of a modern boy named Arthur King. Arthur fakes a heart attack to get out of Maths, and by doing so sets off a chain of events that shows that Arthur is no ordinary, dull lad: he and friend Lawrence discover that they are the spirit of King Arthur and the Knights of the Round Table reborn. And with that, they must save their local wood – Albion Wood – and a rare species of bird that lives there from destruction. OK, so it's not really a reworking that Geoffrey of Monmouth or Thomas Malory would necessarily have endorsed, but *The Legend of Arthur King* does tell Arthurian legend with a modern twist.

Alan Garner's *The Weirdstone of Brisingamen* is a children's book set in the 1960s, but one that draws on the folk tales of early Britain. A key concept in Garner's book is that 140 knights lie in an enchanted sleep in a cave, protected by a wizard and awaiting the call to fight against evil. Although not mentioned in this story by name, this is a clear reference to Arthur's eventual fate.

Arthurian legend has influenced other great fictional creations of the twentieth century, not least the works of J R R Tolkien. Tolkien's famous books *The Hobbit* and *The Lord of the Rings* have much in common with both Arthurian legend and Anglo-Saxon and Germanic sagas from the early medieval period. This should not be surprising, as Tolkien was a distinguished scholar in these fields; his famous Rohirrim warriors appear to have been based on heroic Anglo-Saxon society, and it might also be imagined that there is more than a bit of Merlin in Tolkien's powerful and wise wizard Gandalf.

Yet it must not be imagined that all Arthurian fiction and modern literature is oppressively highbrow. A flourishing trade exists in Arthurian-themed comic books and graphic novels. The most famous of these is Hal Foster's comic strip *Prince Valiant* (which has appeared in American newspapers since 1937), although Barr and Bollund's *Camelot 3000* (published between 1982 and 1985) is also well known – transporting Arthur into the year 3000 to battle an alien invasion encouraged by Morgan Le Fay. Among the other contributions to this genre, Disney managed to contribute *Goofy King Arthur*, in their 'Goofy Through History' series.

Arthur: the movie

No, not the Dudley Moore comedy that forces its way onto your television every Christmas. Given that Arthurian legend leads with a strong plot, lots of sex and violence, and the chance for actors to run around waving swords like maniacs, it's not surprising that many movies have been based around the reign of Arthur.

Without a doubt, the cinema has played a crucial role in maintaining the popularity of the Arthurian legend for modern audiences. People still read books, but the cinema offers a story to a far wider audience – and the possibilities of dubbing and subtitles allow cinema-goers in diverse countries the opportunity to watch the story of Arthur unfold before them.

In cinema, often more is made of the Arthur-Guinevere-Lancelot love triangle than occurs on the written page of Arthurian legend. As a consequence, Arthur is often portrayed as a middle-aged or elderly king, ineffectual against the martial and marital skills of Lancelot; this particular slant on Arthurian legend presents a skewed vision of Arthur's reign, but ultimately presents the correct balance of romance and action for cinema-goers.

Among the many films set in the world of Arthur, a few stand out head and shoulders above the rest; the list below starts with these, before moving on to some of the less memorable contributions I've witnessed in this special niche of cinematic history.

Starting with the best movie of them all, *Excalibur* (1981) should be considered an unmissable film for Arthurian fanatics. Directed by John Boorman, *Excalibur* is broadly based on Thomas Malory's *The Death of Arthur*, but also nods its head in the direction of T H White's mid-twentieth century fiction. Boorman's biggest obstacle in making *Excalibur* must have been trying to compress Malory's *The Death of Arthur* into 135 minutes of cinema. If you've read *The Death of Arthur*, you'll realise what an impossible task he was up against, and that most directors would need 135 five hours. Yet Boorman and his fellow screenwriter Rospo Pallenberg do a great job, and manage to make their screenplay hit the target more times than it misses. Their retelling of Malory's legend of Arthur focuses on the end of Uther's reign and the beginning of Arthur's reign. It then moves on to the arrival of Lancelot, leading in turn to the love triangle of Arthur, Guinevere and Lancelot. Of course, the story of the Quest for the Holy Grail is included, as is a vivid action sequence depicting Arthur's final defeat at the hands of Modred. The entire film has an excellent dark, brooding backdrop, with fog and rain aplenty, contrasting with the shining plate armour of Arthur's warriors (Arthurian knights have never looked finer than in *Excalibur*). For the sake of a streamlined plot, Boorman and Pallenberg sometimes compress the roles of several knights into one character; for example Perceval, rather than Bedivere, throws Arthur's sword Excalibur into the lake as the King lies dying. Magic and mysticism comes to the fore in Boorman's movie – Nicol Williamson plays Merlin with a perfectly judged mix of humour and menace, and Helen Mirren will make your spine tingle as Morgana (Morgan Le Fay). The relatively unknown actor who plays Arthur, Nigel Terry, is well supported by a cast including Patrick Stewart (of *Star Trek* fame), Gabriel Byrne, Liam Neeson and Clive Swift (the long-suffering husband of Hyacinth Bucket in the sitcom *Keeping Up Appearances*). Along with Nigel Terry, *Excalibur*'s love triangle consists of Nicolas Clay playing Lancelot and Cherie Lunghi as Guinevere. Battle is brutal, short and gory in *Excalibur*, and the musical score using Wagner's music is both moving and apt. The best costume is undoubtedly Modred's golden plate armour, with a helmet loosely based on a stunning Roman parade helmet found at Newstead in southern Scotland (dating to AD 80–100). But the highlight of *Excalibur*, matched in no other Arthurian story, is Arthur's conception through Uther's suit of armour at the start of the film. A true landmark both in cinema and human biology!

First Knight (1995) is one of Hollywood's more recent attempts to revive the popularity of the legend of Arthur, directed by Jerry Zucker. Richard Gere stars as Lancelot and Sean Connery takes on the mantle of the great King himself; Julia Ormond plays Guinevere. The film opens with a young Guinevere travelling to meet the ageing Arthur, her prospective suitor. On the way, she is ambushed by the evil Malagant (elsewhere spelt Meleagant and here played by Ben Cross, ably assisted by Ralph Ineson, otherwise known as 'Finchy' from the TV comedy *The Office*). With her escort scattered, Guinevere is only saved by the intervention of Lancelot – in this film he is portrayed not as a knight but as a hired swordsman who works for the highest bidder. They fall in love, although Guinevere remains in denial as she is betrothed to Arthur, marriage to whom will save her lands from the marauding Malagant. Other kidnap attempts are made, and eventually Lancelot must rescue Guinevere from Malagant's ruined castle hideout; later, as the couple embrace, Arthur walks in on them and demands a trial for treason. During the trial, Malagant storms Camelot and is only repelled by Lancelot and the common folk, who remain staunchly loyal to Arthur (this is Hollywood, after all). Arthur receives a fatal wound, Malagant is slain by Lancelot, and the dying Arthur hands the kingdom to Guinevere and her common lover. *First Knight* takes a few elements of Arthurian legend – the familiar love triangle, and, perhaps surprisingly, also Chrétien de Troyes' story of *The Knight of the Cart*. Even with such inspired plots to guide the movie, *First Knight* seems a little sterile to me, and despite the presence of big name stars such as Connery and Gere, the film is very much an 'also ran'.

In contrast to *First Knight*, Nathan Juran's *Siege Of The Saxons* (1963) is an interesting and fun variation on the usual themes explored by Arthurian movies. It is the story of Arthur's daughter, Katherine (specially invented for his film, it would seem, and played by Janette Scott), who is plunged into a fierce fight to protect the kingdom when her father is killed. The film begins in fine medieval style with a joust between the champion of England, Edmund of Cornwall (played by Ronald Howard), and a Saxon champion. Edmund wins, but the high-handed arrogant reaction of the Germans (the Saxons in *Siege of the Saxons* are from Saxony) suggests that there may be trouble ahead. It transpires that England's own Edmund of Cornwall and the Saxons are plotting against the ageing Arthur, so that Edmund may take the crown and act as an ally to the dastardly Saxons. Arthur survives an assassination attempt by a sinister Germanic killer named 'the Limping Man', but his time as King is running out. Edmund of Cornwall's men surprise and kill Arthur, but are dressed as Saxons to disguise their treachery (right down to horned helmets, which Arthur's men wouldn't dream of wearing in this film). Katherine is saved by the timely actions of a patriotic rogue named Robert Marshall (played by Ronald Lewis); Robert comes across as the leather-clad offspring of Errol Flynn and Terry Scott: he has a charming manner and a succession of cheeky one-liners. The relationship between Robert and Kate (as her father the King affectionately called her) is quite amusing to watch, especially when Robert cuts her hair and dresses her like a boy to deceive Edmund's men. The disguise is necessary as Edmund's men stop at nothing to hunt her down – they even line up a row of monks and a bow and arrow armed firing squad shoot them all. Robert Marshall realises that Katherine's only hope is to enlist the help of her father's wise advisor Merlin, and together with the rather unnerving Men of Chatham, who are on the Queen's and Merlin's side, they do so. With Merlin's help, Katherine and Robert sneak into Camelot and foil Edmund of Cornwall's attempt to crown himself. When he is unable to draw Excalibur from it's scabbard as the heir to Arthur should be able to, the nobles side with Katherine (who, of course, can draw Excalibur). Edmund flees to his Saxon allies, who immediately kill him for failing them, and the climax of the film is a battle between Robert and the knights of Arthur on one side fighting 'for Katherine and for England', and those nasty Saxons on the other. It is easy to guess who wins. The kingdom safe, Robert is made Baron of Cornwall and Chatham, his earlier outlawry forgiven, and the film closes with him accepting Katherine's offer to make him her king.

Knights of the Round Table (1953) stars Robert Taylor and Ava Gardner, and is an Arthurian romp of the finest Hollywood tradition, with knights in shining armour, damsels in distress, and more chivalric banter than you could shake a jousting lance at. And watch out for one of Britain's finest actors, Stanley Baker, as Modred, vying for power with Arthur whilst unable to pull the sword from an anvil set in stone. By many measures, *Knights of the Round Table* is typical of the sort of historically based action films made in the 1950s and 1960s. Although the script dips its toe in the waters of Arthurian legend, the characters could, for the most part, be interchangeable with those of any other similar tale such as Ivanhoe or Robin Hood, rather than reproducing Arthurian legend in its purest form.

Lancelot and Guinivere (1962) is also known as *The Sword of Lancelot*, and was co-produced by, directed by, and starred Cornel Wilde. *The Sword of Lancelot* is in many ways a worthier movie than *Knights of the Round Table*, a film that it makes some effort to mirror. The plot is pretty familiar to anyone with even a slight knowledge of Arthurian legend, and there's nothing wrong with it being so. In a nutshell, Lancelot (played by Wilde) is Arthur's most renowned knight and champion, yet he falls for the King's wife Guinevere (Jean Wallace). Brian Aherne, playing the role of Arthur, has to fight to keep his kingdom and his wife. The sword fighting sequences in this film are pretty special – as in so many historical movies from the 1950s and 1960s – but the plot holds precious few surprises for the viewer.

A Connecticut Yankee in King Arthur's Court (1949) stars Bing Crosby, and is a fairly standard musical showcase for him. Despite Crosby's laid back persona and droll humour, this film is a pretty standard remake of

Mark Twain's classic novel. The few changes that were made to Twain's story-line were to allow for a musical without all the political satire that Twain so loved. Rhonda Fleming plays the beautiful Alisande, the love interest of Crosby's character Hank, and Cedric Hardwicke excels as the elderly Arthur, blissfully unaware that he's out of touch with his people. Before this 1949 version was made, Will Rogers starred in a less faithful 1931 film entitled *A Connecticut Yankee*.

In a similar vein to both versions of *A Connecticut Yankee* is *A Spaceman in the Court of King Arthur* (1979); this film is also known by the slightly cumbersome title *The Unidentified Flying Oddball*.

Monty Python and the Holy Grail (1975) was written and performed as a comedy, but it also happens to be as historically accurate as most of the other films in this list – inasmuch as it is not at all accurate! Nevertheless, this is an entertaining twist on the usual stories of Arthurian legend, with many sketches and minor details revealing that the writers had a good knowledge of the medieval tales. Watery 'bints', limbless knights and foul Frenchmen abound, and in many ways, *Monty Python and the Holy Grail* is to the modern world what Twain's *A Connecticut Yankee* was to its late nineteenth century audience.

Another comedic approach to the story of Arthur is *A Knight in Camelot* (1998), starring Whoopi Goldberg, Ian Richardson and Michael York. It's pretty standard fare about a modern day American transported back in time into Arthur's world with theoretically amusing consequences. In most respects, *A Knight in Camelot* is really just a variation on the theme of *A Connecticut Yankee in King Arthur's Court*, updated for the story to revolve around the cultural problems encountered by the female lead role.

The Sword in the Stone (1963) is Disney's treatment of T H White's stories about the young Arthur: *The Once and Future King*. In terms of quality of animation, *The Sword in the Stone* isn't one of Disney's finest films, yet some of the sequences, including the training of Arthur (known by Merlin as 'the Wart') is still very watchable. As the story is based on T H White's fiction, *The Sword in the Stone* remains one of the most off the wall contributions to Arthurian cinema, successfully getting away from the usual Arthur-Guinevere-Lancelot love triangle.

Camelot, would you believe, is a musical starring the late, great Richard Harris. This 1967 cinema version of the Lerner–Loewe musical was panned almost universally by the critics. Still, what the critics say the Oscars ignore, and the film won coveted awards for Costume, Score and Art Direction/Set Decoration. Lerner and Loewe's story is more T H White than Malory, the light-heartedness of which is a far more suitable backdrop for a musical than Malory's instructive text could ever be. *Camelot* begins with the marriage of Arthur and Guinevere and ends with Arthur at the battlements of Lancelot's castle. Focusing on almost every Arthurian movie makers' first choice plot – the love triangle – *Camelot* also stars Vanessa Redgrave as Guinevere and Franco Nero as Lancelot. Despite the Oscars, the set designers managed to make the set appear more like a theatre stage than a film set, giving the whole film a love it or hate it feel.

Indiana Jones and the Last Crusade (1989) stars Harrison Ford and Sean Connery (not an unfamiliar face in Arthurian-related movies). The father and son archaeology tag team battle the Germans for possession of the Holy Grail (after finding the Ark of the Covenant in the first film of the trilogy). The Germans want the Grail to bring them a spiritual advantage in the soon-to-start Second World War, but the Jones' work together to prevent this happening. When it finally appears, the Grail is a simple wooden cup rather than the grandiose vessel of some stories. 1991's *The Fisher King* is another film that builds upon Arthurian themes and their relationship with the modern world, perhaps less successfully for the viewer than the Indiana Jones movie.

Amongst the other varied contributions to Arthurian cinema, mention must be made of *Gawain and the Green Knight* (1973), *Parsifal* (1982) which is a cinematic interpretation of Wagner's opera of the same name filmed by Armin Jordan, *Lancelot du Lac* (1974) which is also known as *Le Graal* or *The Grail*, and *Sword of the Valiant* (1984). Movie versions of the comic strip *Prince Valiant* have been made twice (1954 and 1994), along with an animated series of the same name in the 1990s. Any of the films mentioned here are well worth spending an afternoon in for – whether as a great celluloid experience or an unintentionally funny historical romp depending on the film.

The legend of Arthur has also made it onto the small screen on countless occasions, mostly for children (and adults with nothing better to do): for example, there has been a recent cartoon series of *Prince Valiant*, and the 1949 serial *The Adventures of Sir Galahad*. In 1998, Sam Neill starred in the lead role of *Merlin*. This was a four-hour-long miniseries that retold the story of the rise and fall of Arthur from the perspective of Merlin. Despite his political prowess, the wizard is unable to break the spell that imprisons his lover, Nimue (Isabella Rossellini).

Along the way, Merlin battles against the treachery of Morgan Le Fay (Helena Bonham Carter) and the evil Queen Mab (Miranda Richardson, playing a character borrowed from Irish legend).

Merlin was next played by Rik Mayall (who you'll recognise from *The Young Ones*, *Drop Dead Fred* and countless Comic Strip films) in 2000's TV film *Merlin: The Return*. Arthur (played by Patrick Bergin) and Mordred (Craig Sheffer) are locked in deadly conflict, and Mayall's Merlin uses the power of Stonehenge to banish Mordred from the living world; he then sends Arthur and his knights into an enchanted sleep, ready to rise if ever Mordred should return. Naturally, he does. A modern scientist (Tia Carrere) accidentally releases Mordred, and it's then up to Arthur, his knights, Merlin and a small child to stop their ancient enemy from taking over the world.

Other recent TV appearances for Arthur include *We Are History* (a very amusing spoof history series claiming, amongst other marvels, to have discovered Camelot), and David Brent's song 'Excalibur' in another comedy, *The Office*. Keep your eyes peeled for Arthurian references and themes on TV, as they crop up quite often. Even a Carling Black Label lager advert carried the theme of the Lady in the Lake a few years ago.

Arthurian themes have also featured up in several TV series, including *Babylon 5*, *Bonanza*, *Dark Knight* and *Quantum Leap*. Documentaries retelling the growth of Arthurian myth and history appear on television from time to time, and others are available to buy, among which Eagle Media's *The Legends of King Arthur* (2002) fares quite well. This DVD presents three programmes (one on Merlin, one on the search to find Camelot, and one on Arthur himself), and a series of biographies and questions to test yourself with.

Spiritual Arthur

The twentieth century saw a boom in mysticism and spirituality, and this has continued into the twenty-first century; naturally enough, as one of the world's most famous legendary kings, Arthur – along with his wizard Merlin – have their own special place in this domain.

Merlin is often linked to the ancient society of druids. Despite their popularity in the modern world, we actually know very little about them. A couple of Roman references suggest that druids were either wise men or religious men in Celtic society; we are told that they had a sacred grove on Anglesey, which has been interpreted by many people to mean that they worshipped pagan earth gods and goddesses. Yet we know so little, and certainly not enough to describe the semi-historical Merlin as such a man. Nevertheless, Arthur and Merlin's mystical Celtic connections have seen them firmly ensconced in the world of modern spirituality.

The Holy Grail also holds a special religious or spiritual connection for some people, and Arthurian legend has sat at the edge of many such studies in the past. Modern studies have focused their attentions further away from Arthurian legend than may be expected, perhaps attempting to place distance between the 'fiction' of Arthur and the 'truth' of the Grail.

Playing with Arthur

Never fear – you no longer need to restrict your activity in the Arthurian world to simply reading or watching movies about Arthur. You too can take part in mock battles; you too can adventure in the world of Arthur, saving maidens and slaying giants; and you too can collect 'Arthuriana' in the form of figurines, mugs, tea towels and countless other items.

Since the 1970s, role-playing games and wargames have allowed participants to play a crucial role of their own in the Arthurian world, and this was accelerated in the late 1980s and the 1990s by a rash of computer games allowing the player to do the same.

Arthurian legend is one of the backbones of European mythology, along with Classical and Norse legend. As such, it proved a major influence on the creators and early gamers of *Dungeons and Dragons* and other role-playing games. In a role-playing game, the players each create an imaginary character, and verbally direct the actions of their character in an imaginary world – rather like actors in a play. Each character has its own personality, strengths and weaknesses; when an action with some degree of chance is taken by a character, the character's player rolls a dice to see if they are successful, and this is directly influenced by their ability in that field (be it using a sword, casting a spell, picking a lock, or climbing a cliff face). Another player directs the action, introduces new non-player characters and creatures, and keeps the game's plot moving on. In 1985, a game designer named Greg Stafford went one step further, and instead of just playing Arthurian based games using other rule sets, he created *King Arthur Pendragon*, or *Pendragon*, a role-playing game uniquely set in Arthurian Britain. The sort of quests familiar in medieval Arthurian tales make ideal plots for role-playing adventures, and *Pendragon* allows each player to create a knight or wizard, who may be Cymric (British), Saxon, Roman, Irish, or one of several other cultures, each with their own strengths and weaknesses. Even if you don't wish to play the games, Stafford's *Pendragon* is an excellent sourcebook for the world of Arthurian legend. Other role-playing games can also be adapted to Arthurian settings – the best known game, *Dungeons and Dragons*, is supported by a *Legends and Lore* sourcebook, detailing the characteristics of the main characters from Arthurian legend and many other myths and legends.

Wargaming is often associated with role-playing, but instead of dealing with the actions of a single character, this kind of game allows you to examine the military history and battle tactics of the historical Arthurian period – controlling vast armies of cavalry and foot warriors. Played over a terrain-modelled table, players assume command of an army of miniature figurines, sculpted and painted to accurately portray warriors of the period. Moving your shieldwalls of spearmen and troops of cavalry according to pre-determined battle strategies, combat is adjudicated by dice rolls, which are modified according to various factors such as your army's morale, armour quality and ferocity. When your enemy has taken enough casualties, your opposing leader's warriors lose heart and flee, leaving your own metal miniatures in control of the tabletop. Most games are played using rules that have been created for all ancient and medieval warfare, although *Glutter of Ravens* (the title being a direct reference to Arthur's appearance in the northern British poem *The Gododdin*), and *Goths, Huns and Romans* are two sets specifically designed for Dark Ages battles. Another popular rule set is *Warhammer Ancient Battles*, a game based on Games Workshop's successful wargame formula. Aside from being an unusual pastime, historical wargaming also allows you to find out a great deal about how ancient armies fought battles, and why they might have won or lost. If this hobby appeals, be prepared to suffer eye strain for hours at a time, trying to paint faces on tiny metal figures as your hands tremble with cramp!

Going hand in hand with role-playing games and wargames are miniature figurines and toy soldiers. Produced in different scales, and representing either the Arthur of legend or the Arthur of history, many detailed figurines have been produced over the past few decades, and make for great collections of Arthuriana. There are also countless 'Legends of King Arthur' or 'Camelot' chess sets, too. You too can have your own set of Round Table knights at a very reasonable price!

There have been many Arthurian-themed computer games made available over time (including a *Monty Python and the Holy Grail* game), and it would seem that any listing given here would be completely out of date between the time of writing and publication of this book. The games available can range from simple 'hack and slash' arcade-style games, to longer, thoughtful adventures and mystery games that are so playable and go on for so long that deep vein thrombosis might set in before you're more than halfway through.

If you are a video game player, *Legion: The Legend of Excalibur* is quite good fun; you get to run around as Arthur, and can select other knights including Lancelot, Anguish and Perceval to accompany you on any of twelve set adventures. Merlin and Guinevere (abbreviated to Gwen in *Legion*) also make appearances. The game also has a brief introduction to Arthurian legend for those who buy the game blissfully unaware of such matters. *Legion* could well have prevented this book being written, so watch out if you only have limited free time! Many other arcade-style games also exist, and there's even a fairground attraction named 'Excalibur' – where you attempt to pull the life-sized sword from a 'stone' to test your strength (ranging from damsel, through varlet and knight, right up to king). Sadly, the prize is not the right to rule modern Britain… candy floss or a goldfish are more common prizes in the twenty-first century.

The more adventurous have the additional outlet of taking part in re-enactments of Arthurian life – spending a weekend away under canvas, sword fighting 'Saxons' (who may well be IT consultants or accountants during the week) and experimenting with different ways to make pottery, paint shields, or link chainmail together. And finally, if you favour a slightly more sedentary lifestyle but still wish to bring a little piece of Arthur's world into your living room, replica swords with the name 'Excalibur' are available by the forgeful. Most are clearly fantastical designs, but just imagine sitting back and looking at Arthur's sword, hanging above your fireplace by the picture of granny.

Arthur online

In Chapter One, I mentioned that typing the name 'King Arthur' into an Internet search engine brings up around 295,000 entries. So what are all of these entries about? Once you exclude any adverts for the many companies who choose to use King Arthur's name to sell their products (you can find out more about the sorts of things Arthur has been used to advertise in the 'Arthur's ad' section of this chapter), you will find that the Internet has some really great information about Arthurian history and legend.

Of course, you need to sort out the good from the bad and the ugly. This section includes my suggestions of good places to start surfing.

Arthurian Resources (www.arthuriana.co.uk) includes Arthurian essays, a notes and queries section, and links to other Arthurian pages to visit on the internet.

Arthuriana (smu.edu/arthuriana) is the online version of *Arthuriana: The Journal of Arthurian Studies*. This publication is the quarterly journal of the North American branch of the International Arthurian Society (see the society's own entry later), and stakes its claim as the world's only academic journal on Arthurian studies. Older back issues are freely viewable on this site, although membership is required to view more recent papers.

Arthuriana / Camelot Project Bibliographies (see www.lib.rochester.edu/camelot/acpbibs/bibhome.stcm) lists many lengthy bibliographies for Arthurian subjects.

ArthurNet (www.clas.ufl.edu/users/jshoaf/Arthurnet.htm) is a moderated email discussion group, whereby you can post a question or comment on an Arthurian topic and receive replies from other people in the discussion group. It is sponsored by *Arthuriana* journal (see above), and is a good place to find general discussion with like-minded people.

Britannia (www.britannia.com) includes the former Early British Kingdoms site, and is a great place to start investigating the possibility of a real-life Arthur, the history of Britain during his supposed historical period, and British history in general.

Britannia (www.durolitum.co.uk) is not linked to the above site, and is instead an Arthurian and Late Roman historical re-enactment group. *Britannia* travel across Britain demonstrating their skills and theories about life at this time, and their site comprehensively lists where you might be able to watch them, how to join in, and some further historical information.

Cadw (www.cadw.wales.gov.uk) – pronounced 'Kad-oo' – is the organisation responsible for the preservation of historic monuments in Wales. Cadw's site is a wonderful place to find out more about visiting Wales' important Arthurian heritage, and to see exactly what is being done to record and conserve such places.

Castles of Wales (www.castlewales.com/home.html) tells you everything you may wish to find out about castles (in Wales, naturally, although some are in England too). As well as this, it provides a huge amount of detail on medieval Welsh (and English) history and culture, should you wish to find out what happened to the Britons after Arthur's time.

The Council For British Archaeology (www.britarch.ac.uk) publishes the excellent *British Archaeology* magazine, and has a huge amount of information on archaeology in modern Britain. The e-journal *Internet Archaeology* may also be accessed through this site.

English Heritage (www.english-heritage.org.uk) is the online home of the organisation that looks after England's historic sites. The majority of historical locations linked to Arthur in England are looked after by English Heritage, and this site is a great place to find out more about visiting these places.

The Heroic Age (members.aol.com/heroicage1/homepage.html) is an online journal dedicated to the study of the early medieval period. The journal publishes academic articles on all aspects of history and archaeology during this period, and is free to read.

Historic Scotland (www.historic-scotland.gov.uk) is the Scottish equivalent of English Heritage and Cadw. Some Arthurian sites in Scotland are managed and preserved by historic Scotland, and this is a valuable site to start finding out more about them.

The International Arthurian Society (www.dur.ac.uk/arthurian.society) was founded in 1948, and aims to promote the study of Arthurian legend and literature. A major international conference is held every three years (in Europe), and the society publishes an annual bibliographical bulletin highlighting all publications about Arthur over the past twelve month period.

The Oxford Arthurian Society (arthsoc.drruss.net) was founded in 1982, and since 2001 has been a University of Oxford student society. The site is a good place to find out about joining the society, what they do, and more about their quarterly journal, *Ceridwen's Cauldron*.

The Society of Ancients (www.soa.org.uk) is a site dedicated to the study of ancient and medieval military history and the hobby of wargaming, and as such is a good place to learn more about warfare in the period of the historical Arthur.

Arthur's ad

Arthur has entered our popular imagination so much that this shadowy sixth century warlord has been used make business people large amounts of money and to sell us beer, motor cars and flour (to name but three). Not only this, he is also the figurehead of several tourist boards in the UK. Not bad going for someone who may never have existed!

Arthurian legend has even been used by the British National Lottery, who named their three lottery machines Arthur, Guinevere and Lancelot; the company running the lottery is named Camelot. The very name of the company conjures up images of happiness, stability and wellbeing, and of course, that's what the Lottery is all about. That and winning shed loads of cash. Even so, that the three machines that dish the money out are named after characters from Arthurian legend, and that they are names instantly recognisable throughout the British Isles, shows the extent to which the tales of Arthur and his Round Table have infiltrated the British psyche.

There are also guidebooks to Arthur's world (notably for the south-west of England and across Wales), lectures to attend, themed holiday and coach trips, videos and DVDs to buy, and even songs written about the great King. Rick Wakeman, carried away by the excesses of 1970s Prog Rock, recorded a concept album entitled *The Myths and Legends of King Arthur and the Knights of the Round Table* in 1975. Wakeman followed this up with a live show on ice at Wembley: skaters enacted scenes from the legend on a huge scale, including sword fights. Other musicians, from folk to pop and rock, have instead limited themselves to singles.

And finally, there's just a chance that you might end up staying in a Camelot Guest House. There are many hostelries with this name scattered around Britain, linked by nothing more than the intent to liken their hospitality to that of Britain's most famous king. Just keep a watchful eye on that night porter with the name Modred...

The High King And Usurper Fall At Camlann

Chapter Seven

Will the Real King Arthur Please Stand Up?

Although Arthur was supposed to have lived in the fifth or sixth century, references to him in literature and history are relatively rare before the twelfth century. Despite the scarcity of near-contemporary historical mentions of Arthur, a great many people have spent a great deal of their time attempting to discover the true identity of Arthur, and almost as much time trying to discredit other writers' work.

To be completely frank, it's highly unlikely that we'll ever know for sure who Arthur was. That's assuming that he existed in the first place. (Summing up the views of many, Winston Churchill commented that if Arthur didn't really exist, then he should have.) However, there's no reason to instantly dismiss Arthur on the grounds of slim historical records: only a handful of personal names have survived from the fifth and sixth centuries, so scanty reference can be viewed as preferable to no reference at all. This great hole in British written history means that researchers have relied upon oral tradition and folklore more than is usual in historical research. In oral history, names change and disappear over time, so much so that we cannot always be sure of the names of important and influential leaders, or of the areas over which they held sway. A researcher's path to discovering their very own, real-life Arthur is fraught with difficulty and strewn with many obstacles; nevertheless, many have attempted it, and this chapter presents a selection of theories: old and new, possible and unlikely, well researched and poorly judged.

One of the earliest modern attempts to hunt down the historical Arthur was made by E K Chambers in his 1927 book *Arthur of Britain*. Considering medieval legend and earlier Celtic folklore, Chambers saw Arthur as the last bastion of the civilized Roman world, standing against a tide of barbarian invasion. This has remained a popular image ever since.

Even the most sober of history books mentioning the British Dark Ages will usually include a reference to Arthur; some historians have denied his existence, saying that there is simply not enough evidence from close enough to his lifetime to support him as a historical figure. A more common reference to Arthur in such books is to include him as a footnote (literal or otherwise) to the history of the period, stating that he probably existed and was a Welsh or British war leader who held back Saxon advances into Wales or the South-West. Some writers also mention his traditional connection to the Battle of Mount Badon, and occasionally to his reported death at Camlann, but nothing more. Typical of such histories, and perhaps more generous than most, J N L Myres summed up the search for Arthur in his book *The English Settlements* (published in 1986). Myres said that the ongoing quest for Arthur was the biggest waste of time a historian could ever undertake, and that there was no contemporary or even near contemporary evidence for Arthur's existence. The generous side of Myres' statement is that Arthur may have lived and fought the Saxons, but also affirmed that any addition to that statement moves the case from history into romance.

In the face of popular Arthurian studies by Leslie Alcock and John Morris, who as you will see were two academics who both firmly believed in the existence of Arthur, David Dumville stood firm. As a textual historian, he argued in his 1977 essay 'Sub-Roman Britain: History and Legend' (published in volume LXII of the renowned journal *History*) that the most commonly used Arthurian sources were not strictly historical texts, rather they were compilations of earlier, sometimes unreliable material, and as such were not contemporary records of their subject matter. From an academic point of view, this detracted from the sources' validity, and Dumville stated his case for completely removing Arthur from all serious studies of fifth and sixth century Britain.

To be fair to such historians as Myres and Dumville, these are valid points, and the history of the period is such that there really is no need to focus solely on Arthur: there are plenty of other historically attested-to leaders whose deeds make for fascinating reading. But there is still the nagging thought that some of the writers of sober histories dislike the idea of Arthur as being too 'populist', or dare we say it, too... exciting.

On the other hand, many historians – both academic and amateur – have gone out of their way to shed light on the possible existence of a historical Arthur, spewing out many good and many bad theories along the way. And the discovery of Arthur is not a pursuit limited only to twentieth and twenty-first century historians: Geoffrey of Monmouth certainly intended his Arthur to be considered real, and other medieval sleuths followed in his footsteps.

Medieval detectives

Didn't anyone ever tell you that King Arthur was real – and that a group of monks dug up both Guinevere and himself at Glastonbury at the end of the twelfth century? It was said that shortly before the English king Henry II died in 1189, a bard of British or Breton descent revealed to him the secret location of Arthur's grave, which was at Glastonbury Abbey. Henry was succeeded by Richard I (who ruled for ten years from 1189), and the new King supported the Glastonbury monks' search for the grave, which they found in 1190 or 1191. Within a coffin were held the bones of a huge man (obviously Arthur), along with other smaller bones and a lock of golden hair (Guinevere's, naturally). As luck would have it, an inscribed cross was also found, proving the names of the coffin's tenants: 'Here lies the famous King Arthur in the Isle of Avalon' (another account says that Guinevere was also mentioned on the cross, probably on the reverse).

Could this really have been Arthur and his queen? Of course it could. But then again, Glastonbury Abbey had been devastated by fire in 1184, and funds were desperately needed to rebuild the site to its former glory. A steady influx of Arthurian pilgrims would have helped no end. Very sneaky? Possibly. Also, Henry II (and his successor Richard) stood much to gain by showing that Arthur – the hero of England's enemies, the Welsh – was not sleeping as their legends suggested. By revealing the grave (and therefore the death) of the Welsh hero the English took away a pivotal point of Welsh national pride and political flag waving. Not only that, but showing Arthur to be buried in England meant that the English could lay some claim to the great man as being one of their own heroes.

A drawing of the now lost cross, provided by William Camden in his 1607 edition of *Britannia*, hints that the cross was actually older than the twelfth century (suggesting it was not a contemporary fake), but was also probably not as early as the sixth century. The bones have also disappeared over the centuries, so we cannot even use science to help us out with the true dates of the skeletons.

In all probability, the revelations surrounding Arthur's grave at Glastonbury were probably no more than a tool of the propaganda machine used by the medieval English against their Celtic neighbours, located at a religious site ready to play the game in order to rebuild its wealth and raise its own profile. Yet excavations in the 1960s did show that the monks' earlier dig did take place, and we also now know that Glastonbury was an occupied site in the fifth and sixth centuries. So could this have been Arthur's final resting place after all?

Arthur the High King

The most common modern perception of the 'historical' Arthur is that he ruled with the title High King. In general terms, the idea of Arthur as the High King – the supreme King of all other kings in Britain, ruling the entire land – is based upon the medieval interpretation of how Arthur would have ruled, rather like a king of the entirety of medieval England or France. But it also draws some inspiration from the centuries of rule from Roman, when the land was governed as a single province. This section could just as easily be entitled 'Arthur the Emperor', and if a real Arthur ever did rule with this much power, he would probably have thought of himself as such a figure (emperors of Rome were ten a penny at times in the late Empire).

In the period immediately after the collapse of Roman rule, we know that powerful warlords or civil leaders with military backing snatched power. This happened on the continent, and perhaps also in Britain. Could Arthur have been such a usurper or 'tyrant'? Or perhaps, at a slightly later date, he rose to power amongst the Britons and unified their diverse kingdoms to repel foreign assault?

Welsh royal genealogies and regnal lists, which are so often long and rather too complete to believe (dragging in all sorts of legendary and mythological rulers who really don't belong there), could be expected to note Arthur in them somewhere if he was such an important figure. Yet he is only mentioned three times in the entirety of the lists. Once is as the victor at Badon, once is as a king of the entire island of Britain, and once in a regnal list of former kings of Britain including other pseudo-historical or mythological characters. Therefore these lists are of little historical value, and his absence does not immediately discount Arthur's possible existence.

The modern champion of an all-powerful Arthur, ruling over the majority of Britain, was the late John Morris. Morris lectured in Ancient History at University College London, and founded the journal *Past and Present* in 1952. His book *The Age of Arthur: A History of the British Isles From 350 to 650* was for many years considered the standard reference work on Britain during this period. Now, though, most academic commentators consider that Morris lacked critical judgement of the diverse sources available, and *The Age of Arthur* stands as a testament to his ability to assemble the many and varied sources into a cohesive directory. The sheer quantity of otherwise obscure source material that Morris made readily available to the general reader through this book is nothing short of remarkable, and it is for this, rather than celebrating the book as a reliable history of the period, that Morris' work should be remembered. Morris considered Arthur to be the last Romanised emperor of Britain, ruling from a capital city at Colchester (the Latin name being *Camulodunum*).

Morris' Arthur succeeded Ambrosius as the supreme commander of the armies of the Britons, probably in the 470s and certainly by the 480s, and his succession, according to Morris, coincided with a change in the character of the struggle for Britain. Morris contended that before Arthur's time, politics and warfare revolved simply around the campaigns of the Britons on one side and the Saxons on the other; as Arthur rose to succeed Ambrosius, a southern British leader named Cerdic (almost universally described as a Saxon elsewhere, although it is true that his name may have a British origin) opposed Arthur with the help of Saxon warriors – hence Cerdic's later reputation as a Saxon leader. Arthur managed to subdue Saxon encroachment across the lowlands, using cavalry armies, and then fought his series of twelve battles immortalised by Nennius – including the famous Battle of Badon in or around 495. Morris contends that Badon was fought between Arthur and an alliance of Cerdic, and the Saxon kings Oesc of Kent and Aelle of Sussex, and this pivotal battle took place at Solsbury Hill. Morris saw Badon as the final victory of the Britons, giving way to an era of peace, during which time Arthur rebuilt Britain as a post-imperial successor state, ruling as an emperor. In the usually doom-laden words of the sixth century commentator Gildas, Morris observed praise for the government of Arthur (without referring to him by name), whom he believed managed to restore Britain to a land with imperial structure, solid governmental rule and a revered church. Morris believed that twenty-one years after Badon, in or around 515, Arthur fell in battle against Medraut, a rebellious southern British chieftain perhaps from Suffolk. With Arthur died the short-lived but successful revival of imperial rule – a revival more successful than anywhere else in Dark Ages Europe.

Morris' theory was ingeniously constructed around both traditional history and folk tales of the Celtic nations, cross referenced and tied into more reliable history with meticulous attention to detail. However, as noted above, many academics have since criticised Morris' acceptance of such source material at face value, and, comfortable as Morris' theory is – fitting in as it does so well with the popular image of the Arthur of legend – few scholars accept it today.

Published two years before Morris' book was Leslie Alcock's acclaimed *Arthur's Britain* (published in 1971 and revised in 1989). This book quickly became, and still is, the standard work on Dark Ages Britain, and in it Alcock suggested a similar general overview of Arthur, that of a major British warlord of the late fifth century who controlled large areas of Britain and fought against the encroaching Saxons and Picts. Laying his cards on the table as a scholar who firmly believed in the Battles of Badon and Camlann, and dating them around 490 and 510 respectively, Alcock used modern archaeological research to support his suggestions. Many of the theories that Alcock suggests are based on early Welsh sources, many of which he places a high level of integrity in. Alcock's Arthur was cast in the role of High King or Emperor in all but name: he had the military power to refortify hillforts across the south of modern England and to hold back Saxon advances from the eastern side of the island. Alcock believes that the real Arthur fought the twelve famous battles listed by Nennius, as well as his final, unlisted battle at Camlann. Alcock cannily sited Arthur's headquarters within the ramparts of South Cadbury hillfort, a site he directed the excavation of in the 1960s. The sheer size of fortification at South Cadbury suggests that this hillfort must have been used by a large military force – larger it seems than most armies of the period were. South Cadbury had some tradition linking it with Arthur, although there is nothing in Alcock's excavations to point to the shadowy Arthur any more than several other candidates who may have refortified the site.

Among the other researchers to have touched upon the popular notion of an all powerful Arthur, Geoffrey Ashe in his book *The Discovery of King Arthur* (published in 1985 and revised in 2003), also suggests that Arthur was a British High King or emperor. Ashe's revelations are dealt with later in this chapter.

Arthur the soldier

Arthur is sometimes referred to by a Latin title: *Dux Bellorum*. Although it may sound like an overweight wildfowl, this title actually means

'Commander of Armies' or 'Duke of Battle'. The most common depiction of Arthur in our earliest Celtic sources is as just such a warlord, rather than the classic image of him as a later, chivalrous medieval king. Some early references even know him simply as Arthur the Soldier. It is also worth noting that the early historian Nennius wrote that Arthur fought on the side of the British kings, rather than stating that he was a king himself. So perhaps the true Arthur was a military man, a general with the flair and ruthlessness to inflict a series of defeats upon the enemies who beset Britain from every side.

Perhaps as a relic of our memories of Arthur as a medieval king, many commentators have chosen to depict the historical Arthur as a dashing cavalry commander, racing around the British Isles to defeat Saxon, Irish and Pictish invaders, and directing local resistance in a land beset by barbarian hordes. The professional warriors of the Dark Ages did ride into battle as cavalry – British written sources certainly confirm this – and it has been conjectured that the roads built so long and straight by the Romans would still have been serviceable to a warband organised in a similar fashion to the late Roman mobile field forces. For those people who subscribe to this theory of a roving, warrior Arthur, there is no need to identify his precise geographical location – he based himself at sites around the country. There is also no need to 'reveal' his true name as anything other than Arthur or Artorius, for that was his name. It may also be argued that the many geographical features around Britain bearing his name – such as Arthur's Seat, Arthur's Chair, Arthur's Stone – are memories of a battle won or a garrison posted by the warlord Arthur. Michael Holmes, in his 1996 book *King Arthur: A Military History*, suggested that Arthur was such a leader, fighting on multiple fronts in Britain during the traditional dates set down by early Celtic 'histories' of Arthur.

The statement by Nennius in *The History of the Britons* that Arthur carried the image of the Virgin Mary on his shoulders (or shield), and that by the virtue of Jesus Christ he was able to defeat the pagan Saxons, has led some commentators to suggest that Arthur was some kind of proto-crusader, waging a Christian religious war against his pagan foes. Among the proponents of this theory is Dilys Gater who, in her 1991 book *The Battles of Wales*, offered such an explanation. Gater outlined the theory that the still Romanised, Christian Arthur set up his headquarters and residence at the old Roman site of Caerleon (pointing out that several episodes in the Welsh stories of *The Mabinogion* were set there) and fought his campaign against the Saxons in modern day England. Gater suggests that the only one of Arthur's battles fought on Welsh soil was Camlann, which she identifies as a siege of Caerleon, where Arthur is slain defending his headquarters. Such a theory ignores the fact that our main source for Arthur carrying symbols of Christianity into battle with him came from a manuscript compiled in a monastery, which might have overplayed the religious aspects of Arthur's life. In other early tales of Arthur – notably in the *Lives* of the saints – Arthur is sometimes shown at odds with the church. Even so, the medieval image of Arthur as a pious and thoroughly Christian king, combined with the appeal of 'Christian' Britons fending off the 'pagan' Saxons in the fifth and sixth centuries has meant that the idea of Arthur as an early crusading British warrior king remains popular.

A theory about Arthur's obvious exclusion from historical sources, that rises to the surface every once in a while, suggests that he was indeed a powerful warlord, but that he incurred the wrath of the Church in some way. By doing so, Arthur virtually guaranteed that his name would be written out of history, as the recorders of early British and, later, Welsh annals and chronicles were, almost without exception, religious men. Support for this idea can perhaps be seen in the Celtic *Lives* of the saints, which sometimes portray Arthur as a buffoon or worse. It has been suggested that Arthur relied upon heavy subsidies from the Church to fund his countrywide wars against the Saxons – throughout history, Christian churches have been traditionally wealthy organisations – probably without their consent.

There is very little of historical substance in the idea of Arthur as an omnipotent military force, or a whirlwind of swords and spears. Such a general theory cannot be discounted, yet neither is it particularly enlightening – Arthur cannot be identified beyond the historically debatable early Celtic references to him, nor can his battles be pinned down to specific sites (although many have tried).

Arthur the... bear?

Perhaps he had a big beard (Dark Ages Britons do appear to have loved their beards, moustaches, and tresses in their hair), or was very hairy, yet bear in this instance refers to the warrior's ferocity. Arthur the Bear may well have been the name that another warlord used in battle; those historians who expound this theory suggest that the name 'Arthur' is a combination of the Welsh and Latin names for a bear. The Latin word for bear is *ursus* and the Welsh word is *arth*. If such a combination of words was used, Arthur (or whoever bestowed the name upon him) was a shrewd politician, using the name to give mass appeal to all Britons – both those who considered themselves to be Celts, and those who still imagined themselves to be Roman. It has been suggested that by doing so, Arthur was attempting to unite opposing Celtic and Roman factions, although no firm evidence has survived to support this. It must also be questioned whether, if Welsh speakers used the word *arth*, and Latin speakers used *ursus*, would the composite *Arthur* have registered any bear-like recognition with either linguistic group?

There are other examples of Dark Ages warlords being known by other names. The northern Britons of Rheged knew the Saxon leader who opposed their king Owain by the name of Fflamddwyn, which means Flamebearer; the Saxon king's true name well may have been Ida, or perhaps his son Theodric. Gildas mentions that the meaning of one of his contemporary British kings' names was 'tawny butcher' (Gildas said this of Cuneglasus), although it more likely translates as 'Blue Hound', and it is possible that other British warlords were known by similar titles. Gildas' tirade suggests that another of the King's fathers was nicknamed 'the Lion', and Gildas' contemporary king Aurelius Caninus was probably 'Aurelius the Dog'.

An alternative translation of Arthur's name is to be found in a late twelfth or early thirteenth century copy of *The History of the Britons*. This copy has some additional marginal notes known as the Sawley Glosses, and they explain that Arthur's name translated into Latin as 'horrible bear' or 'iron hammer'. Not a bad battle name for a fearsome warlord.

Think of it as a modern writer would a pen name. Or, perhaps more pertinently, the alter ego of a modern wrestler: Giant Haystacks and The Rock immediately spring to mind. Other modern sportsmen have animal related nicknames that, like the use of a bear to imply ferocity, reflect their own personalities or traits: goalkeeping cats, donkey defenders, and midfield terriers exist in football teams across the land.

It may even be the case that Arthur was not the battle name of one individual, but a rank held by a variety of warlords at different times, rather like the name Vortigern may simply be a title that has passed into the modern world remembered as a personal name. This explanation would certainly explain the wide time frame over which Arthur's deeds are sometimes explained as having taken place, and a succession of battle winning 'Bears' could also explain why the name became so famous in

Celtic folk tales and tradition. Yet there is a complete lack of evidence to make this any more than historical speculation.

Even if we do readily accept that Arthur was simply a battle name, this brings us no closer to identifying the real man behind the name. Yet several commentators have put forward the idea that the name 'the Bear' was used by another, historically secured leader. The reason, they claim, that 'Arthur' is not to be seen in any reliable historical context is that history has recorded him by his given name, not his battle name. This theory has been used to support the claims of Owain Ddantgwyn, Ambrosius Aurelianus and Riothamus as the real Arthur, to name but three contenders who are mentioned elsewhere in this chapter.

Arthur the Roman

The presumed dates for a historical Arthur lie in the late fifth or the sixth centuries, as outlined elsewhere in this book; this period of Dark Ages fell between Romanised British society and Anglo-Saxon society. Therefore, when modern scholars began to research the possibility of a real-life Arthur early in the twentieth century, knowing that the mysterious King was supposed to have fought against the Saxons, several looked for a Roman Arthur – or Artorius, to use the Latin version of his name. This man would probably have been trying to hold on to the rapidly diminishing Roman past, heroically attempting to hold back a tide of barbarian invasion; at least, that's the romantic view this theory conjures up.

Pre-eminent among such scholars was R G Collingwood, who wrote about Arthur and the arrival of the Saxons in the 1930s. He saw Arthur not as a Celtic-British warlord or chieftain, but instead as a Roman army officer, holding the late Roman military rank of *dux* ('Duke') or *comes* ('Count'). Collingwood's Arthur led a mobile field army, rather like that of the later Empire and consisting mostly of well-armoured cavalry, inflicting a series of defeats against invading waves of barbaric Saxons in order to preserve the last vestiges of Roman authority in Britain in the fifth century. The historical basis of Collingwood's theory should be questioned; as is outlined in Chapter Two the change from Roman Britain to Anglo-Saxon England may not have been quite so bloodthirsty as once thought. It may also be that Collingwood's thinking was influenced somewhat by the beginning of the end of the British Empire that was underway as he wrote, and also in his military-based theory by the dark years leading up to the outbreak of war in 1939. The idea of an imperial Arthur, standing valiantly against the 'barbaric' odds might well have had popular appeal in Britain at that time.

WILL THE REAL KING ARTHUR PLEASE STAND UP?

One of the more sensible candidates pushed into the limelight as the 'real' Arthur is Ambrosius Aurelianus. Described by Gildas, one of our earliest sources, as being the victor, or instigator, of the triumphant campaign leading up to the Battle of Badon, Ambrosius should probably be a far stronger contender as the real-life Arthur than he is often credited with. From Gildas' sketchy biography of him, we know that Ambrosius' parents were considered Roman – probably Romanised British officials, or possibly some of the last officials to arrive before Britain became independent. Ambrosius' father may even have been one of the imperial usurpers (Gildas actually says that his parents 'wore the purple' – ostensibly an imperial reference) who sprang up in Britain in the first decade of the fifth century, although this would place him a little early in our accepted chronology; nevertheless, Geoffrey of Monmouth recorded that 'Aurelius Ambrosius' was the son of Constantine III, one such usurper. His parents having died in some calamity (perhaps a Pictish or Saxon raid), Ambrosius was credited by Gildas as uniting the weakened Britons and turning them into a formidable fighting force. We do not have the years of his birth or death, or even any concrete evidence for his floruit, but sensible guesswork places Ambrosius at the peak of his military and political power at some point between about 460 and 480. Tradition also records conflict between British factions led by Ambrosius and Vortigern, culminating in civil war. Many commentators have suggested that Ambrosius led a pro-Roman party, and Vortigern a Celtic Nationalist party, but to concur with this almost certainly oversimplifies the complex political balance of fifth century Britain. Place name evidence suggests a number of sites in the south of Britain that may have been sites for Ambrosius' victories, or areas from which he could have raised warrior bands (place names with the prefix 'Amb').

Ambrosius is the only Briton traditionally linked with Badon aside from Arthur, and his name is one of the few that appears to have passed into the modern world as that of a man of history rather than legend. Vortigern, Hengist, Horsa, Arthur and many more are remembered today for their pseudo-historic actions, whereas Ambrosius is famed as a straightforward Romano-British military leader, with few later legends being pinned to his name. Gildas even goes so far as to bemoan that his contemporary 'tyrants' were not a patch on leaders like Ambrosius. Perhaps such a reputation would be fitting of the real-life Arthur? Counting against Ambrosius, though, is the fact that his name has passed down through time alongside that of Arthur. They are thought of as near enough contemporaries, or occasionally that Arthur was a cavalry commander in Ambrosius' army; would this have happened if the two characters were one and the same? Possibly, but not likely.

Ambrosius also appears to date a little early to fit in with the traditional Arthurian period, although as no dates can be confirmed for either man, this is a weakened argument. Perhaps a more telling comment is that Ambrosius is remembered as a Romanised Briton, whereas the Arthur of early legend was very much a heroic warlord in true Celtic fashion. Perhaps early Arthurian legend changed Ambrosius' character to fit the demands and expectations of what was by that time a less Romanised and more 'heroic' audience, but is it possible that the real-life leader's background would have been so thoroughly rewritten?

Aside from Ambrosius and an otherwise unidentified Artorius, another Romanised candidate exists. Several historians, including P J F Turner and Scott Littleton and Linda A Malcor, have argued that the legendary Arthur was in fact based on an earlier Roman cavalry commander, who was stationed in Britain a couple of hundred years before the widely accepted dates of the Arthurian era. The story of this intriguing soldier is outlined in the next section of this chapter.

Arthur the Sarmatian

In the centuries of Roman rule, many people from the furthest extremities of the Empire came to Britain. They served in the imperial army or travelled for trade or business purposes. I always felt most sorry for the Syrian and Moorish recruits who we know garrisoned Hadrian's Wall in weather conditions completely alien to them – well, would you want to swap such sunny climates for Newcastle or Carlisle on a frozen January morning?

Among the many peoples recruited by the Roman emperors to fight on their behalf were a group of steppe barbarians who suddenly arrived in a huge folk movement towards the eastern fringes of the Empire. Well armoured, skilled on horseback, wielding long two-handed lances, and riding large war horses, the Sarmatians were formidable opponents in battle, and the Roman army must have been extremely relieved when, after a few campaigns, the Sarmatians became auxiliary troops in the imperial army.

In 175, a large force of newly recruited Sarmatian cavalrymen set off across Europe bound for Britain. There were about five and a half thousand of them, and they would have travelled with their own horses, spare mounts, and extra horses for breeding. With them they would have carried their own banners – in the form of a flying dragon (which looked rather like a modern airfield windsock), which was later to become associated with most Roman army units, and presumably also of their successors in the warbands of the British kings... Arthur included.

Incidentally, we still have the name of the Roman general who commanded this formation of heavy cavalry. His name was Arthur. Well, close enough to Arthur: his name was Lucius Artorius Castus.

The first researcher to notice Castus' possible Arthurian connection was Kemp Malone in 1925, and this was combined with a Sarmatian link offered by Helmut Nickel in 1975. As Curator of Arms and Armor at the Metropolitan Museum of Art, New York, Nickel noticed the similarity between Sarmatian heavy cavalry on heavily armoured horses and the later European knight. This connection was to stick in the minds of several other researchers.

Amongst others, P J F Turner and Scott Littleton and Linda A Malcor believe that Lucius Artorius Castus could well have been the real Arthur. But, given that this Roman cavalryman lived a couple of centuries before the commonly accepted dates for the historical Arthur, how likely can this theory be?

Scott Littleton and Linda A Malcor's *From Scythia to Camelot* (published in 2000) is, as the subheading of the book explains, a 'radical reassessment' of the legends of Arthur, the Knights of the Round Table and the Holy Grail. Littleton and Malcor follow the theory that both the Arthurian and Holy Grail traditions did not derive from native British folklore and mythology, but from that of the peoples of ancient Scythia (modern South Russia and Ukrainian Steppes). The authors argue that this folklore was carried to Britain and Gaul from the Steppes by Alan and Sarmatian tribes serving in the Roman army as auxiliary troops. They go on to attempt to show that several characters from Arthurian legend, including the Fisher King, might have been based on historic individuals who lived during the early years of the fifth century.

This may all sound a little far-fetched, but the folklore of the Sarmatian people known as the Ossetes contain a number of familiar sounding themes for the Arthurian reader. The heroes of their folk tales are referred to as Narts, and among the deeds of these Narts can be found a story about a dying warrior king whose sword is thrown back into the water, Excalibur-like. Other Ossetian stories include references to a magical vessel (Grail- or cauldron-like, both of which match Arthurian literature), and a sword in a stone also makes an appearance.

Littleton and Malcor also maintain that Lucius Artorius Castus (the leader of the Sarmatian cavalry who first arrived in Britain) was the real Arthur of history. Despite the lack of positive evidence, Lucius Artorius Castus makes a fine circumstantial candidate as the real Arthur. He was a man with a fine military record, whose name and major life exploits were recorded on a memorial stone. As an officer in the Roman army, he was active in the late second century AD – although this is significantly before the traditional period of Arthur. The gaps in his life have been ingeniously filled by the authors who celebrate him as Arthur, suggesting that he saw action in the eastern regions of the Empire. Here, it is suggested, Castus saw action fighting against the non-Romanised Sarmatian tribes on the fringes of the Empire, and was then appointed as an officer of them when they began to serve the Emperor.

Littleton and Malcor suggest that this Roman general and his Sarmatian troopers were given the task of repelling raiders from the north of Roman Britain, and that Nennius' list of battles (as outlined in Chapter Four) was based on his campaign. Their proposed campaign was a series of running battles fought against an invading army of Picts, who struck south from modern Scotland to York, across the Pennines (fighting battles on the rivers Ribble and Douglas in Lancashire). The Pictish invasion was eventually repelled and forced back into Scotland by Lucius Artorius Castus and his Sarmatian horsemen. With the exception of tentatively identifying York with Nennius' City of the Legion, and the river Douglas with Nennius' Dubglas, there is sadly no firm evidence to support this theory.

Although Lucius Artorius Castus lived a couple of centuries before the traditional dates given for Arthur, it is just possible that he became famed as a Roman warrior fighting for the Britons against barbarian enemies. This would certainly be in keeping with the earliest mentions of Arthur in Dark Ages literature. It may well be that the name Arthur, first popularised in Celtic tales, passed into the medieval world as the name of a warrior synonymous with the Dark Ages, and was misinterpreted as a contemporary of that period. Or perhaps it was convenient for the racially proud and independent Celts to claim this great warrior as one of their own, fighting as he did against one of their chief enemies, the Picts.

WILL THE REAL KING ARTHUR PLEASE STAND UP?

Anthropologist Howard Reid shares the view that Arthur's origins began in a land far removed from Britain. In his book *Arthur the Dragon King* (published in 2001), he believes that the origins of Arthur are to be found among the Sarmatians, Scythians and Alan steppe warriors of Central Asia and Europe. Not quite uniquely, but perhaps surprisingly amongst the authors mentioned in this chapter, Reid does not endorse Arthur as a real-life person. Instead he suggests that the lack of historical and archaeological evidence points to Arthur as a figure of folklore only (although it has to be said that any archaeological evidence for Arthur – a named gravestone for example – would be highly unlikely anyway). Reid instead outlines the possible origin of this legend, and traces his fictitious background to the horse-riding tribes of Eastern Europe: once again, the Sarmatians.

Reid employs the same theory as other researchers suggesting Sarmatian origins for Arthur, namely focusing on a unit of Sarmatian heavy cavalry who served in Britain in the Roman era. Instead of Arthur being a Sarmatian cavalry commander or a direct descendant of one, Reid suggests that Arthur simply travelled in their folklore. In turn, this folklore was absorbed by the Britons who came into contact with the eastern horsemen and in turn became part of the Britons' own lore.

Among the points that Reid argues to support his case, he notes that the Sarmatian recruits were probably not accompanied by womenfolk or families; there are no archaeological traces of the distinctive jewellery that they would have worn, or any other personal items to suggest their presence. Reid suggests that the soldiers would have settled into Britain and taken local wives – something which increasingly happened in the latter days of the Empire – and that this would have allowed British and Sarmatian folklore to fuse succinctly.

As Reid points out, the military movements of the Sarmatian cavalry are quite interesting, given the links between Arthur's military successes and the north of Britain. The Sarmatians were stationed in Britain throughout the third century, and appear to have remained during the fourth century also. Roman veterans were often retired to key strategic sites (there's nothing like a bunch of old, retired soldiers to protect key sites cheaply and effectively, despite what *Dad's Army* might suggest). The Sarmatians appear to have been settled close to the fort of *Bremetennacum Veteranorum*, by modern day Ribchester in Lancashire. This could explain the reason for so much Arthur-related military activity having been sited in modern northern England – the people who were telling the original stories were based there, rather than true historical events having occurred there.

Reid also goes on to suggest a character with an Arthur-like name in recorded history: Eothar (also known as Goar). Active in 446, Eothar was a 'savage king' of the Alans – yet more eastern horse warriors, culturally similar to the Sarmatians who had arrived in Britain (maybe even sharing the same folk tales). His armies fought against the Armoricans in France, which geographically ties him in with some of the later stories about Arthur (not least Geoffrey of Monmouth's influential *History*). The time period just about fits that of Arthur as well. Perhaps, just perhaps, the British and, later, Welsh memories of Arthur were founded as a composite of this historical king and the folk tales of the Sarmatians, although Reid himself plays down the possibility of it being more than just another theory.

There are a couple of stumbling blocks in the Sarmatian theory, which tend to be glossed over by supporters of the idea. The use of the sword in stone legend, the evidence of which is used to suggest links between Sarmatian and British tradition, ignores the fact that swords were important in virtually all European strands of folklore. They were expensive weapons to make, and were the sign of both a nobleman and a true warrior across the continent, and as such, magic blades feature heavily not only in British and Sarmatian stories, but also in German and Scandinavian sagas. Blades being sacrificed into the water are not uncommon, either – hundreds of examples have been dredged from water features over the years both in Britain and Ireland. I also know of no evidence to prove that the Sarmatian legends were written down before the nineteenth century – therefore, these stories of eastern Arthurian promise may have been no more than adaptations of British Arthurian legend in the first place, rather than vice versa. These two points do not automatically discount the Sarmatian connection, but rather serve as a cautionary tale that all that glitters is not (necessarily) Arthurian gold.

Arthur the minor king

Perhaps Arthur was no more than a regional king, ruling an area no larger than a modern British county. Perhaps his reputation and importance to the Britons was blown completely out of proportion after he won a series of victories over his enemies (recorded in Nennius' list of battles, as discussed in Chapter Four). Or perhaps he employed a particularly gifted bard to recite inflated stories about his achievements, stories so popular that they spread throughout the British kingdoms. Perhaps, perhaps, perhaps: but there may be some truth in these ideas.

This is possibly one of the more plausible Arthurian theories, but leaves some questions unanswered – which part of Britain did Arthur come from? Why does his name not appear in any reliable genealogical list of early Welsh or British kings showing exactly who they were related to (and, believe you me, the medieval Welsh enjoyed making extended lists of their Welsh and British predecessors)? How did his name spread so thoroughly throughout the Celtic world, and how was he reinvented as the last hope of the Celtic Britons?

If Arthur was a regional ruler, most researchers have pinpointed him as belonging to one of three regions of Britain: the North, the South-West, or Wales.

Arthur of Wales

Wales is traditionally remembered as the final enclave of the Britons, who defended the hills and valleys against Anglo-Saxon incursion. Eventually the Britons became known by the invaders' word for 'foreigner': 'Wealh', which we know today as 'Welsh man', but which also came to mean 'slave' in the Anglo-Saxon tongue. The Britons, or if you prefer, Welsh, kingdoms of this region outlasted those of the South-West and the North; it was not really until Edward I subjugated the natives in the late thirteenth century that Wales was really conquered. The pre-eminent kingdoms of Dark Ages Wales were Gwynedd in the North, Powys in mid Wales and modern Shropshire, and Dyfed in South Wales. At various times, other smaller kingdoms existed, but these three were the main ones. Arthur was certainly remembered in the folk tales and literature of Wales, but did he really originate and rule there? Several researchers have concluded that he did.

The idea that Arthur was a Welsh king is not a new one. Gerald of Wales undertook a late twelfth century journey around the country, recording the history, culture, and legend and lore of the land. In amongst Gerald's recollections in the pages of *The Journey Through Wales* and *The Description of Wales*, which teem with insightful reflections about the medieval country, Arthur's name crops up on several occasions. Gildas notes the Britons as fighting bravely during Arthur's time, and that the King fought with the image of the Virgin Mary emblazoned on his shield (Gerald knows enough of Gildas and Nennius' works for them to be his sources here). He also suggests that Gildas never mentioned Arthur because the King killed Gildas' brother (as told in Chapter Four), and also gives an account of the discovery of Arthur's tomb at Glastonbury.

Gerald names Glastonbury as Avalon, and says that Arthur's wounds were cared for there by a noblewoman named Morgan, a story that was to become well known in medieval legend. Yet Gerald then scotches any further fantasy by explaining that the Britons (by this he perhaps means the Cornish or Bretons, rather than the Welsh) stupidly still believe that Arthur is still alive. Clearly this view was not unanimous in Gerald's lifetime.

Gerald of Wales' notes may not have been historically accurate, any more so than the many other mentions of Arthur across time. However, his work is important as it reflects an introspective native Welsh view of their hero, and features in a work not wishing to promote only Arthur, but to report on many facets of the land and its people.

That Arthur was a Welshman became a mainstay of many early theorists. Thomas Bulfinch wrote, at the beginning of his excellent retelling of the legend, that Arthur was a prince of the Silures (the Roman name for a tribal area of South Wales). Bulfinch places the Arthur of history in the year 500, and raises him to the lofty rank of Pendragon (a pre-eminent rank among the British nobles) about ten years after this.

One widely read modern theory identifies Arthur (again the point being made that Arthur translates as 'the Bear') as a North Welsh leader who flourished between 490 and 520. His name was Owain Ddantgwyn, although before revealing his name in their book, the authors (Graham Phillips and Martin Keatman) candidly refer to Owain as 'Warrior X'. In this 1992 book, entitled *King Arthur: The True Story*, Phillips and Keatman concluded that the father of one of Gildas' tyrants was the real-life Arthur, and that this descendant of the British warlord Cunedda ruled the kingdoms of Gwynedd and Powys. We know precious little about Owain Ddantgwyn, although Phillips and Keatman concluded that the real-life 'Modred' was another of Gildas' tyrants, and defeated Owain/Arthur in the Camlan Valley close to Dolgellau in Wales. Their Arthur fought against Saxon, Pictish, and Irish invaders, and used the Roman city of Viroconium (the modern day hamlet of Wroxeter in Shropshire) as his power base.

Steve Blake and Scott Lloyd put forward another argument for a Welsh Arthur in *The Keys to Avalon: The True Location of Arthur's Kingdom Revealed*, in 2000. Concentrating on the traditional Arthurian sources, Blake and Scott suggest that modern interpretations of Dark Age Britain's geography had been muddled. For example: Keint was not actually Kent, instead being Gwent, Alban was not Scotland but Powys, and Kernyw was not Cornwall but the Gwynedd coastline. By doing so, the authors attempt to reign in Arthur's geographical spread, suggesting that the majority of legends and early sources connected directly with – and only with – Wales. For good measure, Blake and Lloyd reveal the Grail Castle of legend as Dinas Bran in North Wales. The site of Arthur's court of Kelliwick, they claim, is Gelliwig which is on the Lleyn Peninsula in Wales (rather than the traditional site of Killibury in the South-West) They suggest the same site for Camlann as Phillips and Keatman. A number of sites Blake and Lloyd present for Arthur's courts draw on a list presented in a Triad poem, while further evidence for these North Welsh settings can be found in *Culhwch and Olwen*.

Picking up where they left off, in their second book, *Pendragon: The Definitive Account of the Origins of Arthur* (published in 2002), Blake and Lloyd summarise a variety of Welsh documents to continue their case for a Welsh Arthur. They introduce a lesser known story about Arthur's last battle at Camlann, try to identify a number of his mistresses as remembered in Welsh folklore, detail a number of the characters and events associated with Arthur in Welsh tradition, and suggest a radical alternative for his burial place. Using this information, Arthur is once more pinpointed by the authors as a warlord associated with the North Welsh kingdom of Gwynedd. Describing him as the 'Head Dragon' of Gwynedd, the authors note that a number of his victories must have been fought against fellow Welshmen, just as the native tradition remembers. This is a valid point that so few researchers make when attempting to identify Arthur as a minor king: he would probably have had to step on many toes to become powerful. Welsh kingdoms would have fought their fellow Welsh kingdoms with just as much vigour as they fought the Saxons and the Irish with.

Blake and Lloyd subscribe to the same theory as Phillips and Keatman when it comes to Arthur's final battle at Camlann, identifying the battle site as Camlan (with one 'n'). As they are quick to point out, this theory has been suggested several times since it was first highlighted in an 1872 issue of the periodical *Archaeologia Cambrensis*. Even so, many modern researchers have favoured the site of Camlann at either the River Camel in south-west England, Salisbury Plain or the Roman fort on Hadrian's Wall named *Camboganna*. Blake and Lloyd produce more evidence than Phillips and Keatman to support their identification of this North Welsh Camlan. *The Stanzas of the Graves*, a surviving piece of medieval Welsh literature, suggests that Arthur's loyal warrior Bedwyr (Bedivere in later legend) was buried nearby. Welsh tradition also remembers that there were several survivors of the battle (Cedwyn, Cynwyl the Saint, Derfel Gadarn, Geneid Hir, Morfran ap Tegid, Pedrog, and Sandde Angel-face), and most of these can also be linked through other traditions and place names to the north-west region of Wales. The authors also speculate that the chapel of St Mary at Rhyd Llanfair on the river Conwy, or perhaps more correctly the nearby Dol y Tre Beddau (translating as the Meadow of the Town of the Graves) where around forty stone-lined graves were found in the nineteenth century, may well have been the burial place for Arthur. Another possible site mentioned by the authors is the now forgotten cairn of Carnedd Arthur in Snowdonia, or another forgotten cave known as Ogof Llanciau Eryri (translating as Cave of the Youths of Snowdonia).

Beyond these assertions, in *Pendragon* the authors do not attempt to give dates for Arthur, or name him as another historically-attested figure; to Steve Blake and Scott Lloyd, as to many others, identifying a kingdom of origin for Arthur is achievement enough, alongside a broad 'early medieval date' with no specifics mentioned. This approach is useful inasmuch as it allows the authors to get their theory across, without having to bog themselves down in unsubstantiated detail to justify their claims.

Steve Blake and Scott Lloyd have made a good, up to date addition to the case for a Welsh Arthur; however, using so much Welsh historical and literary tradition at face value leaves them open to criticism by their doubters. It is possible that the Arthur they are building a case for never existed in real life, and that they have instead uncovered a fictitious Arthur of early Welsh literature: realistic enough to give the Welsh hope that this great warrior did once exist in the heart of North Wales, but with no foundation in true history. On the other hand, perhaps Blake and Lloyd's thorough research of their frequently overlooked sources has paid off, and they have indeed found the geographical locale of their man.

Another region of Wales (including areas of modern England) that has Arthurian connections is the old kingdom of Powys, now the mid Wales area of the Welsh Marches. Chrétien de Troyes' medieval account of Arthur picks out Montgomery Castle as the site of Camelot, although Montgomery has now, for the most part, receded from playing any role in the legend. Not far from Montgomery, near to Churchstoke in Shropshire, is the river Camlad, a tributary of the river Caebitra. This is an often overlooked alternative for the site of Arthur's famous final battle at Camlann, but as the river has been known by the names Camalet, Camlet, and Kemelet in the past, it is another possibility for the site of Arthur's court of Camelot, which neatly ties in with Chrétien de Troyes' assertion about nearby Montgomery. Both the Camlad and Montgomery are also situated close to the old Roman fort at Rhyd-y-Groes, which just happens to be one of the main locations featured in the Welsh Arthurian tale *The Dream of Rhonabwy*. Positioned as close to these other possible Arthurian sites as the fort is may just be a coincidence, although there are many other Roman forts in Wales that could have been chosen at random to feature in the story. Sadly, there are no known suitable candidates as the historical Arthur from the kingdom of Powys. Even without any obvious Arthur, it is interesting to note that the Roman city of Viroconium (modern day Wroxeter) underwent a huge rebuilding programme in the fifth century, on a scale so far unlike any other British city of this period. Whether Arthur existed, and whether he existed in Powys at this early date, cannot be proved, but someone had the political power, manpower and organisational prowess to organise this event (aside from Arthur, other suggested candidates for Viroconium's rebuilding include Vortigern and an Irish or British warlord named Cunorix).

One of the more obvious choices of candidate for a Welsh Arthur has to be King Arthwyr of Dyfed (the principal kingdom in South Wales). Arthwyr lived in the late sixth century – perhaps a little too late for the traditional Arthurian dates – but we know very little else about him. Perhaps Arthwyr's father, King Pedr ap Cyngar, named him after the great warlord himself, although whether Arthur was known as a historical or legendary leader at this early date, we cannot tell for sure. It is even possible that some of Arthwyr's now forgotten deeds were later drawn into the folk tales of Arthur, and that the king of legend is a composite of several such men.

Baram Blackett and Alan Wilson subscribe to the theory that Arthur was not just one single, individual warrior in their 1998 book *The Holy Kingdom: The Quest For The Real King Arthur* (assisted by a writer named Adrian Gilbert). Instead, they propose that the Arthur of folklore and legend derived from two real-life men: Arthun (or Anwn), and Athrwys (or Arthwys), a king of the South Welsh kingdoms of Glywyssing and Gwent. Arthun was supposedly the son of the late fourth century Roman rebel Magnus Maximus, and is known in Welsh history as the King of

Greece (which probably is a misreading of his Latin name: Antonius Gregorius). Arthun actually ruled in South Wales, as did Athrwys. Conventional history dates Athrwys as a seventh century king, but with some conviction, Blackett and Wilson argue instead for an early sixth century date.

Sadly, Blackett and Wilson also aired their views that their work was being undermined by academics, who they believe didn't want the true story of Arthur to be told, for whatever reason. Blackett and Wilson felt that they were undertaking their studies against a wall of great opposition from well-qualified but (in their opinion) ignorant academics and heritage organisations; publicly announcing such a feeling can seldom, and should seldom, do the researchers involved or their theories expressed much good. To do so lends little credibility to one's work. Another of the seemingly wilder claims made by Blackett and Wilson is that which suggests they may have found the real Excalibur – and quite possibly the fabled Sword of Constantine of legend – residing in America. The sword they possess is certainly not of the Roman *gladius* type which they claim – which in any case, would be of a type too early for Constantine to have used. Indeed, the sword looks to be of a typology a couple of hundred years too late to have been wielded by a real Arthur. Yet we can all dream.

Just as Blackett and Wilson identify the historical Arthur (or half of him, at least) with King Athrwys of Glywyssing and Gwent, so do Chris Barber and David Pykitt. Their belief is that, after fighting at the famous Battle of Camlann, Athrwys abdicated and travelled to Brittany, where he was remembered not as Arthur but as St Armel (or Arthmael), whose shrine may still be seen at St Armel-des-Boschaux.

There are many other traditions that link the historical Arthur with Wales. Whether there is any basis in these stories, or whether, as the Celtic language was gradually pushed back into the hills and valleys of the west, Arthur's geographical locale shifted with them, we cannot be sure. Traditions take many years to build, so perhaps there is some truth in the idea of Arthur as a king in Wales.

Arthur of the West

The majority of British folk tales about Arthur suggest that he was from the South-West: Tintagel, Glastonbury, and South Cadbury are all sites that are now inextricably linked with the life of Arthur. Anyone who has ever holidayed in Cornwall or Devon will be able to tell you that

WILL THE REAL KING ARTHUR PLEASE STAND UP?

Arthur was an ancient king in this corner of Britain. Or, at least, that's the impression you're left with from even the briefest visit. In some places, you can't walk more than a hundred yards without coming across your next 'Ye Rounde Table Tea Roome' or 'King Arthur Car Park'. Perhaps it's not quite that bad, but Arthur's place in small business and tourism is sealed for life in the South-West… and the King Arthur car park does exist.

Quite a few scholars have agreed that the South-West is a likely area for the true Arthur to have ruled. There is also the great weight of early tradition linking the King to this area – both in folklore and also in place names and known sites. Despite this, there are relatively few solid, detailed modern theories regarding the historical existence of a south-western Arthur.

The south-west of modern England remained in the hands of British dynasties for a significantly longer period of time than the South-East. Modern Somerset, Cornwall and Devon were firmly in British control, and known as the kingdom of Dumnonia, into the seventh century, and although pushed back in the seventh and eighth centuries, Cornwall did not fall under Anglo-Saxon rule until 838. As a result of such a late conquest, much of the Romanised South-West was preserved in the hands of the Britons (Exeter, Dorchester and Ilchester all show signs of having preserved some sort of urban occupation). Such survival may well have been helped along by the strong rule of a fearsome local warlord – the warlord whose memory is preserved in those tea rooms and car parks mentioned above. We Britons certainly know how to commemorate our greatest leaders!

Commentators who favour a south-western Arthur recognise the importance of the early British poem *Geraint Son of Erbin. Geraint* is an important early piece of literature, as it immediately connects Arthur with the South-West in a historical context, rather than the usual tales of folklore and legend. It also shows him to be an influential warrior, whose men fought and died alongside those of Geraint at the Battle of Llongborth, which probably took place at Portchester on the south coast (Langport in the South-West is an alternative battle site).

A number of other medieval Welsh and Cornish stories make reference to Arthur as a great warlord or king of the area; the Life of St Gildas shows him commanding the armies of Cornwall and Devon in a siege of Glastonbury (where Guinevere was being held captive). A number of other early stories link Arthur to this part of the country: *The Dialogue of Arthur and the Eagle* and *Geraint Son of Erbin* are two such tales. Arthur's greatest victory – the Battle of Badon – is often tied into his south-western roots as it is frequently identified (with no secure foundation) as the south-western Roman city of Bath, as 'Badon' would have been pronounced 'Bathon' in the British tongue.

Even Arthur's legendary court of early tales, Kelliwick, is traditionally sited at Killibury in the South-West, and Arthur will forever be associated with the promontory fort and later religious centre at Tintagel. The ongoing connection between Arthur and Tintagel was strengthened in 1998, when a team of archaeologists from Glasgow University found an inscribed slab bearing the name of a certain Artognou, son of Coll. This stone can be securely dated to the fifth or sixth century, but although superficially similar, it is difficult to reconcile the name of Artognou with that of Arthur. Perhaps, as discussed earlier, the names might both mean 'the Bear', which could be a useful link, but we cannot even be sure of this. The excavation, however, suggested that Tintagel was not purely a religious centre at the time that a real Arthur may have lived, but could in fact have been a royal site or hillfort of a British nobleman. If tradition is to be believed, that man may well have been the historical forerunner to Geoffrey of Monmouth's Gorlois.

There is another clue in the early stories of Arthur. Many traditional tales identify Arthur's grandfather as a Constantine, but he is usually suggested to be Constantine III, an early fifth century British usurper to the Roman Empire. Yet one early tradition remembers Arthur as the grandson of Constantine Corneu, a king of Dumnonia, the name of the powerful British kingdom in the south-west of modern England. Three kings of Dumnonia are sometimes said to have ruled at the time of Arthur: Constantine's son Erbin; Constantine's grandson Gereint; and Constantine's great-grandson Cado. If this were the case, Arthur must have been the son of Erbin, and was merely a prince. Quite how a prince came to be elevated to the lofty heights of Arthur's fame in the following centuries is difficult to say. Perhaps if this south-western Arthur of tradition really did exist, some of his deeds were remembered and exaggerated by later poets and bards, sowing the seeds of the later, greater Arthur. But again, there is no solid history to base this assumption on.

Arthur of the North

As well as the possibility of Arthur being a British warlord or king from the west of Britain or Wales, many researchers have attempted to tie the historical Arthur into the British kingdoms of the North. Ranging across the north of modern England and throughout much of modern lowland Scotland, several British dynasties fought against a tide of Pictish, Irish and Saxon inroads into their territories. Pre-eminent among the northern British kingdoms was Rheged, which probably spanned the country from coast to coast, and centred upon Hadrian's Wall. Yet others also existed: Elmet was centred on the Pennines and modern Leeds and Yorkshire, although much of it fell to the Saxons at a fairly early date. The kingdom of Strathclyde sat above Rheged, and was centred round Dumbarton. The kingdom of Gododdin (a name probably deriving from the earlier tribal name 'Votadini') was immortalised in the poem *The Gododdin* – perhaps the earliest source to mention Arthur, this early reference suggests that he may have been a warlord of that kingdom. These northern British kingdoms had probably evolved in the late Roman period, or perhaps the early years of independent Britain at the start of the fifth century; used as buffer zones between the civilized lands of Roman Britain and the barbarian north and Ireland, such regions probably produced the sort of tough warrior you would have gone out of your way to avoid fighting in battle. This, combined with the references to Arthur in early northern literature, suggest that a search for him in the North could be particularly fruitful. And several researchers have done just this.

British history records the names of three northern leaders whose names bear a striking similarity to that of Arthur. A generation before the traditional sixth century dates for Arthur, a king named Arthwys ruled as a descendant of Coel Hen, in the Pennines. The kingdom of Elmet, based in the Leeds area, also spawned an Arthwys, son of King Masgwid Gloff. Little is known of either of these two kings – certainly not enough to build a case for either of them have being 'the' Arthur. The third northern figure was named Artur, he was the son of King Aedan (sometimes styled Aiden) of Dal Riata, the kingdom of the Irish settlers in modern south-west Scotland. Although probably born in the 550s – and therefore perhaps a little too late for the traditional dates for Arthur – Artur was proposed as a suitable candidate by David F Carroll in 1996, and by Richard Barber before him. Barber has suggested that this Artur is the first historically traceable 'Arthur' in British history, and therefore perhaps deserves more attention than most commentators give him. It has been suggested that Artur may have been based at Camelon in Stirlingshire, the name of which may later have corrupted into Camelot. We know so little about the lives of these three would-be

Arthurs, and it is tempting to speculate that some of their deeds may have passed into later folklore as the actions of an Arthur formed as a composite of several warlords. On the other hand, it may be possible that all three were named in honour of a historical or legendary warrior hero, in the hope that his prowess might be instilled in the boy. Perhaps, in the same way that Jason and Kylie were frequently chosen names in the late 1980s (Elvis is less so now than it was in the 1960s and 1970s – although it's still a popular name for owners to give their dogs) the children were named after the central characters of popular culture of the time. For the latter two suggestions to be accurate would mean that Arthur must have been established in folklore or history (or both) at an earlier date than most researchers currently believe, so perhaps the deeds of these three kings really did help to sow the seeds of a later legend.

A number of researchers and scholars have attempted with some success to identify Nennius' list of Arthurian battles with sites in southern Scotland and the Borders, dating to the fifth or sixth century. Among the better attempts are John Stuart Glennie's *Arthurian Localities* (1869), W F Skene's *Arthur and the Britons in Wales and Scotland* (edited and reprinted in 1988 from an 1868 original), and more recently, the well-written history of Arthur and the Borders by Alistair Moffat, entitled *Arthur and the Lost Kingdoms* (1999). By analysing the names of hills, rivers and regions, all three managed to locate suitable sites for the twelve battles listed by Nennius in his ninth century account of Arthur's victories. When combined with the early references to Arthur and some of the characters who later became part of the legend in northern British Dark Ages poetry, and the fact that so little reliable history was recorded for the lands north of the Humber during this period, a convincing case for the real-life Arthur can be made. All three are interesting theories, but the whole case for their authenticity depends upon whether Nennius' battle list consisted of real encounters, whether Arthur really fought in these battles, and whether the authors have correctly identified the battle sites so many centuries after they were first forgotten.

Norma Lorre Goodrich argued in 1986 that Arthur was a northern king, and that his court was at Carlisle and the western end of Hadrian's Wall. Relying heavily on medieval literature as straightforward sources of historical value (which can seldom be a great foundation), Goodrich's work suggested that she saw Arthur as a king of Rheged. A great deal of poetry has passed down to the modern day from the poets and bards of the northern Britons, but there is little in there to suggest that Arthur was linked to the kingdom of Rheged in the centuries immediately after his presumed death.

The case for a 'Scottish' Arthur was made in 2000 by Archie McKerracher, a fellow of the Society of Antiquarians of Scotland. McKerracher identified the site of Arthur's court very precisely: the back garden of 40 Adam Crescent, a terraced house in Stenhousemuir, near Falkirk. This theory relies upon identifying the Round Table made famous in Arthurian legend, which was first mentioned by Wace in the twelfth century. McKerracher argued that the Round Table was indeed real, but that far from being a piece of furniture, the 'round table' was really a round house and that confusion occurred as the original sources were copied, translated and corrupted over the centuries. Thus, in McKerracher's opinion, Wace's 'Round Table' should actually be read as 'table rotunda'. The only building in Britain's history that could ever be identified as such, according to McKerracher, was a beehive-shaped stone building known as Arthur's O'on (deriving from the word 'oven') on his identified site in Stenhousemuir. This building was apparently knocked down in 1743 to repair a dam. McKerracher's theory also suggested that Arthur ruled the north of Britain from Wales to Dumbarton (making him a British king with a modern 'Scottish' residence rather than a true Dark Ages Scot), and that he lived in the fifth or sixth century. McKerracher's Arthur built his 'O'on' as a mausoleum after taking part in a pilgrimage to Jerusalem; doing so would have shown a direct influence from the Middle East. McKerracher went as far as to suggest that the O'on was built to house a secret holy order dedicated to the cult of Mary Magdalene, and that Arthur's later association with Wales and the South-West came about only with Geoffrey of Monmouth's influence. As ingenious as McKerracher's idea was, it would appear to rely too heavily on interpretations of medieval sources, written down over five hundred years after his Arthur's death. It is also unclear whether the site of Arthur's O'on is datable to the correct period in history, or indeed when the association of the site with Arthur's name took place. Nevertheless, we should add it to the growing list of Arthurian possibilities.

In 1935, O G S Crawford suggested that the site of the Roman fort of *Cambloganna* (Castlesteads, on Hadrian's Wall) might well have been the original Camlann (the famous final battle fought by Arthur, where it is recorded that both he and Modred died). There is no strong evidence to support this theory beyond the obvious and fairly brittle linguistic link. Of more interest is the fact that the Northumbrian River Glen, often put forward as one of Arthur's battle sites, was later the site of the fifteenth century Anglo-Scottish battle of Homildon Hill, and sixteenth century Battle of Flodden was also fought close by. Ancient and medieval battles were usually fought at strategically important sites, and the fact that two later battles were fought in the area suggests that the River Glen could well have been a key site in a Dark Ages campaign. The river is also overlooked by the important Dark Ages royal site at Yeavering, so could quite possibly have been fought right outside the real-life Camelot.

Arthur the mercenary
The idea that Arthur may have been of a non-British nationality ultimately derives from a reference in Nennius' ninth century *The History of the Britons*, which translates as saying that he fought *with* the British (meaning *on their behalf*) rather than actually being British himself. The popular theories that suggest that Arthur was of Sarmatian descent typify this, yet there is no reason to limit his nationality to this one group of people. Alliances between different cultural groups were made and broken with alarming frequency in Dark Ages Britain – many British and Saxon kings allied themselves with and enlisted the help of Irish warlords, and the Britons had, of course, at an early date employed Saxons as mercenaries.

Late Roman military policy allowed the mass employment of non-Roman subjects. Goths, Franks, Vandals, Saxons, and many more 'barbarians' fought for the later Roman emperors, and they were paid in money or with land within the Empire. One of the Empire's most successful later generals, Stilicho, was himself a Vandal. The two high ranking Roman commanders who were killed in the Barbarian Conspiracy in Roman Britain were named Fullofaudes and Nectaridus, which are both Germanic names. So it was not unusual for Roman officials to bring outsiders in to fight for them, and we may presume that the same applied to their post-Roman British equivalents. Is it not impossible therefore that Arthur may have been such a warrior? Many of the best certainly were.

The main stumbling block with this theory is whether the Britons and Celtic culture as a whole could have thrown such pride behind a warrior who really didn't belong to them. Could all of those traditions and legends have sprung up about a warrior who fought not for national pride but for money and land?

Arthur and onions

A French King Arthur? *C'est impossible!* Or, according to Geoffrey Ashe and several others, not so impossible, although this Arthur would have actually considered himself a Briton, and would have been based in Brittany. Ashe, in his book *The Discovery of King Arthur* (published in 1985, and revised in 2003) is a firm believer in Geoffrey of Monmouth's statement that his own stories of Arthur were learned from an older book, an earlier history written much closer to the time that Arthur lived. As such, the story of Vortigern, his High Kingship, and his dealings with the Saxons are considered by Ashe to be based on true historical events, as are the tales about Ambrosius. The same applies to some of the details of Arthur's life, which Ashe has unravelled to reveal yet another true life of Arthur. Through some bold and at times ingenious detective work, Ashe believes that the Arthur of Geoffrey of Monmouth's *History* can be identified through his deeds as a British or Breton warlord named Riothamus.

Ashe believes that Riothamus' name may have been a title rather than a personal name – translating as 'Greatest King'. His personal name, argues Ashe, could perhaps have been Arthur. Riothamus is mentioned briefly in contemporary sources as a Briton (probably a king) who crossed to mainland Europe and fought against the Visigoths in the Loire Valley. This happened in 468, and afterwards, he was double-crossed by the Prefect of Gaul, and then disappeared from history. It is possible that Riothamus was exiled to Britain at this time, as a result of the ongoing civil wars amongst the Britons in Brittany. He may later have returned to the continent, and perhaps died fighting Germanic (possibly Saxon) enemies around 470. He disappeared from the historical record near to Avallon in Burgundy, which gives Riothamus an obvious link to the legend surrounding Arthur. Ashe sees Arthur as a *Restitutor* – a restorer of the Roman way of life – whose real motives and deeds were distorted by medieval writers after Geoffrey of Monmouth touched upon his historical actions.

Ashe believes that original documents of Riothamus' life were used by Geoffrey to write his *History* and broadly based the events and locations upon fact; and there are certain similarities between Riothamus' career and that of Geoffrey's Arthur. This version of events appears to have been lost or forgotten in other sources, except for in the *Life of St Goeznovius*, which recalls Arthur fighting in France, and that mystery surrounded his death. This tale also suggested that Arthur had cleared much of Britain and parts of France from Saxon dominance in the fifth century, and it should also be remembered that the original stories of Arthur's famous Round Table might have also originated in Brittany.

Perhaps the two problems most difficult to reconcile with Geoffrey Ashe's Riothamus connection is that the historically recorded events in the warlord's life connect him with Brittany rather than Britain and suggest that his main enemies were Visigoths rather than Saxons. This obviously does not fit with the traditional view of the historical Arthur's life, but there is nothing to suggest that the traditional view is any more correct, beyond the fact that it has been passed down through the centuries. The second stumbling block is that Riothamus' date pushes Arthur back about fifty years from his traditional date; although again, who is to say that tradition is any more accurate than Ashe's bold identification? The date we have for the Battle of Badon seems to correctly fit in circa 500, later than Riothamus' probable death by about three decades, but it is possible that Riothamus-Arthur never fought at Badon at all, and that only later was his name connected to that great victory.

A third question must be asked of Riothamus/Arthur, along with any of the other historically attested characters who have been pushed forward as the solution. The question being that as history allows all of these people to have lived independently of each other, plus many hundreds of thousands more people whom we no longer remember, why must we try to identify the shadowy Arthur as one of the people whom we already know of? Could there not be space for a few more unidentified warlords? We certainly do not know all of their names, so why should we assume that Arthur is one that we do actually know?

Despite leaving these questions hanging in the historical ether, Ashe's original theory is well researched and reminds us that leftfield thought should not always be dismissed out of hand. If the three questions can be satisfactorily answered, Riothamus makes a fine candidate for the historical Arthur.

Geoffrey Ashe isn't the only person to have suggested that Arthur may not have lived in Britain, but instead lived in the recently established British colony of Brittany. Tradition records that Arthur was the grandson of Constantine (Geoffrey of Monmouth himself recorded this in his twelfth century *History*); one theory suggests that this Constantine was the early fifth century British usurper, Constantine III. It has been suggested that Constantine's continental campaigns saw the settlement of British warriors on the mainland, and that Arthur may have descended from these people. This idea is highly dependent upon the unsubstantiated statement linking the historical Constantine to Arthur, and has little to support it apart from that.

Out of the Dark Ages...

And into? The Bronze Age? Outer space? Although most historians place Arthur firmly in the fifth or sixth century, not everyone has limited their research to this two hundred year period.

The occasional author has proposed far more mystical origins behind the legend of Arthur. Arthur is sometimes linked to Druidism, which seems unlikely: Arthur, whether in the guise of a political leader or military leader, is never convincingly tied in to any such religious practices, although we know precious little about Druids (about the same, in fact, as we know about Arthur himself). A pre-Roman, Iron Age setting for the historical Arthur is a possibility, given the occasionally warlike nature of the British tribes during this period, but there is little else to link the great King to this period beyond the sometimes chaotic background of warring tribes.

John Darrah, in his book *The Real Camelot*, boldly attempts to remove Arthur from his usual place in the Dark Ages and shifts him back in time to a Bronze Age setting, a couple of thousand years earlier. Darrah suggests Arthur existed in the second millennium BC, and exists partly as a man and partly as a divine being; in this respect, Darrah follows the well-worn mystical path trodden by Frazer's influential *The Golden Bough*. Stonehenge is Darrah's Camelot, and also the Round Table or temple; he believes that later Celtic traditions borrowed on these half remembered stories, having been passed down by sects of priests.

A number of pseudo-historical, mystical explanations surround the legend of Arthur, yet very few ever touch upon a possible historical parallel. Some researchers, as you will read, have even gone so far as to suggest that Arthur was a god.

Was Arthur a Celtic god?

Some scholars have seen Arthur as more than a mere mortal, suggesting that some Celtic legend hints that Arthur – and a number of his followers – were actually gods. These gods were from a pre-Christian Celtic world and, as such, the only way to incorporate them into the culture of the Christianised Celts was to reinvent them as characters from folklore. Roger Sherman Loomis suggested that Arthur's knights were solar and storm gods.

At the turn of the twentieth century, Sir John Rhys argued that the main characters from Arthurian legend were derived from Celtic gods, goddesses, and associated characters from ancient Celtic myth. He believed that a real Arthur had existed in the fifth century, but that the tales later told about Arthur represented far earlier myths, reset in a more relevant historical world. Rhys' theory was mostly based on the meaning of the characters' names, and now seems quite dated.

T W Rolleston argued along similar lines in his *Celtic Myths and Legends*: he believed that the Arthur of legend was a composite of a Welsh warlord and the ancient Celtic god Artaius. Rolleston's Arthur blended stories about the real-life warlord with the ancient god, and later drew on Breton legend and that of Charlemagne to produce the king known in medieval romance. Rolleston believed that Welsh migrants arrived in Brittany telling stories of a warlord called Arthur, and that this character gradually merged with Artaius, whom Rolleston tells us had altars dedicated to him in France. To support his theory, Rolleston compared his Arthur scenario to that of Ireland's sixth century Saint Brigit, who he envisaged as drawing in elements of the myth of the ancient, pagan goddess Brigindo.

A few of the supporting characters from medieval Arthurian legend may also have originated as gods and goddesses. If so, these early pagan figures would have been incorporated into the Arthurian world as part of Christianity's widespread drive to swallow up other religions' memories into its own. Kay, Bedivere, Guinevere and Morgan Le Fay may possibly be identified as Celtic deities. Gawain has also been cited as a Celtic god incorporated into Arthurian legend. Gawain is one of the earliest characters associated with Arthur in legend and folklore; his original name was Gwalchmai (which translates as Hawk of May), and one tale about a fight between Lancelot and Gawain suggests his possible origin as a deity. Lancelot killed two of Gawain's brothers (Gareth and Gaheris), and a duel between these two, Arthur's greatest knights, took place. During the fight, it is revealed that Gawain has secret powers that increase his strength threefold between the hours of nine and midday, when the sun is at its strongest. I suspect that this news may well have left Lancelot rather vexed. Gawain's direct link to solar energy has suggested to many writers that he originated as a Celtic solar god, although it should also be noted that it could be a direct reference to the light and hope that a gallant knight brings to dark times.

Some commentators have gone even further and proposed that the stories within the *Lives* of the saints indicate that Arthur may have been a demon. And that his continued bating of the saints, testing their religious belief and powers may have represented the battle between good and evil, and that the demonic Arthur was present to measure the faith of religious folk. Beyond some circumstantial evidence in the *Lives*, there is little else to support this rather unusual theory.

Arthur in the landscape

Even now, Arthur's name lives on not just in legend, but in the landscape too. A cursory glance over regional maps of south-west England, southern Scotland and most of Wales will show you how. Many of these sites are simply geographical features, yet some are man-made sites dating to the Dark Ages. Appendix B lists some of the better Arthurian-related sites you can visit, but dotted across many areas of the country (notably in the uplands), you will occasionally pass by an Arthur's Chair, Arthur's Oven, Arthur's Table, or one of several other variations on Arthur's belongings or deeds.

The possibility exists that long-forgotten folk tales linked such sites with the legendary Arthur. Some suggestion has even been made that the presence of Arthurian-named features may have indicated that a garrison of Arthur the Emperor or High King was present during or after his lifetime, as part of a huge defensive network around Britain. More likely, the naming of features after Arthur (especially items of his household furniture) shows the desire by people in different regions to be linked to their greatest folk hero, and in doing so, they also elevate him to the physical presence of a giant. The fact that closer study of these sites reveals that the naming tradition appears to have been ongoing for centuries – certainly from the ninth to the sixteenth centuries – enforces Arthur's appeal to generations of Britons. Yet the presence of Arthurian-named sites in a given area does not bring us any closer to knowing where the King may have ruled, just that the people of that area wished, at some point, to be associated with his greatness.

The Once And Future King Departs To Avalon

Chapter Eight

The Quest for King Arthur

So, to return to the book's initial question, King Who? From terse references in unsubstantiated histories, Arthur's shaky foundations gained a foothold in the histories of both the Celts and the medieval romantic movements, allowing him to become the greatest hero of the European medieval age. But did he really exist? And if he did, was he a king or just a war leader? And was there only ever one Arthur, or a multitude of people whose deeds were joined together to make our later legendary hero?

What is clear is that Arthur – whether he was a real man or not – came to represent leadership in two very different periods of western European history, and was (and still is) so famous that he needed little explanation when introduced into new tales or a new environment. For example, when Camelot launched the National Lottery in Britain in the 1990s, no one asked why they'd given their lottery machines names like Arthur, Lancelot and Guinevere. Arthur, and by association his main followers, are household names, and this phenomenon did not only begin in the twentieth century: in early oral tales, poetry and attempts at history, Arthur's name suddenly sprang into use. He needed no introduction in the earliest of these tales, and the early storytellers and historians who used his name never felt the need to explain to their audience who Arthur was, where he ruled, or that he was a skilled warrior. They just knew – more's the pity for the modern researcher, who has to pluck at straws and ethereal hints of a real man, committed to paper hundreds of years after the tales were originally told.

A search for a real-life Arthur who fits the image created by our medieval chroniclers is destined to fail; in this respect, it is likely that Arthur never existed. We can be sure that any real-life Arthur would not have recognised himself as the hero of medieval chivalry that he was destined to become. An honest, just king of all Britain, who ruled from a Round Table set squarely at the centre of his Gothic-inspired Camelot certainly never existed. A real-life Arthur may well have been surrounded by some of the best warriors in the land, but they would not have adhered to the chivalric code envisaged by medieval romancers – such concepts simply did not exist in the fifth and sixth centuries. His 'knights' would have been warriors, intent on serving their warlord right up to death. Yet the character of Arthur the hero allowed medieval writers to shape him as they wished – such a heroic personality would be malleable enough to shape into the values and virtues of any given historical period, and this explains why Arthur has remained popular since the Dark Ages.

Whether he was a king, a warrior, or never even existed in the flesh, the thriving and ongoing obsession with Arthur among the Britons and the rest of the world has been fuelled by the way in which our hero had been created. He is essentially a shape shifter, who different authors have been able to cast in a variety of moulds to satiate the desires of their audience. That's why we love him. In his earliest form, Arthur was a man of battle who crushed the Saxon enemies of the Britons and Welsh, and went on magical, superhuman quests. He also represented power in Dark Ages society, which evidenced itself for good and ill in the hagiographic tales of Britain's saints. In the medieval period, Arthur came to typify chivalric code and the strength of feudal society, justifying the way in which the target audience of Arthurian stories – the nobility – lived. In the post-medieval world, Arthur became a mystical figure from Britain's enchanted past; with a growing interest in national identity, Arthur came to represent the way in which Britons saw their ancestors, as great and noble leaders. On a localised level, folk tales of Arthur continued to be told, bringing about the regionalisation of Arthur as a 'Welsh king', a 'south-western king' or a 'northern king'. In the nineteenth and early twentieth centuries, Arthur was used as a paragon of Victorian virtue, preaching to readers the ideals to which they should conform. The later twentieth and the twenty-first century sees Arthur fulfilling a number of roles – the hero of a fantasy world in games, a yardstick for heroism and machismo, a link to our ancient and mystical past, and as a heart-throb star of the movies. My own retelling is notably different to that of Geoffrey of Monmouth or Thomas Malory, yet we are all reciting the tales of the same character. As an example, my Grail Quest in Chapter Five plays down the Christian aspect of the adventure, in an attempt to update the tale for a modern, religiously diverse audience; yet the Christian element was the key theme of Arthurian legend to a wholly more religious medieval audience. As such an ethereal character – whose name is perhaps his most famous attribute – we have all been able to bestow upon him whatever personal traits or deeds we wish, allowing him to successfully shift between cultures and eras, all the time still fulfilling the role of the People's Hero.

The shape shifting ability of Arthur, his evolution over time and the way in which his stories can be adapted to emphasise the opinion of an author or a culture's desires may perhaps be seen in some of the medieval Welsh tales of Arthur. In some of these stories, notably a couple of the *Lives* of saints, Arthur acts with noted cruelty or stupidity. There may be a contemporary reason for this. At the same time as tales of Arthur's baseness were being circulated in Wales, he was gaining recognition and popularity in the courts of Anglo-Norman England – the adversaries of the Welsh. So by ridiculing their former hero, the Welsh may have been distancing themselves from the newly emerged Anglo-Norman Arthur. On the face of it, degrading your own national hero because he's become popular with foreigners seems ludicrous, but this theory does go some way to explaining why Arthur received some bad press in Welsh tales.

At some point, even the most ardent believer in a real-life Arthur is likely to conclude that perhaps the man who is their quarry never actually existed. They may not persist with such a denial for any significant length of time (for what are we without hope?), but only the most narrow-minded would fail to consider the possibility. This denial is not just that of Arthur as a larger than life literary hero – as suggested above, we can be certain that this incarnation could never have existed in a historical context – but even as any kind of real-life leader in the fifth or sixth century. After all, what evidence do we really have? A couple of dubious chronicle entries, written down at an uncertain date, and a handful of folk tales and jumbled references that emerged before Arthur's name was whisked away on a flight of Celtic fantasy. It's a fair comment. But placed into historical context, there is no less evidence (as so few sources have survived from the time) for a warlord named Arthur than there is for some of the other British and Saxon leaders of this period, a number of whom most historians would consider real. And would the Welsh, along with their British and Breton kin, have attempted to fit a purely legendary character into a historical context? Other Celtic heroes existed in a timeless age – the great warrior Cuchulain of Irish myth, for example, inhabits a legendary world devoid of real world dates and history. Why would Arthur have been different?

Not every name from the past has been so 'fortunate' as to have their true identity and deeds so scantily documented, and their character has passed down identically from generation to generation based more securely on their real actions and personality. We know of Henry V's deeds, so can never make him anything other than a batterer of the French, and the Duke of Wellington is the same (although his moribund role as Prime Minister is often overlooked). Even legendary British characters like Beowulf and Robin Hood have well-defined roles, making them less malleable for new generations of writers.

The furthest that I would go in suggesting a real-life Arthur is that a warrior who championed the British cause possibly did exist. Not as the Arthur we now remember, but as a warlord whose deeds snowballed over time to create the Arthur of legend – the warrior who could defeat giants, the king who would rule justly, the leader whom the greatest and most noble men in the world would serve. Given the historical circumstances during and after the centuries of his flourit, it is not terribly surprising that no evidence of his life has survived; so few documents exist that we can string together only a scanty narrative of the history of that time. The famous list of twelve Arthurian battles may be one example of his early, real-life deeds, but, in the centuries following his lifetime, the deeds of the warrior Arthur expanded into the realms of legend. In this respect, Arthur is like any number of other pseudo-historical heroes. For example, Robin Hood is likely to have existed, although there is no evidence that he was any more noble than any other brigand; Roland, the valiant paladin of the Franks, was based on a real-life warrior, but again his deeds were blown out of all proportion. Likewise, Bram Stoker's famous Dracula was broadly based on the fifteenth century Wallachian ruler Vlad Tepes ('the Impaler', due to his penchant for dropping his Turkish enemies onto sharpened poles). And William Wallace has been paraded as a hero far worthier than his brutal real-life campaigns deserved ever since the 1995 movie *Braveheart*.

So the most important – but sometimes overlooked – point to make about Arthur is that if he ever did exist, he was not the man of Arthurian literature we think of today. A real Arthur may have had his name and deeds hijacked and turned into the Arthur of legend, but there is no point in looking for an ancient leader who led his chivalrous men from quest to quest, setting the world to rights. Some of the deeds ascribed to Arthur – even the earliest of Celtic tales – may have been carried out by a real man, but in all probability, any historical deeds that have survived in legend are a composite of the actions taken by two or more individual warlords, perhaps many years apart. Not only Arthur, but other characters from Arthurian tradition – Vortigern, Merlin, Kay and many others are also probably composites of real people, mixing their real deeds with copious or judicious amounts of fable. As a composite character, Arthur has been allowed to flourish – any number of heroic deeds or likeable traits may have been incorporated into his reputation, without restriction. It's a child-in-sweet-shop phenomenon: why have just one thing when you can grab at the lot?

However, with few exceptions, almost all writers who believe that Arthur really did exist have agreed on a few very basic facts:

1.   He was a British leader.
2.   He lived in the Dark Ages, more specifically the fifth or sixth century AD.
3.   Whether a king or not, he was a warrior, and he fought the enemies of the Britons.

But that's as far as general consensus goes. From these three statements, several schools of thought have sprung up – Arthur was really a king, Arthur was only a general, Arthur lived in the North, Arthur lived in Wales, Arthur's real name was not Arthur, Arthur won the Battle of Badon in 518 and died at Camlann in 539, and so on. If such variety shows the modern reader one thing, it is that we really do not know enough about the historical or pseudo-historical Arthur to make accurate decisions about him. And let us not forget that there are many doubters of a real-life Arthur, queuing up to shoot the latest theories down. Not a single candidate pushed forward by a modern researcher has yet conclusively been proved to be the real Arthur, whether you're a believer or not.

I've deliberately shied away from making any such astonishing claims that reveal the real King Arthur. Inevitably, writers wishing to promote their own Arthurian candidate have to twist or ignore important tracts of the scanty historical evidence to support their theory, and to do so in such a book as this would be unbalancing. Instead, the historical sections of this book have tried to touch upon some of the warriors and rulers whose historical existence is more certain. The name of Arthur has eclipsed all of these people – perhaps even absorbed some of their deeds – yet their effect on the history (if not the legend) of Britain must be at least equal to Arthur's.

It is interesting to note that the integration of historical figures into Arthurian legend focuses mostly on warriors from the late sixth century AD, who had strong connections with northern British kingdoms. Perhaps these people were contemporaries of a real-life Arthur, who fought alongside him, gradually filtering from folklore and oral history into the legends that sprang up around Arthur in later centuries. Perhaps a real-life Arthur existed in one of the northern kingdoms, as many historians have suggested; the date would be slightly later than Arthur's traditional date, but this would not necessarily be a serious stumbling block.

It also seems a strong possibility that those historians who search for a British leader named Arthur are chasing their own Questing Beast. Given that some other warlords in the Dark Ages were known by battle names or nicknames, the bear-like connotations of his name may suggest that 'Arthur' is there under our noses, recorded by his real name. Perhaps Ambrosius is a strong candidate, or Riothamus fighting in France, or Geraint who fought at Llongborth. Perhaps he was another king of whom we know very little – there are plenty of candidates who fit such criteria in the fifth and sixth centuries. Perhaps we could even offer up a great warlord such as Urien of Rheged as 'the Bear' of legend, suggesting that some later confusion worked his true name into the tales independently when the connection between his personal name and battle name had long been forgotten. He certainly exerted influence over lesser contemporary kings and died at the hands of a fellow Briton. Furthermore the link to later sixth century northern British kingdoms mentioned above would support Urien as a candidate, remembered now by both his own name and his battle name. But again, this would be no more than mere speculation and theorising.

No matter what you conclude, one thing is certain: if a historian or archaeologist was ever able to prove or disprove Arthur for certain, the world of legend would instantly become a less memorable, less eye opening wonderland.

Appendix A

The Arthurian Companion

Space does not allow me to exhaustively list every character ever mentioned in the many and varied stories of Arthur, so this appendix instead gives a potted history of the most important and some of the more interesting characters from Arthurian legend. It draws on many diverse Arthurian sources, but focuses on medieval Arthurian literature more than Celtic or modern tales. I have limited the list to characters from legend only, rather than history; as a concession, I have noted any parallels between the characters as listed and any historical figures whom they may be based upon.

A number of knights are listed as being a Knight of the Round Table. These have been drawn together from Sir Thomas Malory's work and the Vulgate Cycle, and not all of the knights were present at the same time – some were late-comers, others died and were replaced by one of the other worthy knights listed.

Aglovale – One of the Knights of the Round Table, a son of Pellinore who is slain in battle by Lancelot.

Agravaine – One of the Knights of the Round Table, and a son of King Lot. Sometimes known as 'the Arrogant' or 'the Proud', Agravaine is the least likeable of Lot's sons; a talented and skilled knight, he lacked the personality to go with it, and is usually depicted as an envious man.

Working alongside Modred, Agravaine helped to reveal the secret love between Lancelot and Guinevere, and was eventually slain by Lancelot.
Agwisance – Also known as **King Anguish of Ireland**. One of the Knights of the Round Table, who began as an enemy of Arthur when the boy was crowned. Anguish plays a leading role in the medieval romance of *Tristan and Iseult*.

Ambrosius – Also known as **Ambrosius Aurelius, Aurelius Ambrosius** and **Ambrosius Aurelianus**. The leader of the Britons before Arthur, Ambrosius' parents were said to be of Roman blood. Some pseudo-historical stories place Arthur as Ambrosius' cavalry commander, who succeeded his commander at a later date. He would appear to be a historical British leader, possibly the warlord who defeated the Saxons at the famous Battle of Badon, a victory which in legend is often attributed to Arthur himself.

Anna – Geoffrey of Monmouth identifies a sister to Arthur named Anna who, like the King himself, was the child of Uther and Igraine. She is known in later tales as **Morgan Le Fay** (and you can find out more about her under that entry in this appendix).

Arthur – The High King of Britain, and son of Uther Pendragon. You should know quite a lot more about him if you've got this far in the book, so I won't dwell on him any further here.

King Auguselus – The King of Scotland, who Geoffrey of Monmouth mentions as one of the notable knights present at Arthur's court in the City of the Legion.

Bagdemagus – One of the Knights of the Round Table, and King of Gore after his uncle Urien. Bagdemagus tried to rescue Merlin from his enchanted imprisonment, but failed. He also failed on the Grail Quest, struck down by an angelic knight.

Balin – Also known as the **Knight with the Two Swords**. Balin fell out of favour with Arthur when he beheaded an enchanted maiden. He later regained Arthur's trust, and at the climax of several adventures, killed his brother Balan in a duel where neither brother realised who he was fighting.

King Ban – King of Benwick, brother to Bors, and father of Lancelot. A major ally of Arthur during the High King's early years, assisting him in the Battle of the Eleven Kings, and delivering Lancelot into the care and training of the Lady of the Lake.

Baudwin of Britain – One of the Knights of the Round Table, and a stalwart follower of Arthur early during the boy's reign, for which he was made Constable of Britain. An early tale remembers three vows he made: never to fear death; never to deny anyone meat and drink; and never to be jealous of his wife or other women.

Bedivere – Also known as **Bedevere** and **Bedwyr**. One of the first Knights of the Round Table, but made famous as one of the last: Bedivere was the survivor of Camlann, who returned Excalibur to the Lady of the Lake. Sometimes referred to as being one handed.

Bellinor – One of the Knights of the Round Table, who took the seat of Bors at the Round Table when Bors left Camelot with Lancelot.

Bors – One of the Knights of the Round Table, renowned as a pure and modest knight. When he politely spurned the advances of a lady, she threatened to jump out of a tower with all of her ladies in waiting; Bors' purity meant that he had to stand by and watch, rather than accept her advances. Bors survived the Grail Quest, accompanying Perceval and Galahad; he later sided with Lancelot in the war against Arthur.

Brastias – One of the Knights of the Round Table. Originally a knight of Gorlois, Duke of Cornwall, Brastias served Arthur well and fought alongside him in the High King's first campaigns. He travelled to Benwick to enlist the help of King Ban on Arthur's behalf.

Breunis Saunce Pité – Also known as the **Brown Knight Without Pity** and **Breuse Sans Pitié**. Enemy of Arthur's knights and imprisoner of ladies; he had collected thirty such women before Gareth defeated him. Not a nice chap – the name says it all.

Cador of Cornwall – The Duke of Cornwall during Arthur's reign. One of the Knights of the Round Table, and an erstwhile companion to Arthur and capable British warlord in Geoffrey of Monmouth's History. Cador was the father of Constantine, who ruled after Arthur's death.

King Carados of Scotland – One of the Knights of the Round Table, although he originally fought against the newly crowned Arthur.

Clariance of Northumberland – One of the Knights of the Round Table, although this Duke or King of Northumberland originally sided against Arthur at the start of the High King's reign.

Colgrevance – One of the Knights of the Round Table, who assisted Arthur in his early campaigns against the rebel kings. Colgrevance has the rare and dubious honour of two deaths: once during the Grail Quest at the hands of Lionel, and later by Lancelot when the secret affair of Lancelot and Guinevere was outed by a group including Colgrevance. No information explains what happened in between his two deaths, and it may well be that there were two characters with the same name.

Constantine – One of the Knights of the Round Table, not to be confused with earlier rulers of the same name in Geoffrey's *History*. Constantine was the son of Cador of Cornwall, and became King after Arthur's death. Malory wrote that he was left as joint governor of Britain when Arthur campaigned against Lucius on the continent (along with Baudwin of Britain), and that he tried to keep Bors, Ector de Maris, Bleoberis and Blamore as companions of the Round Table when he was King. Constantine may well be based upon a historical king mentioned by the monk Gildas, writing in the mid-sixth century; if they are one and the same, Gildas did not hold him in high esteem (but then again, Gildas held no contemporary secular leader of his in high esteem).

Culhwch – Also known as **Kilwich**. Pronounced 'Keelhookh'. The tale of *Culhwch and Olwen* is one of the greatest tales of Welsh literature, and is one of the earliest stories presenting Arthur in a fabulous light. Culhwch was a cousin of Arthur's, and asked him for assistance in winning the hand of his future wife, Olwen. Arthur and his knights obliged, helping Culhwch to achieve his goal.

Cynon – Arrived at Arthur's court as a young and inexperienced knight. His tale of defeat by The Lord of the Fountain led Ywaine to take up the quest, eventually becoming the Lord himself.

Dagonet – Arthur's fool or courtly jester, and a favourite character of Tennyson's poetry.

Dinadan – One of the Knights of the Round Table, who displayed good humour on several occasions (quite an unusual feat among the dour Round Table crew). Despite saving both Modred and Agravaine on an earlier adventure, they killed him during the Grail Quest.

Dinas – One of the Knights of the Round Table, originally a follower of King Mark. He sided with Lancelot in the war against Arthur.

APPENDIX A: THE ARTHURIAN COMPANION

Dornar – One of the Knights of the Round Table, and a son of Pellinore.

Dubricius – Archbishop of the City of Legions in Geoffrey of Monmouth's *History*, who crowns Arthur at Silchester. Dubricius also addresses the British army before their victory at Badon, giving confidence to the Britons in advance of this hugely important victory.

Ector – Arthur's foster father. An honest, decent and humble knight, entrusted by Merlin with the task of bringing up Arthur, the future King of the Britons. Ector remained loyal to Arthur throughout his life.

Ector de Maris – Also known as **Hector**. One of the Knights of the Round Table, and half-brother of Lancelot, who followed Lancelot to fight the evil knight Turquin. Ector was defeated by Turquin and lashed with thorn bushes. He married the niece of a dwarf, took part unsuccessfully in the Grail Quest, and sided with Lancelot against Arthur.

Elaine of Astolat – Also known as Elaine le Blank and the Lady of Shallot. Elaine is part of a sad romance of Lancelot's, and she starved herself to death when the great knight spurned her advances.

Elaine of Carbonek – Another Elaine who fell in love with Lancelot. An enchantress tricked Lancelot into sleeping with Elaine, and the child of their union would grow up to be Galahad.

Enid – Wife of Geraint, and described as being so beautiful that nature would never better her. Despite this, she was extremely loyal to her husband and may well have been a model of medieval feminine virtue.

The Fisher King – Also known as the **Maimed King** and sometimes as **Pellam**, he was the guardian of the Holy Grail.

Florence – One of the Knights of the Round Table (despite having a girl's name!). Son of Gawain, and one of the party of knights who revealed Lancelot and Guinivere's love.

Gaheris – One of the Knights of the Round Table, and a son of King Lot. A friend of King Mark, Gaheris took part in several adventures that damaged his reputation, and he was eventually killed by Lancelot.

Galahad – One of the most famous Knights of the Round Table, and son of Lancelot. The perfect knight, unmatched by any other, not only in strength but also in purity and courtesy. This stood him in good stead on the Grail Quest, at the end of which the saintly Galahad had the true secrets of the Grail revealed to him, allowing him to die in peace, there and then. In many ways, Galahad epitomised the idealism of later medieval and Victorian Arthurian chivalric values.

Gareth – Also known as **Beaumains**. One of the best known Knights of the Round Table, and one of the best knight in arms of Arthur's realm, certainly remaining more loyal than some of his brothers. Gareth is a personal favourite of mine, as the hero of some rather good stories. Arriving at Camelot as a kitchen boy, he volunteered to escort Lady Linnet to rescue her sister from the clutches of the evil Red Knight. This he did in the face of tremendous rudeness from Linnet, and he was eventually revealed as Gareth, son of King Lot, and brother to Gawain. He was eventually slain by Lancelot.

Gawain – Also known as **Gwalchmai, Gawaine** and **Gauvain**. One of the greatest Knights of the Round Table, nephew of Arthur and son of King Lot. Gawain was a mighty warrior, and one of Arthur's finest champions before Lancelot arrived on the scene; at some point, he was widely expected to succeed Arthur as High King, and also held the right to wield Arthur's sword Excalibur. He was eventually killed in battle fighting Modred. Gawain is the main character in the medieval English tale *Gawain and the Green Knight* and in some Celtic tales as a companion of Arthur, and may have originated either as a Celtic god (his strength was directly linked to solar energy, and he was at the height of his considerable strength at midday) or as a now forgotten Dark Ages warrior hero.

Geraint – Also known as **Gereint** or **Erec**. One of the Knights of the Round Table, and husband to the stunningly beautiful Enid, whose relationship with Geraint is the focus of a medieval romance. Geraint is not mentioned by Malory, but features in the Welsh tales of *The Mabinogion* and in Chrétien de Troyes' *Erec and Enide*. Both stories may have been drawn from an older, common source.

Gorlois – Gorlois was the Duke of Cornwall who rebelled against Uther Pendragon, and whose wife ultimately became the mother of Arthur. Gorlois' son and successor, Cador, was a great ally of Arthur in Geoffrey of Monmouth's *History*.

Griflet – Also known as **Girflet**. One of the Knights of the Round Table, who makes several cameo appearances in the tales of some of the major Arthurian characters without ever taking a starring role himself.

Grummore Grummursum – One of the Knights of the Round Table, from Scotland.

Guinevere – Also known as **Gwenhwyfar** and **Guinivere**. Arthur's beautiful wife and queen, described by Geoffrey of Monmouth as being of Roman blood and brought up by Cador of Cornwall. Later described as being the daughter of King Leodegrance, who gave Arthur the famous Round Table as a wedding present (the table had originally been given to Leodegrance by Uther Pendragon). Unusually for a female character in Arthurian legend (with the exception of the enchantresses), Guinevere comes across as a strong-headed woman with her own views; her adultery with Lancelot is the catalyst for the fall of Arthur's kingdom.

Gwrhyr Gwalstat – A knight of the Round Table, who mastered every language of the known world, as well as the speech of many animals. He plays a role in the tale of *Culhwch and Olwen*, adapted from an earlier Welsh story.

Harry le Fise Lake – One of the Knights of the Round Table, who fought against and was defeated by the evil knight Breunis Saunce Pité.

Idur – A young knight of Arthur's court, who killed three giants on the hill of Brent Knoll in Somerset.

Igraine – Also known as **Ygerna**. Mother of Arthur, who married Uther Pendragon after he made her pregnant with the aid of Merlin's magic; she was previously married to Gorlois, Duke of Cornwall, who was killed in battle against Uther's men.

Iseult – Also known as **Isolde**. The daughter of King Agwisance (or Anguish) of Ireland, who healed and fell in love with Tristan, but ultimately married his uncle (sometimes father) King Mark, setting the scene for one of medieval Europe's finest romantic tragedies.

Karados of Estrangor – Possibly the same knight as **Cador of Cornwall** or **King Carados of Scotland**. One of the Knights of the Round Table, who also served Uther before Arthur's rise to power.

Kay – Also known as **Cai** or **Cei**. One of the Knights of the Round Table, son of Ector and therefore adopted brother of Arthur. Kay became Arthur's Seneschal steward when his adopted brother was crowned; Kay is often portrayed as hot-headed, cynical and coarse, but he was essentially a good and loyal knight. Kay died fighting against Modred on Arthur's behalf. In the form of Cei, one of the earliest companions associated with Arthur in Celtic folklore.

King of the Hundred Knights – Also known as **Berrant le Apres**. One of the Knights of the Round Table, although originally opposed to Arthur's rule.

Kyndelig – A knight of the Round Table, who had never lost his way on a quest. For this reason, he accompanied Arthur in the story of Culhwch and Olwen, adapted from an earlier Welsh story.

Lamorak – One of the Knights of the Round Table, brother to Perceval and son of Pellinore. Closely linked to Tristan as a worthy opponent in jousts, Lamorak also fell in love with King Lot's wife Morgause. This love caused Lot's sons (with the exception of the more principled Gareth) to kill their mother and then Lamorak himself.

Lancelot – Also known as **Launcelot du Lake** or **Lancelot of the Lake**. Probably the most renowned of all the Knights of the Round Table, trained as a knight by the Lady of the Lake, and father to Galahad. The greatest fighter in Arthur's court, even surpassing Gawain, although he was also renowned as a lover. A series of maidens named Elaine, and of course Guinevere herself, were entranced with him. His relationship with Guinevere was exposed by the spiteful Modred and Agravaine, and this led to the downfall of Arthur's realm.

Lavaine – One of the Knights of the Round Table, and brother to Elaine of Astolat. He saved Lancelot's life by taking him to a hermit when Lancelot had been badly wounded, and sided with Lancelot against Arthur towards the end of Arthur's reign.

King Leodegrance – Also known as **Leodegarius**. Father of Guinevere, who was given the famous Round Table by Uther Pendragon. He later presented the table to Arthur as a wedding gift; Arthur had originally come to Leodegrance's aid against his enemy King Ryons, and met Guinevere when he arrived at Leodegrance's castle.

Lionel – One of the Knights of the Round Table, and nephew of Lancelot. Fought and lost to the evil Turquin, eventually being rescued by Lancelot.

Loholt – Arthur's son. In the Vulgate Cycle, Loholt slays a giant but in turn is killed by Kay, who wishes to take the credit for the giant's death.

King Lot – King of Lothian and Orkney. Father of Gareth, Gaheris, Agravaine and Gawain, and married to Arthur's half-sister Morgause. Lot opposed Arthur's right to rule, and eventually died at the hands of Pellinore; despite this his sons went on to be key members of Arthur's court.

Lucan the Butler – One of the Knights of the Round Table, and one of the earliest warriors to fight for Arthur. He held the honoured post of Butler at Camelot, remained loyal to Arthur throughout his reign, and fought for him at Camlann (some stories show Lucan to survive Camlann, along with his possible brother, Bedivere).

Lucius Hiberius – The Roman governor against whom Arthur fought in Europe, after the Romans demanded tribute from the British High King.

Marhaus – One of the Knights of the Round Table, an Irish knight. Unlike Gawain, Marhaus' power increased as the day wore on, and because of this, he managed to defeat Gawain in a friendly duel.

King Mark – King of Cornwall and uncle of Tristan, and generally an all round bad egg. Often associated with **King Cunomorus**, who is commemorated on the Dark Ages Tristan Stone in Cornwall.

Meleagant – Also known as **Meliagrant** and **Malagant**. One of the Knights of the Round Table, and kidnapper of Guinevere in the French Romance *The Knight of the Cart*; defeated by Lancelot who rescues the queen. Probably evolved from the Melwas of Welsh folklore, who kidnapped Arthur's wife in a pseudo-historical story.

Merlin – Counsellor and sometimes magician to the kings of Britain, including both Uther and his son Arthur. An able politician and seemingly the ultimate civil servant, Merlin was eventually prevented from aiding Arthur when ensnared by Nimue. Curiously, despite all of the good work he did, Merlin had the habit of appearing on the scene a little too late to really influence the action; his real prowess was with potions and political advice.

Modred – Also known as **Mordred** and **Medraut** (a Welsh variant). One of the Knights of the Round Table, although better known as Arthur's treacherous nephew (or, by the time of Malory's seminal work, Arthur's bastard son), who landed the fatal blow on Arthur.

Morgan le Fay – Also known as **Morgana** and **Morgan the Wise**. Mother of Ywaine and wife of Urien, and half-sister of Arthur, being born to his mother Igraine and her husband before Uther, Gorlois Duke of Cornwall. From humble and rather anonymous beginnings in Geoffrey of Monmouth's *History*, she became a malevolent magical enchantress who ensnared a series of knights in adulterous affairs, and an arch enemy of Arthur's.

Morgause – Arthur's other half-sister (Gorlois' other daughter), and voluptuous wife of King Lot of Orkney. She seduced Arthur through sorcery, and from this relationship was born Modred, according to the work of Malory.

Nimue – Also known as the **Lady of the Lake** and **Vivian**. The water-bound enchantress who aided Arthur by providing Excalibur and Lancelot for his cause, although she later blotted her copybook by enticing and ensnaring Merlin.

Olwen – Beautiful daughter of Ysbaddaden the Giant, who was courted by and eventually married Culhwch after he completed a series of near impossible tasks with the help of Arthur and his men.

Ozana le Cure Hardy – One of the Knights of the Round Table, who could have chosen his friends better – he is usually associated with the plots of King Mark and Modred.

Palomides – A Saracen knight who was a member of the Knights of the Round Table. When Pellinore died, he took up the hunt for the Questing Beast.

Patrise – One of the Knights of the Round Table, hailing from Ireland. He died when he ate a poisoned apple at a feast, intended for Gawain.

Pelleas – One of the Knights of the Round Table, and according to Malory, one of only six knights who could defeat Gawain. He fell in love with Nimue, and by the time of Modred's rebellion, she had taken him away to live underwater with her.

Pellinore – One of the Knights of the Round Table, father of Perceval, who was first introduced to Arthur during Pellinore's ongoing hunt of the supernatural Questing Beast; Pellinore believed himself to be the only man alive able to slay the beast. In a duel with Arthur, he broke the King's sword, thus leading to the acquisition of Excalibur; he then became a loyal follower of the High King.

Perceval – Also known as **Percevale** and **Parzifal**. One of the Knights of the Round Table, and a hero of the Grail Quest. Also son of Pellinore. Perceval led a sheltered early life as a country boy, but came into his own during the Grail Quest, where he saw the Grail procession at the Fisher King's castle. However, he failed to ask a vital question that would have allowed him to secure it for Arthur, and was present with Bors and Galahad at the end of the Quest.

Peredur – Geoffrey of Monmouth mentions Peredur as being present at Arthur's court in the City of the Legion, and he also features in medieval Welsh literature; later his name became synonymous with Perceval. Probably based on the historical Peredur, one of the last British kings of York in the sixth century AD, who died in 580.

Persant – One of the Knights of the Round Table, after being defeated by Gareth and summoned to serve Arthur. He also tested Gareth's chastity by ordering his own eighteen year old daughter into Gareth's bed; Gareth's chastity prevailed as the daughter returned untouched.

Pertolepe – One of the Knights of the Round Table, although this was also the name of the behead-able green warrior in *Gawain and the Green Knight*, who was otherwise known as **Bercilak**.

Sadok – One of the Knights of the Round Table, hailing from Cornwall. Originally served the cruel King Mark, but being a chivalrous knight, Sadok disobeyed orders in order to save a life, and joined Arthur's court instead.

Sagramore – One of the Knights of the Round Table. Frequently unhorsed in jousting by some of the greater knights around him, although he was said to suffer from a battle lust that powered him on in combat with almost superhuman strength.

Segwarides – One of the Knights of the Round Table, and brother to the Saracen Palomides.

Tor – One of the Knights of the Round Table, and illegitimate son of Pellinore. Tor had two complete adventures before being admitted to a seat at the Round Table; he also jousted with the Cornish Tristan, after being in a trio of knights indulging in jokes about Cornish knights. Eventually slain by Lancelot.

Tristan – Also known as **Tristram** and **Tristam**. One of the Knights of the Round Table, and nephew (sometimes son) of King Mark, hailing from Cornwall. The tragic love story of Tristan and Iseult evolved as a story in its own right before being absorbed into Arthurian legend, remembered as one of the classic romances of medieval literature. Probably the **Drustan** or **Drustanus** commemorated on the Tristan Stone in Cornwall, or perhaps a Pictish prince named **Drust**.

Turquin – One of the chief enemies of Arthur's knights. Not a nice chap, as he was forever entering into violent conflict against the good king's knights, including Lancelot, Lionel and Ector de Maris.

Ulfius – One of the Knights of the Round Table, previously having served Uther and introduced Merlin to aid Uther's union with Igraine. Ulfius served Arthur well in the early years of the High King's reign, but was probably an elderly man by this time and does not feature later in Arthur's reign.

Urbgennius of Bath – Geoffrey of Monmouth mentions him as one of the notable knights present at Arthur's court in the City of the Legion.

Urien of Gore – One of the Knights of the Round Table, although initially he was a rival to Arthur; father of Ywaine and husband to Morgan Le Fay. Urien and Morgan fell out after Morgan attempted to murder him, and Urien remained loyal to Arthur throughout his reign. Almost certainly named after Urien of Rheged, one of the greatest historical northern British kings, who successfully held back Saxon advances during the sixth century; he was assassinated by rival British warlords on the eve of a battle that would have pushed the Saxons from the shores of Britain.

Urre of Hungary – One of the Knights of the Round Table, who travelled widely in search of adventure and arrived in Britain to serve Arthur.

Was seriously wounded in a tournament, receiving seven near fatal wounds although he killed his opponent; his opponent's mother, an enchantress, cast a spell to ensure that Urre's wounds would never heal until touched by the greatest knight in the world. A number of Knights of the Round Table were approached, and Lancelot succeeded; Urre sided with Lancelot in the war against Arthur.

Uther Pendragon – Arthur's father and ruler of Britain before him. Uther was a great warrior, unifying the Britons and keeping the Saxons at bay. In some versions of the legend, Uther accomplished this by himself; in others, he was assisted by or following in the footsteps of his brothers and Merlin. Merlin also produced a potion for Uther, allowing him to sleep with Gorlois Duke of Cornwall's wife, thus begetting Arthur. The potion allowed Uther to take on the appearance of Gorlois.

Vadalon – One of the Knights of the Round Table, a brave but cruel man who gained a place at the Round Table when Lancelot and his supporters left Arthur.

Vortigern – Along with Modred, Vortigern is one of the arch villains of Arthurian legend, who entered into an alliance with the treacherous Saxons. He is possibly based upon a real-life ruler of post-Roman Britain of whom we now know nothing except legend.

Ysbaddaden – Chief of the Giants and father of Olwen, he terrorised the people who lived in his realm.

Ywaine – Also known as **Uwaine, Owain, Ivan** and **Owen**. One of the Knights of the Round Table, and son of Urien and Morgan Le Fay. A brave and adventurous knight, who rescued a lion from a dragon's attack, befriending the lion from that point onwards. Killed fighting for Arthur at Camlann. Probably based on the historical Owain, the real-life son of Urien of Rheged, who continued to resist Saxon invasion after his father's death.

Appendix B

Arthurian Sites in the UK

Reading about the historical and legendary feats of Arthur and his followers is a wonderful way to pass your time. What's even better, though, is getting up off your sofa and going to visit some of the places that Arthur's people actually lived in or built (both historical and legendary ones). Britain has a wonderful cultural and historic heritage, and we're lucky enough to still be able to visit so many of the important sites in Britain's history. This appendix highlights some of the most spectacular, important and picturesque places associated with the legend of Arthur and/or early medieval Britain. Good luck with some of the hills!

ENGLAND

Avon

Bath
Historical and legendary site

Bath is famous for two things: its beautifully preserved Roman baths, and the ongoing tradition that it may have been the site of the Battle of Badon (Arthur's greatest victory). Geoffrey of Monmouth suggested this, and modern researchers have often agreed with him, pointing out that the correct pronunciation of the British name 'Badon' is 'Bathon'. If this theory is correct, the most likely site for the battlefield is not in the city of Bath itself, but instead at the hillfort of Little Solsbury Hill (Badon, remember, is recorded as being a siege), a couple of miles to the north-east of the city.

Cheshire

Alderley Edge
Legendary site
You have to be quiet if you visit Alderley Edge – Arthur and his knights lie sleeping beneath you. When they are needed, a white horse will arrive to lead them into the present day. Apparently.

Chester
Historical site
Roman city of *Deva*, which may or may not have been the infamous City of the Legion described by Nennius as the site of one of Arthur's battles. Regardless of the truth behind this, a battle between the Britons and Saxons certainly took place here around 616, which resulted in the wholesale defeat of the Britons.

Cornwall

Arthur's Bed
Legendary site
A large stone with a hollowed out centre, one of several such geological oddities connected to Arthur by name. No known connection exists.

Camelford
Legendary site
This village is one of the sites put forward as a possible site of Camelot, although there is, in reality, little to recommend the site beyond the slight name similarity and the fact that the village is in Arthur's traditional homelands of the South-West.

Castle Dore
Historical and legendary site
A hillfort usually identified as the seat of power of Cunomorus, often claimed to be the King Mark of Cornwall of Arthurian legend. Previously occupied before the Romans arrived, it was reoccupied at some point between the fifth and eighth centuries, when a new timber hall was constructed.

Chun Castle
Historical site
A reused Iron Age ring fort, occupied once more in the sixth century, consisting of two concentric dry-stone walls, which apparently still stood to a height of fifteen feet in the seventeenth century. Also looks great from the air, should you be so lucky as to take a flight route over it.

Dozmary Pool
Legendary site
One of the most atmospheric Arthurian locations, the bleak Dozmary Pool has frequently been named as the lake into which Bedivere threw Excalibur after the Battle of Camlann.

Killibury
Legendary site
Killibury is an Iron Age hillfort that is mentioned in Welsh folklore as a court of Arthur's. It is often the location from which Modred was said to have abducted Guinevere.

Merlin's Rock
Legendary site
This prominent rock sits close to the shoreline by the beautifully named village of Mousehole. When a few Spanish ships anchored at the site in 1595 and proceeded to raise Mousehole to the ground, the site had no Arthurian connection, so it is a rather late entry into Arthurian folklore.

Slaughter Bridge
Legendary site
Famously situated close to Camelford, Slaughter Bridge is a traditional location for the Battle of Camlann, where both Arthur and Modred fell. It was identified as such by Geoffrey of Monmouth, and although a ninth century battle was fought between the Cornish Britons and the Anglo-Saxons, there is little reason to believe that Geoffrey's identification is correct. Nevertheless, it is an important site in Arthurian folklore.

Tintagel Castle
Historical and legendary site
Tintagel's setting is perhaps the most romantic of all Arthurian locations. Geoffrey of Monmouth identified the castle on this rocky outcrop as the birthplace of Arthur, and former seat of Gorlois, Duke of Cornwall. Today, the shell of a thirteenth century castle occupies the site, but beneath this, traces of a Dark Ages settlement with trading links to the continent have been found. Among Tintagel's attractions are a tenth century church, Arthur's footprint (in a rock – possibly used in an early rite of kingship), and the view from the site itself. Below the cliffs of Tintagel is Merlin's Cave, a naturally formed site for which the Merlin connection can only be traced back to the nineteenth century. In recent

years, the discovery of an inscription carrying the name 'Artognou' has hit the Arthur-related headlines.

The Tristan Stone
Historical and legendary site
This seventh century inscribed stone once stood near to Castle Dore, but was moved to sit on the Fowey–Lostwithiel road. It carries an inscription to Drustan, son of Cunomorus (often identified as Tristan and Mark in Arthurian legend). Regardless of the possible Arthurian connection, the Tristan Stone is a worthy historical monument in its own right.

Cumbria

Arthuret
Historical and legendary site
Presumed site of the Dark Ages Battle of Arderydd, which is recorded as causing the madness of Myddrin, the historical forerunner to Merlin.

Carlisle
Historical and legendary site
Carlisle was one of the principal courts of Arthur in literature, and Malory made it the place where Guinevere was sentenced to death after her affair became known to Arthur. Carlisle was a Roman town, strategically situated at the western end of Hadrian's Wall, and British occupation continued into the post-Roman period, when the town was probably the most important in Rheged. St Cuthbert visited the town in the seventh century, and apparently saw a working fountain – suggesting that the aqueduct was still in operation, which in turn suggested a continuing post-Roman history of the town.

Hadrian's Wall – *see separate entry under Northumbria*

Pendragon Castle
Legendary site
Pendragon Castle is of Norman construction, although local tradition claims that it sits on the site of a fort built by Arthur's father, Uther Pendragon. Uther apparently attempted to divert the River Eden to create a moat for his fort, but this was unsuccessful.

Dorset

Badbury Rings
Legendary site
A candidate for the site of the Battle of Badon; a pre-Roman hillfort, the ramparts of which still survive, was later replaced with a Roman military station, and it may well have had a continued military presence in the Arthurian era.

East Sussex

Pevensey
Historical site
A beautiful site to visit, Pevensey Castle was a Roman shore fort named *Anderida*, which the Saxons Aelle and Cissa stormed in 491, killing all of the Britons within it. Later associated with William I and the Norman landings in 1066.

Hampshire

Portchester
Historical site
This Roman shore fort is often identified as the Llongborth of Dark Ages British poetry, and today is one of the most impressive Dark Ages sites to be found in the British Isles, if not the whole of Europe.

Silchester
Historical and legendary site
Geoffrey of Monmouth recorded that the old Roman city of Silchester – *Calleva Atrebatum* – was the site of Arthur's coronation. Of equal interest, Silchester is one of two large Romano-British cities that never grew into modern cities (Wroxeter being the other), and excavations have uncovered the foundations of the town, including the city walls. The city appears to have continued to be occupied into the fifth and sixth centuries.

Winchester
Historical and legendary site
King Arthur's Round Table may still be seen hanging in the Great Hall

of the city once popularly imagined to have been the real-life Camelot. Sadly, the Round Table is several hundred years too young to have coincided with a real-life Arthur. The city is, however, full of history and well worth visiting, and the Round Table mentioned in Chapter Six is very impressive to see up close (not that close, though, as it hangs high on a wall).

Herefordshire

Arthur's Stone
Legendary site
This prehistoric burial chamber has a chequered history in Arthurian legend, variously named as the burial site of Arthur, the burial site of a rival king slain by Arthur, and the burial site of a giant slain by Arthur.

Kent

Barham Down
Legendary site
Geoffrey of Monmouth claimed that Modred and Arthur fought a prelude to the fateful Battle of Camlann here, although there is no surviving historical documentation to support this theory.

Dover
Legendary site
According to Thomas Malory, Arthur's men fought against Modred at Dover, in a prelude to the Battle of Camlann. The castle – a brilliant site which encapsulates two thousand years of British history – contains an 'Arthur's Hall', although there are no other traditions linking Arthur to the castle. Despite this, anyone with an interest in Britain's history, from the Iron Age to the Nuclear Age, should make time to visit Dover Castle.

North Yorkshire

Catterick
Historical site
Catterick, a modern garrison town, may well have been the site where the three hundred warriors immortalised in the British poem *The Gododdin* rode to their deaths against their Saxon enemies. It is a likely site of the Catraeth named in the poem, not least for the similarity in name, but also for its strategically important position in northern England.

York

Historical and legendary site

York was an important city in later Roman Britain, named *Eboracum*, and its importance appears to have continued into the Dark Ages, well before the Vikings arrived and renamed it Jorvik. Parts of the Roman walls may still be seen today. As an important medieval English city York was worked into Arthurian legend, although at an earlier date one of the city's last British kings, Peredur, became entangled in Arthurian legend as Perceval.

Northumbria

Bamburgh Castle

Historical and legendary site

On a dramatic outcrop of volcanic rock, Bamburgh Castle looks out over sand dunes to the North Sea. Before the medieval castle was built, the rock of Bamburgh was occupied by a British and then Saxon fortification, becoming the ancestral home of the kings of Anglo-Saxon Northumbria. The British name for Bamburgh may have been 'Din Guyrdi', which may be identified with Lancelot's castle and burial place: Joyous Gard. Thomas Malory instead identified Alnwick, which is close by, as Lancelot's burial place.

Hadrian's Wall

Historical and legendary site

Arthurian sites along Hadrian's Wall include: Castlesteads (*Camboglanna* – a possible site for Arthur's final battle, Camlann); High Rochester (*Bremenium*, a Roman fort identified as a possible site for one of Nennius' Arthurian battles); and Sewingshields Crags (the location of a cave where Arthur is said to lie in sleep, awaiting his call to rescue Britain in times of danger).

Yeavering

Historical site

The site of a seventh century Saxon Northumbrian royal centre, possibly replacing an earlier British centre at the same site. Although no longer to be seen, a great hall and an unusual 'grandstand' construction have been excavated at the site; the use of the 'grandstand' has been suggested as a gathering point for the nobles to listen to their king, or perhaps a viewing platform used for early Christian conversions. The site may have been burned down by Cadwallon of Gwynedd in the 630s before a later rebuilding programme took place.

Shropshire

Wroxeter
Historical site
Some of the remains of the Roman city of *Viroconium* are still visible today. Unprecedented rebuilding took place in the fifth century, and the city has been suggested as a possible administrative centre of Vortigern's and later Arthur's reign.

Somerset

Brent Knoll
Historical and legendary site
Brent Knoll was a hillfort, and may well have been an island in the Dark Ages, as it is close to the Bristol Channel and on the Somerset Levels. In Arthurian legend, Brent Knoll was the site where Idur killed three giants.

Chalice Well
Legendary site
Sited over a spring that ran from Chalice Hill to Glastonbury Tor, this well may well have been mentioned in medieval literature as being visited by Lancelot, and has been put forward as the final resting place of the Holy Grail.

Glastonbury
Legendary site
Glastonbury is alleged to have been Arthur's burial place in the medieval period; it is also connected to the story of the Holy Grail and Joseph of Arimathea.

South Cadbury
Historical and legendary site
Although the hillfort at South Cadbury is a site from the historical period of Arthur, it is perhaps most famous as the legendary 'Camelot'. So

many people have written so much about 'Cadbury/Camelot', but although it is certainly a huge fortification for this period of history, and was certainly refortified for use (presumably by the Britons for protection against the Saxons, and then by the Anglo-Saxons themselves at a later date), there is little solid evidence to link the site to Arthurian legend before the sixteenth century. Leslie Alcock played up the Arthurian connection in his excavations from 1966–1970, and he discovered a large timber hall, a gatehouse possibly styled on late Roman models, and indications of a dry-stone wall around the perimeter, all from the 'Arthurian period'.

Suffolk

Sutton Hoo
Historical site
One of the most famous images associated with British history is the face-masked Sutton Hoo helmet, found at this site close to Woodbridge. Sutton Hoo was an important Anglo-Saxon burial ground, and to this day, the remains of several impressive burial mounds may still be seen.

West Sussex

Chichester
Historical site
Chichester was once the important Roman city of *Noviomagus*, and sections of the city walls may still be seen today.

Wiltshire

Amesbury
Legendary site
Named by Geoffrey of Monmouth as the location of the treacherous Night of the Long Knives. Malory recorded that Guinivere lived in the abbey after the Battle of Camlann.

Liddington Castle
Historical site
Liddington castle is an old hillfort, suggested by some modern commentators to be a likely site for the Battle of Badon.

Merlin's Mound
Legendary site
This prehistoric burial mound stands in the grounds of Marlborough College; it has been suggested that Marlborough may have been a corruption of the name Merlin.

Stonehenge
Legendary site
Perhaps the most famous monument in Britain, it is only natural that Stonehenge is related to Britain's most famous legend in some way. Merlin supposedly erected the stones as a monument to British leaders slain by the Saxons in the Night of the Long Knives. Stonehenge actually dates back to several building phases from 2900–1650 BC.

SCOTLAND

Borders

Eildon Hills
Legendary site
The rounded hilltops of Eildon rise up to dominate the borderland around Melrose. Arthur and his knights apparently lie asleep under the hills, waiting to rescue the British people in their hour of need; other folk tales abound, mostly relating to fairies. Alistair Moffat identifies the area around Melrose and these hills as a possible site for the historical Arthur in his 1999 book *Arthur and the Lost Kingdoms*.

Edinburgh

Arthur's Seat
Historical site
A steep volcanic rock dominating Edinburgh's city centre, Arthur's Seat (a name first mentioned in the fifteenth century) was a fortified site in the Dark Ages period, and may well have been the court of the warriors mentioned in the poem *The Gododdin*. The modern site of Edinburgh Castle sits over another fortified site from this period. Edinburgh may also have been the site of Nennius' Mount Agned, one of Arthur's famous victories.

Orkneys

Orkney Islands
Legendary site
The Orkneys carry a strong link to Arthurian legends of the medieval periods, being the homelands of King Lot and his famous sons – Gawain, Gareth, Gaheris and Agravaine. No serious connection to Dark Ages British culture can be made, but the islands still carry strong Norse connections.

Stirlingshire

Arthur's O'en (Oven)
Legendary site
The back garden of 40 Adam Crescent, a terraced house in Stenhousemuir, near Falkirk, has been identified as Arthur's Round Table by Archie McKerracher, a Scottish historian. This precise location is not a widely held belief, and we cannot be certain of the date that the site became known as Arthur's O'en.

Strathclyde

Ben Arthur
Legendary site
A mountain named after Arthur in the southern Highlands. No known connection exists.

Dumbarton Rock
Historical and legendary site
Referred to as 'Arthur's Castle' in a fourteenth century manuscript, and also remembered as the legendary birthplace of Modred. Known to the Britons as *Alcluith*, excavations have revealed Dark Ages fortifications on this craggy administrative centre of the Kingdom of Strathclyde. Similar sounding 'Dun Barton' means 'Fort of the Britons'.

Loch Lomond
Legendary site
This beautiful loch was identified as the site of one of Arthur's early victories by the medieval writer Geoffrey of Monmouth; here the King besieged his enemies on the islands in the loch.

WALES

Anglesey

Arthur's Quoit
Legendary site
This name has been given to several prehistoric Welsh stone assemblages, usually burial chambers. Others are located in Caernarvonshire, Pembrokeshire, Carmarthenshire and Merioneth. No known connection beyond the name has been established at any of these sites.

Clwyd

Moel Arthur
Legendary site
'Arthur's Hill' is a pre-Roman hillfort, with no known Arthurian connection beyond his memory in its name.

Pillar of Eliseg
Historical site
The Pillar is an inscribed stone, although now badly eroded. It carried a ninth century inscription explaining that it was a memorial to Prince Eliseg, and claimed that he was a descendant of Vortigern.

Denbighshire

Craig Arthur
Legendary site
'Arthur's Rock' is situated at the end of a craggy North Welsh ridge, close to Dinas Bran. No relationship to Arthur has been proved.

Dinas Bran
Legendary site
A stunningly sited medieval Welsh castle sometimes identified as the Grail Castle of Arthurian legend.

Dyfed

Cardigan
Legendary site
Some medieval romances recorded that Arthur held court at Cardigan.

Carmarthen
Legendary site
Noted by Geoffrey of Monmouth as Merlin's birth place, and theoretically named after him (Kaermerdin – 'Fort of Merlin').

Merlin's Chair
Legendary site
Close to Carmarthen is Merlin's Hill, which is peaked by a summit known as Merlin's Chair. Local folklore remembers that Merlin is sleeping under the hill.

Pen Arthur
Legendary site
A Welsh folk tale records Arthur throwing a boulder from the top of this hill into the River Sawdde a mile away. Some commentators have suggested that Pen Arthur is also the site where Arthur and his men fought the great boar Twrch Trwyth in *Culhwch and Olwen*.

Gwent

Caerleon
Historical and legendary site
Caerleon was, in the Roman period, the fortress of the Second Legion, and is perhaps the site intended by Nennius as the 'City of the Legion', where Arthur won a great victory (the other very strong candidate for the site of this battle is Chester). Caerleon was traditionally one of Arthur's courts in Welsh folklore, and the remains of the Roman amphitheatre became known as Arthur's Round Table; there is some possibility that the story of the Round Table is culled from half-remembered memories of such a site. Geoffrey of Monmouth also identified Caerleon as a court of Arthur's.

APPENDIX B: ARTHURIAN SITES IN THE UK

Gwynedd

Bardsley Island
Legendary site
According to some legends, Merlin lives to this day on Bardsley Island, located just off the tip of the Lleyn Peninsula.

Caer Gai
Historical and legendary site
A pre-Roman hillfort that also held a Roman garrison during the years of the Empire; ramparts are still visible. The name translates as 'Fort of Cai', which is a reference to one of Arthur's earliest companions, Kay.

Carn March Arthur
Legendary site
Situtated on this hill is a stone bearing what is claimed to be the hoof-print of Arthur's horse; no other connection to Arthur is known at this site.

Dinas Emrys
Historical and legendary site
This bleak crag in North Wales was once the fortified home of a high status Dark Ages Welsh noble. In Arthurian tradition, it is remembered as the site of Vortigern's ill-fated castle, under which Ambrosius (or Merlin) reveals two fighting dragons, which represent the Britons and their Saxon enemies.

Powys

Montgomery
Legendary site
The castle that dramatically overlooks the town, dating to 1223, was described by Chrétien de Troyes as his idea of Camelot. Coupled with this, the north gate of the town walls was known as Arthur's Gate, and the main street in the modern town retains the name Arthur's Street, suggesting that medieval tradition may have linked Montgomery more strongly with Arthurian legend than we now remember.

West Glamorgan

Arthur's Stone
Legendary site
A prehistoric chamber close to Reynoldston, legend remembers the large capstone as a pebble thrown from the shoe of a giant-sized Arthur, from a distance of seven miles away.

Appendix C

The Arthurian Bestiary

One element of Arthurian legend that can capture a reader's imagination is the fantastical and varied number of beasts that oppose Arthur and his knights at the most inconvenient moments, or that appear to give flavour to a story. This appendix features some of the greatest beasts of fantasy literature, along with some unusual views from the Celtic and medieval periods about some more everyday animals, which now seem outlandishly elaborate.

Badgers
Gerald of Wales noted that badgers would use each other as slaves and as earth carriers when building a new set, dragging the spoil-carrying slave out of the excavation on its back to empty the excess spoil away. Anyone who saw this, Gerald exclaimed, was astonished.

Beavers
Gerald of Wales, amongst others, claimed that the testicles of the beaver made a very powerful medicine. When closed in on by hunters, the beaver would apparently castrate itself and fling the testicles towards the hunters, thus allowing the beaver to escape with its life. Gerald, writing in the twelfth century, also noted that beavers would use others of their kind as slaves when building a new dam.

Cranes
Due to its secretive nature and trance-like way of resting, the crane was considered by the Celts to be a magical creature from the Otherworld.

Dragons
Also referred to, in varying guises, as **Serpents**, **Wyrms**, and **Wyverns**. Although fairly frequent in British folk tales, dragons and other serpents were relatively rare in Arthurian legend. Ywaine defeated one such monster when it was about to kill a lion, and various other tales included knights ridding regions of similar creatures, but giants and dwarves seem to have been more popular mythical creatures in medieval tales. Dragons only seem

to become popular in post-medieval British folk tales; nevertheless, if a Knight of the Round Table did come across such a reptilian creature, he knew he would be in for a tough fight.

Dwarves

Dwarves pop up all over the place in Arthurian legend, mostly as servants, and sometimes as the squire of a knight. Dwarves often show cunning, and quite a strong bond could be formed between master and dwarf (as in the case of Gareth, who forced an apology to his dwarf from a wayward, violent knight). Female dwarves could become lovers of knights, as shown in the Vulgate Cycle; male dwarves, if serving in the role of a squire, do not appear to have been expected to fight. Arthurian dwarves have little in common with the magical dwarf folk skilled with metalwork who lived underground, as portrayed in Scandinavian and Germanic sagas and Tolkien's work.

Faeries

Sometimes appearing as elegant and occasionally cruel elves, at other times as 'Little Folk' in woodlands, faeries appear in some Arthurian legend, and in British folklore in general. Renowned for their healing powers, and for the way in which time passes very quickly or slowly when in their company, faerie knights also existed, with magical powers, enchanted weapons, and gleaming armour.

Giants

Traditional British folklore suggests that giants ruled the island before Brutus arrived and forced them out to live in the hills, swamps and wastelands. Their size could vary greatly – some were not much larger than a well-built human, yet others were considerably bigger: one giant of Arthurian legend managed to split a female victim in two during intercourse. Giants were generally clothed in roughly hewn hides and furs, carried clubs, and were extremely aggressive towards humans, especially women. Giants are also often portrayed as cannibalistic; they are often slow witted and clumsy, vulnerable to attack by a quick thinking, fast talking, or dextrous knight. In the tale of *Culhwch and Olwen*, Olwen's father was described as the Chief of the Giants, suggesting a form of social hierarchy hitherto unexamined.

Griffin

The Griffin had the back half of a lion and the wings, head and fore-body of an eagle. Very large and partial to horse flesh, the Griffin lived in mountainous regions and was a thorn in the side of questing knights.

Hedgehogs

Not content simply with rolling on their backs to steal apples from orchards on their spines, Geoffrey of Monmouth recited that one such apple-loaded hedgehog would rebuild Winchester. Birds would flock to the town, attracted by the smell of apples, and the hedgehog would add a huge palace and a city wall with 600 towers, and then tunnel under the city. This, according to the prophecy, would make London envious. It's a funny old world.

Lions

Perhaps surprisingly, the lion appears several times in Arthurian legend, not least the lion which befriends Ywaine. Perceval aids another lion during the Grail Quest, four of them escort a magical swan in a procession, and a pair of lions live in the Tomb of the Lions. Beyond their strength and loyalty, no other symbolic prowess is emphasised. Panthers and lynxes appear occasionally in Arthurian legend, and the Cat of Palug, mentioned in early Celtic Arthurian tales as being slain on Anglesey by Kay, may well have been one of these.

The Questing Beast

A creature specific to Arthurian legend, hunted first by Pellinore and then by Palomides, the beast's true name was Galtisant. Galtisant had the head of a serpent, the body of a leopard, hind legs like a lion and feet like a hart. The sound of thirty hunting hounds echoed from its belly except for when the beast drank. Galtisant was never recorded as doing any evil to man or beast, and it appears that the hunt for the beast was purely a ritual, undertaken for the thrill of the hunt, rather than any desire to slay it. Nevertheless, Galtisant was never captured.

Ravens

One of the earliest mentions of Arthur connects him with this bird; at a battle featured in the poem *The Gododdin*, a warrior named Gwawrddur 'gluts the ravens', although he does not do so as well as Arthur would have. Glutting – or feeding – ravens was a poetic term for slaying one's enemies on the battlefield. The stench and carnage of a recently fought over battlefield would have seen ravens and other scavenger birds in their element, with the carcasses of the dead to feed on. As such, the raven was associated with death and slaughter; the Celtic deity Bran may have originated as a raven-like god.

Swans

A medieval commentator observed that swans, through their act of singing when at death's door, taught Man that the troubles of death should not concern us. Irish legend has several examples of deities who could turn themselves into swans.

Unicorns

Unicorns looked like elegant white horses, with a straight horn projecting from the centre of the head. A symbol of purity, and unusual among magical beasts for being good-natured and shy (almost every other mythical creature, you will notice, wished to kill humans). Although usually avoiding humans, a unicorn could be attracted by a female virgin, whose sense of purity could entrance the unicorn; the horn and body parts of a unicorn were sought after by alchemists and magicians, as they contained strong magical powers.

Appendix D

A Guide to Welsh Pronunciation

Once you've mastered the system below, you should be able to pronounce the Welsh names you come across in Arthurian legend. Good luck!

Consonants

Most letters are pronounced in the same way in Welsh as they would be in English; however, there are a few exceptions to this rule:

c	always the **k** sound as in *cull* or *kill*, never *s* as in *city*
ch	always as the **ch** in the Scottish *loch*, never as in *stock* or *church*
dd	always sounds like the **th** in *breathe* or *this*
f	always the **v** sound as in *venison* and *of*
ff	has the same sound as **ph** and as in the English *off*, never the *v* sound
g	always hard as in *get*, never soft as in *gentle*
ll	made by producing an **l**, but breathing out both sides of the tongue
ng	has the sound of the English **ng** in *singing*, though in a few exceptions the **ng** is pronounced **ng** + **g** as in the English *finger*
r	this is trilled like a strong Scottish **r** or as in Spanish
s	same sound as the **ss** in *moss* or the **s** in *sill*, never the **z** sound as in *hose*
th	has the same sound as the **th** in *thin*, never as the **th** in *the*

Vowels

There are more vowels in the Welsh language than in English. They are of the kind often known as pure vowels, being more akin to those found in Spanish or Italian.

a	short	as in **a**pple
	long	as in **ra**ther
e	short	as in **e**gg
i	short	as in p**i**n
	long	as in mach**i**ne
o	short	as in n**o**t (not as in note)
u		as the first **y** in m**y**stery
w	short	as the **oo** in sh**oo**k
	long	as the **oo** in m**oo**
y		In monosyllables and in the final syllable of a word, it has the same sound as **u** (see above). In other positions, it has the same sound as both the **u** and the **e** in **u**nd**e**r.

Emphasis

In Welsh, words are usually stressed on the penultimate syllable; where the stress falls on the last syllable, a hyphen is usually inserted. There are some exceptions where established names and places with emphasis on the last syllable are written without the hyphen.

Bibliography

The Arthurian Reader

Where to go from here? Attempting to encompass 1,500 years of literary development and historical studies into a book of this size would be truly impossible. Instead, here follows a list of the books I've found most useful or most enjoyable in my own exploration of the world of Arthur. The level of scholarship and accuracy in each of the books varies greatly, and there are many other books on Arthur out there, but these are the ones I've found I keep returning to time after time. Several books exist in various editions and have been produced by various publishers, so the edition dates given here are not set in stone.

Early Arthurian texts

Barron, W R J and Weinberg, S C (eds.), *Layamon's Arthur: The Arthurian Section of Layamon's Brut*, 1989.

Bede, *A History of the English Church and People* (trans. Sherley-Price, L), 1955.

Bromwich, R, *The Welsh Triads/Trioedd Ynys Prydein*, 1978.

Bryant, N (trans.), *Merlin and the Grail: Joseph of Arimathea, Merlin, Perceval – The Trilogy of Arthurian Romances Attributed to Robert de Boron*, 2001.

Burns, J E, *Arthurian Fictions: Reading the Vulgate Cycle*, 1986.

Chrétien de Troyes, *The Complete Romances of Chrétien de Troyes* (trans. Staines, D), 1990.

Chrétien de Troyes, *Arthurian Romances* (trans. Owen, D D R), 1987.

Coe, J B and Young, S, *The Celtic Sources for the Arthurian Legend*, 1995.

Geoffrey of Monmouth, *The History of the Kings of Britain/Historia Regnum Britanniae* (trans. Thorpe, L), 1966.

Gerald of Wales, *The Journey Through Wales and the Description of Wales* (trans. Thorpe, L), 1978.

Guest, C E (trans.), *The Mabinogion*, 1906 (reprinted 1997).

Layamon, *Brut* (trans. Allen, R), 1992.

Lofmark, C, *Bards and Heroes*, 1989.

Malory, T, *The Death of Arthur/Le Morte d'Arthur* (ed. Cowen, J), 1969.

Marsden, J, *Northanhymbre Saga: The History of the Anglo-Saxon Kings of Northumbria*, 1995.

Padel, O J, *Arthur in Medieval Welsh Literature*, 2000.

Pennar, M, *Taliesin Poems*, 1988.

Short, S (trans.), *Aneirin: The Gododdin*, 1994.

Sommer, H O, *The Vulgate Version of the Arthurian Romances*, eight volumes, 1909–1916.

Stone, B (trans.), *Sir Gawain and the Green Knight*, 1959.

Wace, *Roman de Brut, A History of the British* (trans. Weiss, J), 1999.
Webb, J F, *Lives of the Saints*, 1965.

Arthurian legend
Ashe, G (ed.), *The Quest for Arthur's Britain*, 1968.
Ashe, G, *Mythology of the British Isles*, 1990.
Barber, R, *King Arthur: Hero and Legend*, 1993.
Barber, R, *Myths and Legends of the British Isles,* 1999.
Barron, W R J (ed.), *The Arthur of the English*, 1999.
Beardsley, A, *Beardsley's Le Morte Darthur: Selected Illustrations*, this edition 2001.
Brimacombe, P, *Knights of the Round Table*, 1997.
Bronwich, R, *The Arthur of the Welsh*, 1991.
Cruse, A, *The Golden Road in English Literature*, 1931.
Davis, C, *Celtic Beasts: Animal Motifs and Zoomorphic Design in Celtic Art*, 1999.
Doel, F, Doel, G and Lloyd, T, *Worlds of Arthur: King Arthur in History, Legend and Culture*, 2000.
Ebbutt, M I, *British Myths and Legends*, facsimile edition 1994.
Evans, A, *Brassey's Guide to War Films*, 2000.
Hamilton, C, *Arthurian Tradition: A Beginner's Guide*, 2000.
Johnson, C and Lung, E, *Arthur: The Legend Unveiled*, 1995.
Jones, R, *Myths and Legends of Britain and Ireland*, 2003.
Karr, P A, *The Arthurian Companion*, 2001.
Mancoff, D N, *The Return of King Arthur: The Legend Through Victorian Eyes*, 1995.
Matthews, J, *King Arthur and the Grail Quest,* 1994.
Matthews, J, *The Unknown Arthur: Forgotten Tales of the Round Table,* 1995.
Mersey, D, *Legendary Warriors: Great Heroes in Myth and Reality*, 2002.
Ousby, I, *The Cambridge Guide to Literature in English*, 1993.
Parker, M St J, *King Arthur*, 1995.
Rhys, J, *Celtic Folklore*, two volumes, 1901.
Rolleston, T W, *Celtic Myths and Legends*, facsimile edition 1994.
Saul, N, *The Batsford Companion to Medieval England*, 1983.
Snell, F J, *King Arthur's Country*, 1926.
Snyder, C, *Exploring the World of King Arthur*, 2000.
Stafford, G, *King Arthur Pendragon*, 1999.
Tolkien, J R R, *Finn and Hengest: The Fragment and the Episode* (ed. Bliss, A), 1998.

Arthurian fiction
Berger, T, *Arthur Rex*, 1978.
Bradley, M, *The Mists of Avalon*, 1982.
Bulfinch, T, *The Age of Chivalry*, 1997 (originally published in 1858).
Chant, J, *The High Kings*, 1984.
Cooke, B K, *The Quest of the Beast*, 1957.
Cornwell, B, *The Winter King*, 1995.
Cornwell, B, *Enemy of God*, 1997.
Cornwell, B, *Excalibur*, 1997.

BIBLIOGRAPHY

Cutler, U W, *Stories of King Arthur and his Knights*, 1905.

Frankland, E, *Arthur: The Bear of Britain*, 1944.

Green, R L, *King Arthur and His Knights of the Round Table*, 1953.

Guerber, H A, *Myths and Legends of the Middle Ages*, 1919.

Hulpach, V, *King Arthur: Stories of the Knights of the Round Table*, 1989.

Karr, P A, *The Idylls of the Queen*, 1982.

Lang, A (ed.), *Tales from King Arthur*, this edition 1993.

Matthews, J and Matthews, C, *The Arthurian Book Of Days,* 1990.

McSpadden, J W, *Stories from Wagner*, 1905.

Ousby, I (ed.), *The Wordsworth Companion to Literature in English*, 1992.

Riordan, J, *Tales of King Arthur*, 1982.

Robinson, E A, *Merlin*, 1917.

Robinson, E A, *Lancelot*, 1920.

Robinson, E A, *Tristram*, 1927.

Steinbeck, J, *The Acts of King Arthur and His Noble Knights*, this edition 1979.

Stewart, M, *The Crystal Cave*, 1970.

Stewart, M, *The Hollow Hills*, 1973.

Stewart, M, *The Last Enchantment*, 1979.

Stewart, M, *The Wicked Day*, 1984.

Stobart, J C, *The Tennyson Epoch*, 1907.

Sutcliff, R, *The Lantern Bearers*, 1959.

Sutcliff, R, *Dawn Wind*, 1961.

Sutcliff, R, *Sword at Sunset*, 1963.

Tennyson, A, *Idylls of the King*, 1961 (originally published in 1888).

Tennyson, A, *The Holy Grail* (introduction by Macaulay, G C), 1908.

Twain, M, *A Connecticut Yankee at King Arthur's Court*, this edition 1971.

White, T H, *The Sword in the Stone*, 1938.

White, T H, *The Queen of Air and Darkness*, 1939.

White, T H, *The Ill-Made Knight*, 1940.

White, T H, *The Once and Future King*, 1958.

White, T H, *The Book of Merlyn*, 1977.

Wilkinson, D, *The Legend of Arthur King*, 2003.

Arthurian history

Alcock, L, *Arthur's Britain: History and Archaeology AD 367–634*, 1971 and 1989.

Alcock, L, *By South Cadbury, is that Camelot… Excavations at Cadbury Castle 1966–70*, 1972.

Anderson, R, *The Violent Kingdom*, 1989.

Bidwell, P, *Roman Forts in Britain*, 1997.

Brett, V, *Winchester*, 1999.

Campbell, E, *Saints and Sea-kings: The First Kingdom of the Scots*, 1999.

Carver, M (ed.), *The Age of Sutton Hoo*, 1992.

Carver, M, *Sutton Hoo: Burial Ground of Kings?*, 1998.

Dark, K, *Civitas to Kingdom*, 1994.

Dark, K and Dark, P, *The Landscape of Roman Britain*, 1997.

Dixon, K R and Southern, P, *The Roman Cavalry*, 1992.

Elliot-Wright, P J C, *Living History*, 2000.

Evans, S S, *Lords of Battle: Image and Reality of The Comitatus in Dark-Age Britain*, 1997.

Foster, S M, *Picts, Gaels and Scots*, 1996.

Frere, S, *Britannia: A History of Roman Britain*, 1967.

Gater, D, *The Battle of Wales*, 1991.

Halsall, G, *Early Medieval Cemeteries*, 1995.

Halsall, G, *Warfare and Society in the Barbarian West 450–900*, 2003.

Harrison, M, *Anglo-Saxon Thegn 449–1066 AD*, 1993.

Heath, I, *Armies of the Dark Ages, 600–1066 AD*, 1980.

Ireland, S, *Roman Britain: A Sourcebook*, 1986.

Johnson, S, *Hadrian's Wall*, 1989.

Lowe, C, *Angels, Fools and Tyrants: Britons and Anglo-Saxons in Southern Scotland*, 1999.

MacDowall, S, *Late Roman Infantryman 236–565 AD*, 1993.

MacDowall, S, *Late Roman Cavalryman 236–565 AD*, 1995.

Maund, K, *The Welsh Kings: The Medieval Rulers of Wales*, 2000.

Mersey, D, *Glutter Of Ravens: Warfare in the Age of Arthur*, 1998.

Millett, M, *Roman Britain*, 1995.

Morgan, K O (ed.), *The Oxford Popular History of Britain*, 1993.

Morris, J, *The Age of Arthur: A History of the British Isles from 350 to 650*, 1973.

Myres, J N L, *The English Settlements*, 1986.

Newark, T and McBride, A, *Ancient Celts*, 1997.

Nicolle, D, *Arthur and the Anglo-Saxon Wars*, 1984.

Nicolle, D, *Medieval Warfare Source Book Volume I: Warfare in Western Christendom*, 1995.

Ottaway, P, *Archaeology in British Towns*, 1992.

Palgrave, F, *History of the Anglo-Saxons*, 1876.

Piggott, S, *Ancient Britons and the Antiquarian Imagination: Ideas from the Renaissance to the Regency*, 1989.

Pollington, S, *The English Warrior from earliest times to 1066*, 1996.

Radford, C A R and Swanton, M J, *Arthurian Sites in the West*, 2002.

Rahtz, P and Watts, L, *Glastonbury: Myth and Archaeology*, 2003.

Richards, J, *Stonehenge*, 1991.

Savage, A (trans.), *The Anglo-Saxon Chronicles*, 1997.

Shadrake, D and Shadrake, S, *Barbarian Warriors: Saxons, Vikings, Normans*, 2000.

Snowden, K, *Great Battles in Yorkshire*, 1996.

Snyder, C, *Sub-Roman Britain: A Gazetteer of Sites*, 1996.

Snyder, C, *An Age of Tyrants: Britain and the Britons A.D. 400–600*, 1998.

Southern, P and Dixon, K R, *The Late Roman Army*, 1996.

Stephenson, I P, *Roman Infantry Equipment: The Later Empire*, 1999.

Underwood, R, *Anglo-Saxon Weapons & Warfare*, 1999.

Wagner, P, *Pictish Warrior AD 297–841*, 2002.

Webster, L and Brown, M (eds.), *The Transformation of the Roman World AD 400–900*, 1997.

Welch, M, *Anglo-Saxon England*, 1992.

BIBLIOGRAPHY

Williams, G, *The Iron Age Hillforts of England*, 1993.

Williams, G, *Stronghold Britain: Four Thousand Years of British Fortifications*, 1999.

Arthurian theories

Ashe, G, *The Discovery of King Arthur*, 1985 and 2003.

Barber, C and Pykitt, D, *Journey to Avalon: The Final Discovery of King Arthur*, 1997.

Blackett, A T and Wilson, A, *King Arthur: King of Glamorgan and Gwent*, 1981.

Blake, S and Lloyd, S, *The Keys to Avalon: The True Location of Arthur's Kingdom Revealed*, 2000.

Blake, S and Lloyd, S, *Pendragon: The Definitive Account of the Origins of Arthur*, 2002.

Chambers, E K, *Arthur of Britain*, 1927 (later reprint 1966).

Clancy, J, *Pendragon: Arthur and His Britain*, 1971.

Collingwood, R G and Myres, J N L, *Roman Britain and the English Settlements*, 1937.

Cummins, W A, *King Arthur's Place in Prehistory*, 1997.

Darrah, J, *The Real Camelot*, 1981.

Dunning, R, *Arthur: King in the West*, 1988.

Gilbert, A, Wilson, A and Blackett, B, *The Holy Kingdom*, 1998.

Glennie, J S S, *Arthurian Localities: Their Historical Origin, Chief Country, and Fingalian Relations*, 1994 (originally published in 1869).

Goodrich, N L, *King Arthur*, 1986.

Holmes, M, *King Arthur: A Military History*, 1996.

Littleton, S and Malcor, L A, *From Scythia to Camelot*, 2000.

Moffat, A, *Arthur & The Lost Kingdoms*, 2000.

Phillips, G and Keatman, M, *King Arthur: The True Story*, 1993.

Reid, H, *Arthur the Dragon King*, 2001.

Reno, F D, *The Historic King Arthur*, 1996.

Skene, W F, *Arthur and the Britons* (ed. Bryce, D), 1988.

Turner, P J F, *The Real King Arthur: A History of Post-Roman Britannia A.D. 410–A.D. 593*, 1993.

Acknowledgements

At the age of seven, I was forced into playing the famous King Arthur at a school fete – largely, I fear, due to my inability to learn the maypole dance. The sound of children half strangled by a maypole ribbon still echoes in my ears to this day. The exciting tales of King Arthur and his knights make great stories for kids, and I loved them. Maypole dancing has quite rightly taken a back seat in my life, but my interest in Arthur in both literature and history has continued, and I hope this book is a great introduction to the man and the myth for newcomers to the tales.

First of all, I'm indebted to Geoffrey, Thomas and all of the other storytellers, for making sure that King Arthur's name wasn't lost over the centuries. Credit goes to my artist Deanna Tyson, who created the wonderful images of our Arthurian world in her artwork that you'll spot as you turn the pages of this book. I'd also like to acknowledge the authors of the stories of Arthur that enchanted me as a kid, the influence of whom must have been far greater than I realised at the time. My thanks also go to my mum and dad for helping me to become interested in Arthur, books and history in general.

The expert and brilliant team at Summersdale Publishers are due a great deal of credit; to Liz Kershaw and Sadie Mayne for seeing merit in my vision of the book and to Carol Baker for editing my Nennius-like 'heap' into a readable text. And for being fun to work with throughout, which is a rare talent in the publishing world. Further thanks are due to those people who have discussed the history, archaeology and literature of Arthur with me over and over again, for helping me to decide exactly what I wanted to write about the Once and Future King.

And, finally, my gratitude goes out to my friends and family who helped me maintain my sanity through the writing process, whether it was by forcing me to go to the pub, chatting on the phone, or watching our team lose yet another football match.

ACKNOWLEDGEMENTS

This book is dedicated to Symmie, who kept everything in the house working and alive, and waited so patiently for me to get almost halfway through the writing of each sentence of the book before interrupting me to ask if the scabbard story had gone in yet.

Daniel Mersey
Sussex
Summer 2004

www.summersdale.com